KEEPING THE LIGHTS ON FOR IKE

*DAILY LIFE OF A UTILITIES ENGINEER AT
AFHQ IN EUROPE DURING WWII; OR, WHAT
TO SAY IN LETTERS HOME WHEN YOU'RE NOT
ALLOWED TO WRITE ABOUT THE WAR*

REBECCA DANIELS

SUNBURY
P R E S S
Mechanicsburg, PA USA

Published by Sunbury Press, Inc.
Mechanicsburg, Pennsylvania

SUNBURY
P R E S S
www.sunburypress.com

For information about special discounts for bulk purchases, please contact Sunbury Press Orders Dept. at (855) 338-8359 or orders@sunburypress.com.

To request one of our authors for speaking engagements or book signings, please contact Sunbury Press Publicity Dept. at publicity@sunburypress.com.

ISBN: 978-1-62006-114-5 (Trade paperback)

Library of Congress Control Number: 2018964336

FIRST SUNBURY PRESS EDITION: January 2019

Product of the United States of America
0 1 1 2 3 5 8 13 21 34 55

Set in Bookman Old Style
Designed by Crystal Devine
Cover by Terry Kennedy
Edited by Alyssa Vorbeck
Managing Editor: Jennifer Cappello

Continue the Enlightenment!

To my amazing parents, Alec and Mary Daniels,
whose wartime correspondence and post-war stories
took me on the journey of a lifetime.

CONTENTS

ACKNOWLEDGMENTS

Thanks to St. Lawrence University for generous technology grant funding at the start of this project in 2008, which allowed me to digitize and clean up the slide and scrapbook images for inclusion in this book (with thanks to Chris Watts, director, Newell Center for Arts Technology (NCAT); Josephine Skiff, assistant director, NCAT; and NCAT student workers extraordinaire, Alexandra Collins, '09, and Joseph Pomainville, '10). Thanks also to St. Lawrence for additional support in 2009, to subsidize my research travel to explore Army records in the National Archives, College Park, MD, and in 2018, in the form of a small grant for editorial consulting.

Much gratitude goes to my women's writing group led by the ever-encouraging and always-astute Jane Roy Brown, especially a few members of this group (Rosemary Caine, Carole Fuller, Marilyn McArthur, Sherrill Redmon, and Karen Spindel) who heard most of the chapters as they were first developed between April 2016 and May 2017 (with a special shout-out to Sherrill Redmon who heard every single one) and who offered excellent feedback and encouragement all along the way. Special thanks to Jane Roy Brown, not only for facilitating a remarkable writing group but also for being my independent editorial consultant on the project and helping me shape the final manuscript before it was submitted to the publisher.

Thanks as well to the fantastic team at Sunbury Press, especially Lawrence Knorr, founder and CEO; and Jennifer Cappello, managing editor, for their belief in the importance of this book and their attention to the details of getting it in front of the reading public. I was also privileged to work closely with a patient and always-helpful editor, Alyssa Vorbeck; book designer, Crystal Devine; and cover designer, Terry Kennedy.

Special thanks to my brother and sister-in-law, Toby Daniels and Debbie McKeown-Daniels, for their ongoing encouragement, and to their sons, my nephews, Christopher and Andrew, who never got the chance to meet their wonderful grandfather in person. Thanks, also, for the ongoing encouragement of my step-daughter and son-in-law, Kensey and Tim Batchelder. There are a number of friends and other family members who read various pieces (sometimes even all) of the manuscript and offered encouragement and emotional support: Mary Mountain (my cousin, whose mom has a cameo appearance in one of the letters), Jim and Edna McKeown (who knew and loved Mom, and not just because she and Edna were sorority sisters from different schools and years), Wayne Richards, and Joshua Walker. Thanks, also, to those many folks who, while they never had the chance to read the manuscript in progress, offered research suggestions, encouragement, and support for this endeavor at various stages throughout its development over a decade, notably my ever-encouraging dramaturg and close friend, Zachary Dorsey. Even the smallest comments helped me keep this project alive through those many years, especially during the dark months after I was unexpectedly widowed in the fall of 2010.

Finally, particular thanks to my late husband and avid historian, Skip Stoughton, who was my primary cheerleader and constant encourager when I began this project after my mother's death in 2006. Sadly, he didn't live to see the project to its completion, but I know he would be proud of what I've created by using my parents' words to tell their remarkable story.

INTRODUCTION

In the European Theater of World War II, for every four combat soldiers, there were approximately another six support troops who provided administrative, logistical, and infrastructure support. This is the story of one of those support troops: Harold Alec Daniels, a utilities engineer serving under Dwight David Eisenhower and his successors at Allied Force Headquarters (AFHQ) in various locations in and around London, England; Algiers, in North Africa; and Caserta Palace near Naples, Italy. Alec, as he was called by family members and friends, told most of the story in his own words through his letters home to his wife, Mary. It is also the story of how Alec and Mary, who were my parents, managed to hold their young marriage together over the three-year separation—without any of the electronic communication of today. All that was available at the time was the postal service, an occasional cable, or an even rarer phone call, so mail became incredibly important during that separation. According to the National Postal Museum at the Smithsonian Institution, "For members of the armed forces the importance of mail during World War II was second only to food. The emotional power of letters was heightened by the fear of loss and the need for communication during times of separation. Messages from a husband, father, or brother, killed in battle might provide the only surviving connection between him and his family. The imminence of danger and the uncertainty of war placed an added emphasis on letter writing. Emotions and feelings that were normally only expressed on special occasions were written regularly to ensure devotion and support."[1]

Harold Alec Daniels was born on June 24, 1915, in Portland, Oregon, to a first-generation Swedish immigrant father, and a mother with English and German heritage. They were a working-class family, and part of how Alec financed his college education

1

was to join ROTC. He was commissioned when he graduated as a second lieutenant in the Army Reserves on May 26, 1939, though no one, certainly not young college graduates in the western United States, had any real expectation of war at this point in their lives. After all, it had only been about 20 years since World War I, and no one was expecting another any time soon. Mary Park Cockrell was born on November 18, 1915, in Oregon City, Oregon, a southwest suburb of Portland, to an English father and a Welsh and Irish mother. Though the Cockrell family could claim early Colonial heritage, the rest of the ancestors on both sides of the family were newer immigrants and of the sturdy pioneer stock, typical of folks living in the Pacific Northwest in the early part of the twentieth century. Alec was the older of two brothers; Mary was the third of four sisters.

The story I share in *Keeping the Lights on for Ike: Daily Life of a Utilities Engineer at AFHQ in Europe during WWII; Or, What to Say in Letters Home When You're Not Allowed to Write about the War* is based in several primary sources. First, and most important, are Alec's letters home from his three years overseas, which Mary kept for more than 65 years. Second, Mary's youngest sister, Carol Cockrell, kept Mary's letters to their family when Mary and Alec lived in Bremerton, Washington—Alec was working as a civilian engineer at the Puget Sound Navy Yard & Intermediate Maintenance Facility there—and during the couple's residence at Fort Leonard Wood in Missouri and Fort Riley in Kansas, where Alec underwent basic training in the Army. Third, because Mary aspired to be a writer throughout her life, she left her many short stories and essays, most of which were written many years after the war was over, rarely titled and never dated, in which she shared some of her wartime experiences. Finally, I have childhood memories and stories they shared with me about this time in their lives; although, like many of their generation, they shared these sparingly. Though Mary's side of the wartime correspondence didn't survive (Alec moved around enough that he discarded her letters each time he had to move again), it's clear by his many references and responses to what she wrote that the correspondence was reciprocal and the romance intense. They were working at keeping their marriage alive through acts of imagination: memories of their brief past together and dreams of the future when they would be reunited at war's end.

Newlyweds, Alec and Mary Daniels, with their dog, Pete, in Bremerton, WA, before the war (1941).

Due to strict censorship rules, Alec couldn't write about the details of his job as an Army utilities engineer or reveal anything he might have known about the battles going on near where he was working, so he wrote instead about his day-to-day existence at AFHQ—including his interactions with fellow soldiers as well as the locals he encountered in all three locations to which he was assigned—and some of the details of his electrical jobs, his thoughts about the countries in which he was stationed, politics at home, the Army and its culture, women in the military, war in general, and love and marriage. He also shared details about the health challenges he experienced, including sandfly fever and trench mouth, which were common among many of the soldiers, as well as his experiences with those around him going through what we now call PTSD, but which then was called mental or combat fatigue or soldier collapse. And much more.

I've also consulted secondary sources to place the letters and stories in the context of the campaigns and battles of WWII in Europe, focusing primarily on events of significance in the areas of the European Theater where Alec was stationed. I've given special prominence to two volumes in Rick Atkinson's acclaimed Liberation Trilogy: *An Army at Dawn: The War in North Africa* (Pulitzer Prize winner, 2003) and *The Day of Battle: The War in Sicily and Italy 1943-1944*. I chose these books because Atkinson's writing style is engaging and accessible for someone who is not a historian of the period. His tone is also a good match for the personal material in which my parents' wartime story unfolds.

Because of a major fire in 1973 at the National Archives at St. Louis that resulted in the loss of 80% of Army records from 1912 to 1960, I cannot be sure of Alec's exact assignments, and my correspondence with the National Personnel Records Office confirms that they have none of his military record on file. However, after the war, he told Mary that he was working in a support group for Eisenhower's command group at headquarters, wherever that might be, until Ike was sent to London in 1943 to plan the Normandy invasion, at which point Alec remained at AFHQ.

I have presented the story and the letters in roughly chronological order, though I sometimes take ideas slightly out of order to focus on a particular topic. Alec also had rather idiosyncratic systems for identifying his letters, first using numbers, and then using the number of days since he last wrote. This seemed to be for Mary's benefit, so she would know if she wasn't getting all his letters, but he wasn't always consistent within his own systems. After trying several "systems" (he was, after all, an engineer), he finally settled on simply dating each letter, though sometimes he didn't know the exact date for certain. I have done my best to identify specific dates and, when necessary, slightly longer time frames—sometimes a month or season—as clearly as possible, based on the context of other contents of each letter. The letters have been cross-checked for accuracy with the originals and any errors present in my parents' quoted material are true to their actual letters. I have opted not to interrupt the flow of the reading experience with distracting notes, as the meanings are clear even if the English isn't always "perfect."

Alec was a private person, and he would be mortified to know that his most loving and erotic thoughts (however euphemized for censorship purposes they might have been) about his beloved Mary would be read by complete strangers, or even his own children. Mary, however forward thinking she was in some ways, was also constrained, even Victorian, in her emotional expressions—a lady never, ever shows her feelings, much less kisses and tells.

4

While she wrote in a straightforward manner about certain things, her intense emotions can be read under the surface.

The images used in this book were nearly all taken by Alec or Mary and span their years in Bremerton before the war, their time at Fort Leonard Wood for Alec's basic training, and his time overseas. Both of them were photography aficionados, both before and after the war, and many of the original images were color slides. Amazingly, they have survived for over 65 years, due to Mary's careful storage and handling. Some of the images show the contents of the scrapbooks that Mary kept, both during and after the war.

In spite of growing up experiencing many of the hardships of the Depression, Mary and Alec both had, more or less, conventional and happy childhoods and young adulthoods. This part of their story focuses on the 1940s when they were a young married couple deeply in love and starting to build a life together at the same time the entire world was in the process of going to war for a second time in less than thirty years. And how do I know this story? I'm the older of the children they hoped for and tried to conceive for nearly ten years before turning to adoption after the war years. This is the story of how their marriage survived both infertility and a three-year separation because of WWII. It's also the story of what happened in those years to a young soldier abroad serving as a utilities engineer at AFHQ in England, North Africa, and Italy, and to his wife, waiting not so patiently at the home front. And it's the story of a love that transcended those obstacles to survive and even thrive when the war was over.

1

HOW IT ALL BEGAN

SPRING 1938 – DECEMBER 1941

The story I heard my whole life about how my parents first met was this: In the fall of 1934 and the spring of 1935, two young people attended the same high school in southeast Portland, Oregon, sharing the same halls with the loves of their lives, even graduating in the same class, but never actually realizing it because the school was so large. Besides, they were both shy and didn't interact much with the opposite sex, even at home, as Alec had a brother and Mary had three sisters. Much later, as an adult, Mary wrote in a story entitled "Dear Grandkids" about why she and Alec never met in high school:

> When I went [to Franklin HS] it was the years of the Great Depression. My family was even more depressed than most, I expect, because my dad had bought a drugstore just in time for the banks to fail.
>
> Franklin was the nearest high school, about three miles away, and transportation was by streetcar—not paid for by the school district, either. . . . There were no sports for girls. There was no, absolutely none whatsoever, social life.
>
> You didn't really know who was in your class until the last half of the senior year when they let the seniors come together in three rooms above the auditorium. That is why, when I

Alec was commissioned as a second lieutenant in ROTC upon his graduation from Oregon State in June 1939.

first met the Oregon Stater I married, in the course of getting acquainted we were amazed to find out we had graduated in the same Franklin High School class. He transferred to Franklin his senior year, but there were no special events to bring us all together except for the actual commencement exercises, so we never met. . . . not until four years later.

It was then that Fate—tired of waiting for the pair to meet on their own—intervened in the form of a college roommate and fellow engineering student who thought his buddy needed to meet more girls and decided to set him up with Mary, a nice girl he had known since high school. Mary, Alec, and Jimmy Tice were all in the same year in college, but at that point, Mary didn't even go to

Alec and Mary's wedding photo, March 1940.

the same school the guys did; in fact, the Oregon State Beavers and University of Oregon Ducks were fierce rivals on the athletic fields, and the two campuses were 50 miles apart. Jimmy had a strong presentiment that his friends would make a good couple, so he persisted and finally got them to agree to go on a double date with him and his then-girlfriend during their Class of 1939 senior year. His hunch was right; Alec and Mary fell immediately in love. Since they lived at separate campuses, Alec courted Mary with special delivery letters carried by a uniformed postal service employee and costing ten cents—a princely sum at the time. Apparently, this was part of what impressed her about him.

Mary majored in journalism in college and wanted to be a writer more than just about anything else, except for a mother. She studied journalism because creative writing was not an option at the University of Oregon, but mostly she loved writing short

9

2- OCT 1940

From: Commandant, Puget Sound Navy Yard
To: Harold A. Daniels, 3504 Fairmount,
                Vancouver, Washington

Subject: Probational Appointment

        Having been certified to this Navy Yard as eli-
gible for appointment, as shown by the certificate of the
Manager of the Eleventh Civil Service District, dated August
30, 1940, you are hereby appointed on probation as Junior
Electrical Engineer, P-1, in the Industrial Department (Planning Division), Navy Yard, Puget Sound, Washington, with pay
at the rate of $2000 per annum, appropriation "Replacement of
Naval Vessels, Construction and Machinery" (limitation for
pay of Group IVb employees, etc.), effective when you enter
upon duty, on which date you will execute the required oath
of office.

        Your retention in the service after expiration
of the probationary period shall be equivalent to absolute
appointment.

                                C. S. Freeman,

                                Alex M. Charlton
                                By direction

(Add) position authorized 8-27-40 -
Job Classification Sheet #1865)

- -

                        1st Endorsement
                Puget Sound Navy Yard   SL3-CWW-Bn-Lg
                Bremerton, Washington   October 8, 1940

From: Labor Board
To: Harold A. Daniels
                VIA: Manager

        1.   Forwarded. You executed the required Oath of
Office and entered upon duty October 7, 1940.

                                W. R. Dowd
                                Senior Member

                                By direction

This is Alec's original appointment letter to his job at the Puget Sound Navy Yard in Bremerton.

stories, poetry, and letters and continued doing so until near the end of her life. Alec, on the other hand, an electrical engineer who trusted more in numbers and diagrams than feelings and ideas, was a rather reluctant correspondent, forced into writing letters because of the separation created by the circumstances, but nervous about his lack of ability with words, especially when newly married to an aspiring professional writer.

After the blind date and courtship that followed, Mary and Alec were married in March of 1940, less than a year after his

Alec beside Puget Sound in 1940 or 1941.

college graduation. They lived in Portland near their families at first, and Alec spent several months reading electric meters in Portland's Chinatown, something well below his skill level. In the fall of 1940, he accepted, sight unseen, a civil service job as a junior electrical engineer at the Puget Sound Navy Yard's Industrial Department/Planning Division in Bremerton, Washington. The PSNY was established in 1891 as the first repair facility in the Northwest capable of handling large ships and has been in continuous use ever since, both repairing and building large ships. During WWII, its primary mission was the repair of Pacific Fleet warships damaged in battle. After the war, the shipyard's mission changed from repair work to the deactivation and storage of

Pacific Fleet vessels, and it remains the largest and most diverse shipyard on the West Coast and one of Washington State's largest industrial complexes, earning a place on the National Register of Historic Places in 1992.[1] Bremerton, a ferry ride across the Puget Sound from metropolitan Seattle, was a place they had never been before, but like many young professional families in their generation, off they went on this exciting new adventure.

The newlyweds, "with the audacity, ignorance, and innocence of babes," as Mary described them in one of her short stories, packed their things into their station wagon along with their dog—a German shepherd named Pete, recently adopted from the pound—and they moved to a nice little house on Hood Canal outside Bremerton. Hood Canal is actually a fjord-like arm of Puget Sound and, in spite of its name, is a natural formation, not a man-made canal.[2] On one side of the canal is the Olympic Peninsula, home of the Olympic Mountains, which can be seen from many points around the region and where the rainforests in the west-side valleys of Olympic National Park are the wettest spots in the continental United States.[3] On the other side is the mostly water-surrounded Kitsap Peninsula, where Bremerton is situated. Other than the fog, the weather and topography would have been similar to what they were used to in northwestern Oregon, especially those temperate summers and rainy winters, which created nearly as many shades of green in the landscape as the tourist bureaus boast about in Ireland. Mary described their new community in another of her stories as

> a sort of cross between Shangri-La and Brigadoon. From the
> first time we saw it, it always awed us—that sudden view
> of great Navy ships lined up one after another down the
> waterfront. Carriers, battleships, cruisers, tugs, and all day
> and all night, the sounds of the Navy Yard—whistles and bells
> and horns and target firings. Besides the hustle and bustle
> of the Yard, there was the beauty of the country. The sounds,
> everywhere the water, sometimes as blue as Crater Lake and
> sometimes so wrapped in fog it was like groping through wet
> cobwebs.

In the same week that Alec started his new job, a different adventure took over the headlines. The brand-new Tacoma Narrows Bridge, nicknamed Galloping Gertie by the construction workers because of the extreme movement of its suspension span—the third largest in the world after the Golden Gate and George Washington Bridges—collapsed dramatically in a high wind only four months after it first opened.[4] That bridge didn't re-open until after the war, and while it didn't affect Mary and Alec on a daily basis, it did make the trip to visit their families in Oregon lengthier and more difficult for the rest of their time in Bremerton. After that initial excitement, and the usual challenges of a new job and new community, things seemed to settle down, and they started to make friends and develop their life and work routines.

In her letters to her family during the first year they lived there,* Mary shared lots of social anecdotes that made it clear that they found some very good neighbors and friends while living in Bremerton. It was obvious from Mary's letters during the early 1940s that most of the young wives in her circle of friends didn't work, and she wrote often to her parents and sisters about her mundane daily household chores and how she went shopping with her girlfriends (money was tight for most of them so bargains were to be bragged about), shared meals and plants from their gardens with neighbors, went to lively parties with other young couples they knew, and in general seemed to be having a good time of it in their new community. When the wives had lunch together, it wasn't dining out in a restaurant. Instead, one wife would make her own sandwich and bring it over to her friend's house where they would eat together and talk. This was, after all, the generation that came of age during the Great Depression and who learned to enjoy ketchup sandwiches on white bread when there was not much else in the cupboard. Mary seemed to be resourceful with small appliance repairs, though there were stories about Alec having to take things apart for her to get them to work again when she couldn't manage the fix on her own. One of her stories mentioned his near obsession with wanting to know why and how things worked, occasionally embarrassing her by pulling things apart in public and having to ask for help to put them back together again.

There were few two-car families in those days, especially among their young married friends. Mary drove Alec to work and back each day in order to have access to a car for errands and

---

* Mary didn't date her letters, and her sister saved them without envelopes, so approximate dates have come from the contents of the letters and what I already know of family history.

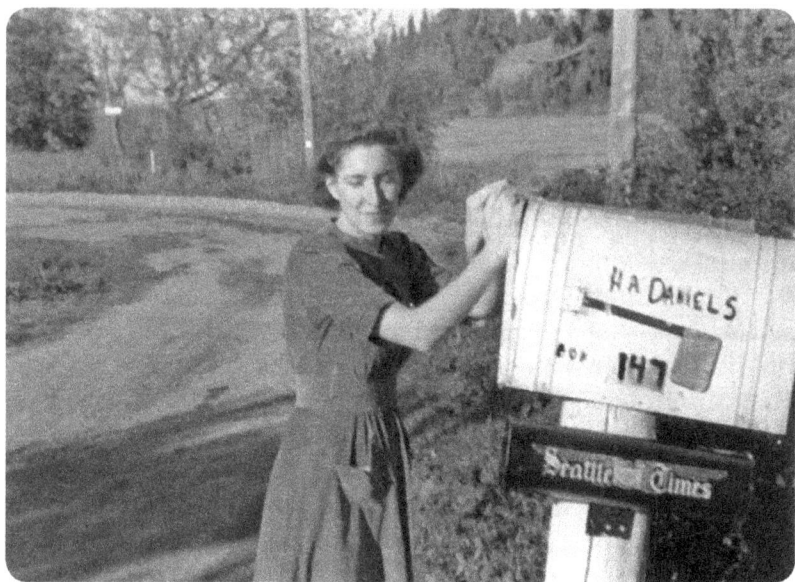

Mary at their mailbox in their first house in Bremerton. On the back of the photo she wrote, "I painted the name on the box."

visiting with her friends, and she wrote to her family of several adventures with their car after dropping him off, most of them involving pushing it or having to find help to get it started again. I remember that Alec worked on every car we had while I was growing up and was adept at keeping used cars running against all odds. Mary developed a lifelong habit of visiting thrift stores and told her mom and sisters about several bargains she was proud of, including an antique beer stein that had etched glass in the bottom so that you only saw the picture once you had finished your beer. There were also many references to pictures they had each taken or film they were getting developed. Both Alec and Mary had significant skills as amateur photographers, and many of their wartime letters also reflected their shared interest in photography equipment. The other things Mary saved from Alec's time overseas were hundreds of slides he took over there; most were of the people he met and scenic views that had nothing to do with combat. There were strict limits on the kinds of photos he could take while in or near a combat zone, and he was careful about his subjects, but it didn't get in the way of his love for and fascination with photography.

Pete, their handsome and much-loved German shepherd, on his chain in Bremerton.

At some point in the spring or summer of 1941, the house they were renting on the canal went up for sale; so, many of Mary's letters to her family talked about their impending move to an apartment complex where many of their friends already lived in Manette, Washington (which became part of Bremerton in the mid-twentieth century). At this point, they also started to plan the dream house they would build when they got their finances in order, a house Mary described in another of her essays as one "with secret doors and floors on different levels and things." The move to Manette seems to have bewildered the dog at first, but with help from their friends they were able to move everything in their old woody station wagon, and they were happy there.

Because of the shipyards and all the big ships and planes that were brought in for repairs, the war touched Bremerton more directly than many other communities, even though the United States wasn't officially fighting in 1940 or 1941. A British ship damaged in the Battle of Crete was brought to town for repairs in the summer of 1941 and was the subject of one of Mary's letters. For some unknown reason, Alec took an Army Extension Course in mess management and got his certificate in November of 1941. The course included budgeting and inventory management and may have been part of his ongoing responsibilities as an Army reservist and a junior officer.

Like many other young marrieds at the end of the Depression, they struggled with finances, and it seemed as though they were in chronic debt to her parents: five dollars here, ten dollars there, and occasionally more for something special, like a new piece of furniture or a radio. Clearly, they were living from paycheck to paycheck, and almost every one of her letters included some cash in repayment of various small loans. In one of her short stories written later in her life, Mary wrote about being poor as an important coming-of-age journey:

> Just starting out—new marriage, new life.
>
> Frankly I hope you had a chance, too, to be poor. And if you're up there in a respectable number of years, then you know how it was when you were. You know how it was to baby your second, third, or fourth-hand car to keep it running. To go wistfully by eating-places that had signs in their window that said they would give you ham and eggs and coffee and flap jacks for one dollar and a quarter. But you didn't stop. Not that you weren't hungry, but because if you spent that money with the day so young, how were you going to get through the day to dinner?
>
> You were camping, of course, imagining you were on a vacation, and along with wistfully passing up breakfast at Joe's Diner, you were looking ahead to also passing up one of those auto park cabins, at a dollar and a half, because you were sleeping in the car.
>
> Being poor—rock bottom poor—was the way you started out your new marriage . . .
>
> I hope you two felt that being poor was no barrier to having a great time, to going many places, and making many new friends. If newlyweds, you might feel that being poor was the kindergarten part of your new marriage. And soon, of course, you would go onto the higher grades and climb the rungs of this ladder and instead of living from paycheck to paycheck you'd—well, you'd be better off, anyways. It would take much to reach that pleasant state.

I hope, indeed, that you seized your day, picked up the ball, so to speak, and ran with it, and made your touchdown before that stunning broadcast on December 7th 1941, because after that as far as income went, you were probably never poor again, and it was hard to remember being young.

I suspect everyone from that generation remembers exactly where he or she was when hearing the news about the Japanese attack on Pearl Harbor. Mary and Alec, on a Sunday morning, while he was changing the tire on their car, heard the news on a neighbor's radio "turned up loud enough to penetrate the walls," as she described in another of her stories. There had been military planes and ships in the harbor for months for "modernization" and other kinds of servicing, but this was different. The United States had been directly attacked.

Mary wrote to her family about the immediate community response: "A neighborhood meeting was organized that afternoon. It was decided that Bremerton was a likely target and the men should stand watch day and night for Japanese planes. We would, of course, have an immediate blackout. Men who worked at the yard in the daytime were excused, but sailors awaiting their ships were glad to do the watch duty" (December 1941). Soon barrage balloons were grounded all over town, and Mary was sending photos to her family and describing their peculiar appearance,

One of Mary's "illegal" photos of the Puget Sound ferry, taken shortly after the Pearl Harbor attacks.

explaining that they were "funny looking things" if you weren't expecting them when you came upon them suddenly. But fairly quickly, certain kinds of photos were simply not allowed because of the fear of an impending attack on the mainland.

She also explained how all the Puget Sound ferries now had armed FBI officers on board who would shoot into the water ahead in case they encountered enemy mines, and she worried about what might happen if their bullets actually did hit an explosive device in the water right in front of a passenger ferry. She also told them,

> I broke the law when I took a picture of two ferries. At least it is against the law now. It's against the law to even have a camera in the area facing any part of the inlet to Bremerton or the waterfront in Seattle. You can't take any pictures of any boats anywhere. You can't take a camera on the ferry. You can't have a camera within six blocks of the Yard. What on earth people will do who live in that radius and have a camera, I don't know. They probably won't enforce the law, which was just passed this week. Alec thinks that more than anything else, they don't want anyone keeping track of the coming and going of the boats. (undated, probably December 1941 or January 1942)

Another view of the Puget Sound ferry in another one of Mary's "illegal" photos.

Everyone in town seemed to know that at least some of the damaged fleet from Hawaii would be coming to the shipyard for repairs and restoration, and in one letter she wished her father could drive up from Oregon to see the visiting fleet. Due to the demise of Galloping Gertie and the need to go around the sound instead of over it, the drive would have taken nearly a full day from Portland, so it proved impossible in the end. (This was prior to the creation of the Interstate highway system, which would shorten the drive between Portland and Bremerton to 2.5 hours.) She also shared that Alec was unhappy to hear of the sinking of the battleship *West Virginia* because the ship had been expected at the yard in a month for refurbishment and repair. He and his team had been working on plans for it, which they had just finished, and which were now totally useless.

After a few weeks, things quieted down in the town itself. Bremerton night patrols were dropped, but because of the arrival of the ships from the Hawaii fleet that could still travel, the work at the shipyards intensified exponentially. And for Mary and Alec, it was just a matter of time before the reservist would be called up to active duty.

2

BASIC TRAINING ADVENTURES

SPRING AND SUMMER 1942

It turns out they didn't have long to wait before Alec was called up for active duty, though in the weeks between Pearl Harbor and his orders, another interesting option was presented to him and the other reservists working in civil service jobs at the Puget Sound Navy Yard. In early March of 1942, the Army sent the folks at the Navy Yard a communication telling them to expect the resignations of all Army reservists working there in Bremerton. Shortly after that, the Navy started making their own offers to the Army reservists who, like Alec, had become an important part of the work they were doing. They would be able to stay at the shipyards instead of being called to active duty. Alec, however, wasn't interested, and Mary wrote to her family about his decision to reject the Navy's offer with a flush of patriotism and pride:

> I married a hero. The first day after the Army sent its letter
> to the Navy about [the] resignation of officers, the Navy wrote
> each officer a separate resignation letter and brought them
> around, and all the boys had to do was sign on the dotted line.
> Well, only one of them did. But the next day quite a few more
> did, and the day before yesterday everyone in Alec's group
> signed but him. Another group had one man who didn't sign.
> All the rest were only too glad to get out of the Army. As one
> of our friends said . . . the other boys at the office think the
> officers who resigned were all slackers. It seems most of them

had been going around declaring loudly that they could hardly wait to get into a tank and get a crack at some Japs. But to me, the crowning touch is that they all think that if they come up finally for drafting they'll all get their officer's commissions back. It will mean quite a cut in pay for us just when we were looking forward to having almost a thousand more a year, and heaven knows Alec would be very unhappy getting up so early in the morning in the cold and maybe having to do physical labor—he who wants a field instead of a yard so he won't have to mow the lawn—but I'm glad he didn't resign. (undated letter, probably early 1942)

Soon after this, Mary shared that she and Alec had just been to see the film, *Sergeant York,* starring Gary Cooper. Seeing the story of a reluctant soldier who turned into a battle hero prompted her to suggest that perhaps she should have ordered Alec to resign his commission immediately, but now it was too late because

Thursday he got his orders from the War Department. Any time after March 15 he is to be ready for active duty—if needed. So here's hoping he won't be needed. He was the last one of the bunch of officers [with whom he worked] to get his notice, but he had the earliest date of all of them, so they call him their test case. He is the only one who belongs to the engineers. The others belong to the coast artillery, etc. According to Life [Magazine], the engineers are the ELITE of the army. I'd rather he'd be in the finance corps. (undated letter, probably early March 1942)

After getting his original notice, Alec took and passed the Army physical exam, but the waiting continued through the winter months. Eventually, he got his letter from the War Department on March 26, 1942, ordering him to report immediately to Fort Leonard Wood in Missouri. The fort had been newly constructed and completed in June 1941. It was originally designated as an infantry division training area, but by the spring of 1942 when Mary and Alec arrived, it had become home to a new Engineer Replacement Training Center as well.[1] The War Department letter told Alec that dependents should stay home, as there would be no housing allowance for them and that housing would be hard to find in any case, since there had been little available for the

R E S T R I C T E D

SYMBOLS: DP - By direction of the President
TDN - Travel directed is necessary in the military service
WP - Will proceed to
AD - Active duty

SPECIAL ORDERS)
NO.........59)

HEADQUARTERS SECOND MILITARY AREA
225 U. S. Court House, Portland, Oregon
March 13, 1942

1. DP 2ND LT RAY JAMES PARKER 0361382 Inf Res Hq. Co. 4th Inf., Ft. Richardson, Anchorage, Alaska, is ordered to AD effective March 22, 1942. WP Fort Mears, Alaska, and report to the CO 37th Infantry, for duty. He will rank from March 22, 1942. TDN. While Traveling in Alaska, officer will be allowed $6.00 per diem. FD 1499 P 1-06 A 0410-2 and QM 1601 P 61-07 A 0525-2.

2. DP each of the following named Reserve Officers is ordered to AD effective March 26, 1942. WP Fort Leonard Wood, Missouri, and report to the CO, Engr. RTC, for duty. Each officer named will rank from the date set opposite his name:

DATE OF RANK

1ST LT JAMES EDMUND COMBLR 0343116 Engr Res
14952 - 18th S.W., Rt 7, Box 228 B, Seattle, Washington March 26, 1942
1ST LT MORRISON ELIOT SIMMONS 0326557 Engr Res
Rt. 2, Box 350 A, Bremerton, Washington March 26, 1942
1ST LT WILLIAM RICHARD TAYLOR 0351431 Engr-Res
6225 Princeton Way, Seattle, Washington March 26, 194
2ND LT FRED RUSSELL CHEATHAM 0408733 Engr Res.
706 California, Pullman, Washington March 26, 1942
2ND LT HAROLD ALEC DANIELS 0378002 Engr Res
56 Jones Drive Apt. 6, Manette, Washington March 12, 1942
2ND LT SOL DURBIN 0367465 Engr Res
1533 N.E. 28th Avenue, Portland, Oregon March 12, 1942
2ND LT ROBERT MORRIS EDHOLM 0391775 Engr Res
13th & Highland Street, Clarkston, Washington March 26, 1941
2ND LT HAROLD ALFRED KIDBY 0366214 Engr Res
2014 S.E. 46th Street, Portland, Oregon March 12, 1942
2ND LT LESTER STANLEY KING 0394289 Engr Res
100 Galvan Drive, Apt. C, Westpark, Bremerton, Wn. March 26, 1942
2ND LT BERNARD MAURICE 0363103 Engr Res
42 Schley Blvd., Eastpark, Bremerton, Washington May 15, 1941
2ND LT HARRY WILBER RICHARDS 0366220 Engr Res
233 5th Street, Bremerton, Washington March 12, 1942
2ND LT CLYDE KEENER SHERMAN 0366221 Engr Res
1733 Gregory Way, Bremerton, Washington March 26, 1942

TDN. FD 1499 P 1-06 A 0410-2 and QM 1601 P 61-07 A 0525-2.

3. DP Paragraph 8, Special Orders No. 56, this hq., 1942, pertaining to the AD of 1ST LT CHARLES FRANCIS PRIDE 0286090 Inf Res Rt. 1, Box 260, Bremerton, Washington, with permanent station to be Signal Corps Replacement Pool, Fort Monmouth, New Jersey, and temp. duty at Fort Lewis, Washington, is revoked.

R E S T R I C T E D   (OVER)

Alec's letter ordering him to report to Fort Leonard Wood immediately for active duty. His name is fifth on a list of other reserve officers in Oregon and Washington also being called up.

construction workers who built the fort the year before.[2] Mary, of course, ignored that order, adamantly refusing to be separated from her soldier, and she started to make plans to drive to Missouri with him and Pete in their used station wagon, a woody they called the "pneumonia box," presumably because its heater

Mary and Alec's "pneumonia box."

didn't work well. If Mary had been born in the South instead of in Oregon, she would most certainly have been characterized as a steel magnolia, a woman known for her determination to do all she could to hold her new family together and stay close to the man she loved in the face of adversity. Out West, however, they would simply have called it her "pioneer spirit."

Though off-base housing wasn't plentiful and definitely lacked the amenities they were used to in Bremerton, the young couple eventually managed to find places to live in Missouri—three of them, to be exact, in less than six months. In one of her short stories written decades after the war, Mary remembered their housing adventures:

> We were forewarned that living conditions around Army camps were fierce, and the order specifically stated that dependents were not authorized to travel, still it was quite a shock to find that we were literally going to have [to] camp out in Waynesville, a small town with lots of color and backwoods character and no water system . . .
>
> Our first home in Waynesville, the little town six miles from Fort Leonard Wood, was a shack behind the Shell station (that

we called the shanty). It had—the housing, I mean—a sink with cold running water, a hot plate, and no bathroom. The Shell station, our landlord, was the town bus stop for Greyhound and had a restroom with four or five stalls. It was handy, if you got there between busses.

Our second home in Waynesville was an upstairs room in a real house, and here we again had a sink with cold water and a two-burner hot plate, but no door. I made a door from three plywood panels. It wasn't really a door, but a folding screen. We shared this house with [seven others, including two children]. Our dog . . . well, we couldn't leave him behind, could we? Your first dog is practically your first child. He lived and slept in the car. Once in a while, when we had a fierce rainstorm, with thunder and lightning, I'd sit in the car and hold his paw. . . .

Our third try at housing (after returning from a month at Fort Riley in Kansas, where we rented a motel room with a bathroom and a two-burner hot plate) was a little farm six miles from the town. Now we had a fenced yard, a kitchen with a kerosene range that had an oven, a drilled well, and an outhouse that had a resident foot-long lizard. It also had beautiful fireflies at night, and the woods blazed red and pink from the redbuds and dogwoods.

Waynesville, Missouri is a town along the legendary Route 66 in central Missouri.[3] It's also in the heart of the Missouri Ozarks, a high plateau in the center of the United States, and near the center of the state, a location described as the "meeting place of the eastern timberlands and western prairies and of the southern cotton fields and the northern cornfields."[4] Mary's letters to her family throughout the time they spent in Missouri are full of comparisons between the weather and the plant life in the Ozarks and those of the Pacific Northwest. She liked the Missouri countryside, which around Waynesville would have been mostly prairie, and she was especially fond of the plentiful Missouri wildflowers, but she still hoped they would be able to leave after the initial eight to twelve weeks of basic training.

However, Mary especially hated the hot, humid weather, complaining that she didn't dare get behind on the laundry because

Alec sweat through two shirts a day and had only five uniform shirts to begin with, so she sometimes had to pull a shirt from the dirty laundry and iron it for him if she hadn't kept up with the almost-daily washing. I find myself wondering about the personal hygiene of those soldiers whose wives obeyed the order to stay at home since basic training kept them so busy that they clearly had little time for doing their own laundry. It must also have been challenging in that humidity to get clothes dry since everything would have been line dried. Mary also noted in a letter to her family that "you can't do anything in a hurry in this country. The sun

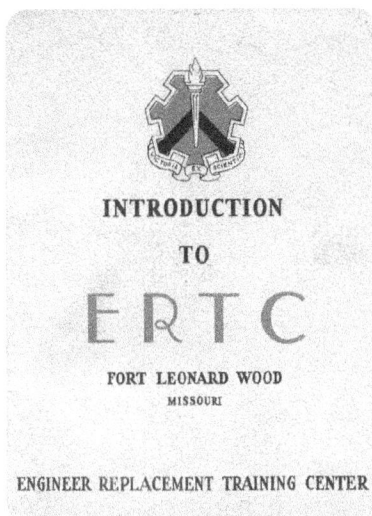

INTRODUCTION

TO

E R T C

FORT LEONARD WOOD
MISSOURI

ENGINEER REPLACEMENT TRAINING CENTER

Cover of the introductory brochure Alec received on his arrival at the Engineer Replacement Training Center at Fort Leonard Wood in Missouri.

is so intense you feel a little light-headed by the time you get to town anyway. . . . I have discovered what every southern girl knew long ago—that there's nothing as cool as a good old cotton slip in the summer. I bought one in Waynesville, and it's wonderful. It doesn't stick to me" (spring 1942).

The Army wives who followed their husbands to the fort in defiance of the military directive seem to have created an immediate sense of community while their husbands were undergoing training, and Mary told her family she would "not lack for entertainment" while at Fort Leonard Wood. She described the people she'd been meeting and events she'd been attending and confided in her parents that "no matter what rank their husbands are, they all have a hard time living on their salaries." Apparently, rents were so high that it was hard for anyone to be able to afford a desirable place to live, and she noted that the officers were "quite the drinking crowd, [which] takes a lot of money" (undated, probably spring 1942). Clearly, Mary and her friends were overcoming serious obstacles, not the least of which was the Army itself, in order to stay with their husbands, and an intense camaraderie between them was the natural result of their situation.

Alec at basic training at Fort Leonard Wood.

While Mary was enjoying social life in their new community, there was much for the young officer to learn. In addition to his own training, Alec was also training others as time passed from spring into summer. He was training with the Army's new repeating rifles, one of which had a recoil that left bruises on his shoulder. One day, after maneuvers, Alec showed Mary his bayonet, which she described to her family as "a most unhealthy looking thing."

After the first month in Missouri, Alec volunteered for special training at the Cooks and Bakers School at Fort Riley in Kansas (an extension of his mess management training the previous fall), and off they went for another new adventure. He studied nutrition—she admitted to helping him with at least one of his homework papers—and mess management and budgeting. While in Kansas he heard that some of the officers he knew at Fort Leonard Wood were being assigned to airport construction, which made him think he might like to request that duty when they returned since it could actually involve some "real engineering."

She wrote,

> Sometimes they give you a choice and sometimes they just send you out because you are needed somewhere. Fort Wood is a training center, and as long as we're there, he'll be training new recruits, which is hard work. This seems like a vacation here [at Fort Riley], after the kind of work Hub did at Fort Wood. The trouble is, he'll be all softened up when he gets back and will have to get broken in all over again, marching and doing rifle and bayonet drills and building bridges, etc. (undated, probably May 1942)

It's likely that Alec preferred the office and engineering work to the more physical aspects of soldiering.

Mary happily told her family that the folks in Kansas were friendly and helpful, and she and Alec were pleased to be housed in a motel with indoor plumbing and its own private bathroom while at Fort Riley, though she missed the Missouri wildflowers, which would have been a riot of color at that time of year. The biggest excitement at Fort Riley was the gossip among the Army wives that Gloria Vanderbilt and her new husband were supposedly also at the fort, so the wives spent most of their free time playing "looking for Gloria." The trouble was that none of them really knew what she looked like. A month later it was time to return to Fort Leonard Wood, so the celebrity search game was over . . . for the moment.

When Mary and Alec returned to Missouri, they rented a room in a large house, but in spite of the available niceties, Mary missed "the shanty," even with its lack of amenities, because Pete had to stay outside, "so sad and doleful on his chain," and there wasn't much privacy. She also told her parents that they recently received a letter from the Navy Yard, telling Alec that his job would be waiting for him when he got back from his military duty. Trouble was, he didn't want it. Instead, he was hoping to be restored to the civil service lists after the war in hopes of getting some other civil service job elsewhere. In this same letter, Mary also had some good news about her own professional aspirations: an article she sent to *Good Housekeeping* had been returned to her with a request to revise and resubmit, so she was hopeful of becoming a published author soon.

Alec (back row, center) with other soldiers, presumably his fellow officers at Fort Leonard Wood.

The next thing her family heard was that if they continued to stay at Fort Leonard Wood, Alec and Mary would be on a list for some new housing that would be available in August. It wouldn't be furnished, other than a pull-down Murphy bed, and it would be farther out of town, but it sounded like the privacy, along with a real stove and a bathroom they wouldn't have to share with anyone else, was worth the price to them. Alec returned to his training duties, which seemed at this point to consist primarily of training units of "colored" soldiers. (Considered offensive today, the terms "colored" or "Negro" were then the self-designations preferred by people of African heritage.*[5]) Of their future at the fort, Mary wrote:

> The adjutant and Alec's company commander both told him he wouldn't be here long [this time]. Since he's been gone, every other lieutenant in the company has left: one to Fort Lewis, one

---

* According to Kee Malesky of New England Public Radio, "[Colored] was adopted in the United States by emancipated slaves as a term of racial pride after the end of the American Civil War. It was rapidly replaced from the late 1960s as a self-designation by Black and later by African-American."

to Florida, one to Massachusetts. They are replacing the white
officers with negro officers in the negro outfit just as fast as
they can, which is the reason they told Alec he would be leaving
soon, but it might be that he would just be moved to a white
company. At any rate, we hope it will be someplace entirely
different. (undated, probably summer 1942)

In the several months Alec spent assigned to Fort Leonard
Wood, it was clear that he was one of the junior officers they kept
around longer than the required eight to twelve weeks because
he had skills they needed. There was the special training in mess
management, and Mary explained that he was also sent off for
several days to "pontoon school" to learn how to build bridges
with his battalion; but the most interesting part of his job duties,
and the one Mary wrote about often because it put them in a
complicated position in relation to some of their new friends, was
that he was charged with training new infantry recruits in the
Negro division.

Nearly 80 years after the end of the Civil War, the Army was
still segregated at the start of WWII, and in spite of some small
experimentation with mixed companies during the later years of
the war, segregation in the armed forces remained official policy
until President Truman changed it in 1948.[6] In the early days
at Fort Leonard Wood, the officers in the Negro regiments were
generally white, and many of the black soldiers were relegated to
non-combat service, being seen as unfit for combat duty. Black
junior officers were trained and commissioned, but they were assigned exclusively to the Negro regiments and not allowed to command white soldiers under any circumstances.[7] Alec's training in
mess and inventory management likely was part of the reason he
was kept at Fort Leonard Wood for so long, because supply maintenance, transportation, and food service in the military would
have been among the major non-combat jobs the Army deemed
acceptable for soldiers of color during WWII.[8]

Missouri, a former slave state, was part of the segregated
South, and in the early 1940s, courts were still upholding segregation laws in Missouri as they did elsewhere in the South, in
spite of regular civil rights challenges.[9] It wasn't until years after
the war was over that integration started to become a reality. Mary
and Alec were always tolerant of and open to people from other
races, but they were in a situation where reaching across the

Mary and Alec at Fort Leonard Wood.

racial divide wasn't accepted on either side and possibly would have posed risks to any blacks they befriended.

And, of course, there were challenges in the Army's expectations for soldiers of color as well. In a letter written after their return from Fort Riley, Mary shared some of the issues in Alec's work with his troops:

> They're having quite a time teaching their colored boys how to shoot. Yesterday the Company Commander's group shot for record and he was very much disappointed in how few of them qualified. Alec hopes his will do better. Anyway it is normal in the white companies for about 80% to qualify, and the colored boys never do better than 30%. Alec thinks they don't make the training elemental enough for the boys and rush them through too fast.

THE CAVALRY SCHOOL MESS
FORT RILEY, KANSAS

May 4 1942

SUBJECT: The Cavalry School Mess.

To: *2nd Lt Harold A. Daniels C.E.*

1. I am directed by the Board of Governors to inform you that you automatically become *Temporary* member of The Cavalry School Mess upon reporting for duty at Fort Riley.

2. The initiation fees and dues set forth in the Constitution and By-Laws, a copy of which is attached.

Temporary members are not required to pay an initiation fee.

3. If you are now a non-active member of the Mess, please give the approximate date of your original membership, by indorsement hereon.

4. The Mess activities include:

Hops, Hunts, Races and Horse Shows,
Golf, Polo, Tennis, Trapshooting,
(including skeet course), and
Swimming.

5. The Bar and Dining Room are open daily and are available to officers, their families, and their guests.

6. It is a custom of the Service for an Officer upon joining a station to affiliate himself with the Mess of that station. Exception to this custom may be made in individual cases.

7. If you do not desire to avail yourself of the privileges of the Mess, request return of this letter with an indorsement through your immediate Commanding Officer to that effect within seven days from date.

Secretary & Treasurer.

Ft. Riley, Kans. 2-9-42—810—1000.

Letter regarding Alec's temporary status at Fort Riley in Kansas.

The way Mary refers to the colored soldiers as boys may sound like casual racism from a contemporary vantage point, but she actually called all young soldiers "boys," never men, in her letters home, making no evident distinction between black and white soldiers. It's also likely that the lack of shooting skills among black servicemen was partly the result of the post-Civil War "black codes" that banned Blacks from owning guns in a number of southern states and were not rescinded until the 1950s or 60s.[10] She explained that, in the early weeks, Alec got the Negro

Mary in her Fort Leonard Wood T-shirt.

soldiers when they were about halfway through their training. Eventually he was training them from the beginning of their time at the fort, which meant he had to check them in, get their histories, assign them to barracks, and generally get all their details arranged. After he met his newest crop of recruits, she reported more experience and education in this group than before, including a college graduate or two, and even one soldier with a master's in chemistry and another who was a graduate of Tuskegee Institute. Shortly after the arrival of this new group, Mary and Alec were both invited to dinner with the colored soldiers, which she described with enthusiasm:

> We had dinner with the colored boys in their mess at their invitation. The Company Commander and wife were there, too, as well as a whole carload of girls from St. Louis (colored girls, of course, and good looking, too). They introduced the two officers and all the colored girls, but not the two officers' wives, which made us feel a little slighted. We had a good dinner with fried chicken and no napkins. The ladies table rated tablecloths and government-issue china. The rest of the boys ate out of their mess kits. The cups are so big you have to hold them with both hands and they have no handles. This was lots of fun, we thought, and the boys must have been impressed with the swell

way they got treated in the army. You see, this was about their second meal here.

Though she didn't mention it often in her letters, there were clearly some tensions between the white and black battalions on base. In another letter about a soldiers-only party after company maneuvers one day, she shared her experience and thoughts about those tensions while she was waiting for Alec in the car outside:

> They had a turkey dinner and beer and soda pop and then they sang a lot of lovely spirituals including Swing Low, and I sat there and sang, too, and everyone had a good time. My, how the colored boys can sing! Afterwards while I was still waiting for Alec, one of the colored lieutenants came out and talked to me until [he] came. There are three colored officers, just as friendly as puppies, and they always come out and talk until Alec comes. One of them is getting married soon. I enjoy them, but I live in mortal fear that Grace [another officer's wife] will see me talking to them some day. Weldon's company [presumably Grace's husband] is right across the road from Alec's. They had a big pow-wow at the club the other night trying to decide what to do about keeping the colored officers from coming in. As the constitution stands, any officer is entitled to the privileges of the club. We drove Alec's company commander back to the barracks with us from the company the other night, and he said he'd been doing a lot of reading up on the colored situation and no one has found a bit of difference between colored and white blood or colored and white minds or anything else. He's from California, and I guess out there on the coast we don't have the feeling about negroes they do back here. Alec said that when the colored officers (there are three of them, all in Alec's company) come into the mess, the table where they sit stays vacant except for them until every other seat is taken. So, it's a bad situation with our sympathies going to them.

Though the race relations on base worried her, soon Mary had other worries to write about: Alec was being sent overseas. In spite of Mary's persistent hope for a posting on the West Coast at Fort Lewis in Washington State, especially so she and Pete could stay nearby, they were notified in early September of 1942 that,

Close-up of Alec in his day-to-day uniform.

after more than five months in the Midwest, Alec was ordered East. Most likely he would ship out from there to somewhere in Europe. They were told they must pack separately and be ready to move at a moment's notice. This news didn't please Mary at all, and she was probably trying to figure out a way to be able to follow Alec, wherever he went. The idea of separation from her beloved husband was something truly unthinkable for her, no matter how proud of his patriotism she might have been. When she wrote the first letter home about his deployment, they didn't have his real orders yet, and her fear was palpable:

> We don't know yet where Hub is going or from where he'll be sent, but we'll probably know the port of embarkation tomorrow. Of course he might be there a day or a week or more; you can't tell about anything at all. . . . I tell Alec that

HEADQUARTERS
ENGINEER REPLACEMENT TRAINING CENTER
Fort Leonard Wood, Missouri

Aug 4, 1942

SUBJECT: Sunstroke

TO : All Unit Commanders, ERTC

1. At the first formation after receipt, the following will be read to each platoon by platoon commanders:

I. Two deaths have resulted from sunstroke in this center last month. To prevent further deaths, it is desired that all personnel be prepared to recognize early symptoms and render the most effective immediate first aid.

II. Early symptoms:
a. A person who has been perspiring, ceases to perspire, and skin becomes dry and hot.
b. A person who does not perspire among others who are perspiring freely.
c. Headaches.
d. Dizziness.
e. Vomiting.
f. Delirium.
g. Unconsciousness.
h. Convulsions.
These symptoms may develop fairly gradually over a period of about 3 or 4 hours or all may develop suddenly.
Upon noticing the early symptoms, the man should be immediately removed to the coolest shady place, stripped completely, and cooled off by sponging face, head, and body with cold water, while fanning body with anything available. Call for medical help or ambulance and transport person to hospital. The man's insistence that he feels all right should be disregarded.
Due to damage to brain and nervous system by the high temperature, later treatment may be of no avail. Cooling the body immediately and thoroughly is of the utmost value in saving life.

III. Precautions:
a. While exposed to direct heat, i.e. out in sun, troops should be clothed,--wear hat, jacket, or shirt.
b. Troops should not be worked for long periods of time, at least not more than one hour, on hot sunny days without opportunity to seek shade and cooling.
c. On hot days, troops should be provided with additional allowance of cool water, at least double the allowance on marches and training details.
d. Ice water must not be served to heated troops, but may be put in canteens for later use.
e. Troops should be instructed and reminded to take additional salt on hot days. 4 to 6 salt tablets taken, one at a time, at intervals, or heavy seasoning of food with salt.
f. Men in the older age groups who come from sedentary occupations are more prone to develop sunstroke.

By order of Colonel BESSON:

G. N. ANDERSON,
Captain, Corps of Engineers,
Adjutant.

DISTRIBUTION: C-4

Reproduced at Hq., 7th E. T. Group   6 August 1942

Letter given to all officers at Fort Leonard Wood, warning of the signs of sunstroke.

if he gives me a month or so maybe I'll get so I can talk about it (instead of just crying). There's not a thing in the world to be done about it. It would have happened later if not now, of course. . . . Everyone is getting scared stiff now they seem to be sending so many out.

She explained that a friend's husband was being sent in the same company, and she was glad to have a girlfriend with whom to travel and commiserate as they tried to stay as close to their husbands as possible until the last possible minute. She made arrangements for her mother to come out to Missouri to get the dog and their car and take them both back to Oregon, while she followed Alec east to New York City: to Fort Hamilton and the New York Port of Embarkation in Brooklyn, to be exact. Fraying nerves, transportation mix-ups, and communication delays caused Mary quite a bit of stress on the way from Kansas City to LaGuardia airport, and she was extremely disappointed at never being able to see the lights of New York City because of the constant blackouts. But in the middle of all the tension, she finally saw Gloria Vanderbilt and her husband at the Kansas City airport on her way to New York. Although she was too shy to speak to Gloria, many years later Mary wrote a story about their chance encounter in the ladies' room. Clearly the chance meeting made an impression because though Mary rarely titled her stories, she called this one "How I Almost Meet Gloria, or Ships That Pass in the Night." She first set the stage of a bustling airport and the handsome and obviously wealthy young couple who entered the waiting area, attracting lots of attention there, including Mary herself, who was just beginning to realize who she was watching:

> After a few minutes, I strolled into the ladies' lounge and stood in front of the mirror putting on my lipstick, and the girl I had been watching came in, too. We were alone there, and we stood together with our lipsticks, and we smiled at each other and then we went out. . . . Later, on my plane to New York, Gloria and I had an imaginary conversation as we stood side by side looking in the mirror of the Kansas City Airport Ladies Lounge:

> "I see you're from Fort Riley," I said to her impulsively.
> "How did you know that?"
> "Your husband's boots (Fort Riley was home to a cavalry unit)."
> "Oh, yes."
> "We were there this spring. We loved the place. Are you being transferred?"
> "Oh, no. We fly to California for the weekend."
> "I'm going to New York. If I'm lucky, my husband will still be there when I arrive. He has his overseas orders."

And then she would say, "Oh, you poor dear! Do you have a
   place to stay in New York?"
"I'll check in at some small hotel."
"But, listen," she would say, "you could stay at my house.
   There's lots of room."

Such a lovely daydream! When Mary got to New York, Alec
was still there, so she was able to share her exciting celebrity encounter with him directly. More importantly, they had two more
weeks together before he had to sail, which probably felt a bit like
a dream to both of them. They found a room to rent in Brooklyn
near the fort and spent some time exploring the city together on
days when he was not called to the fort for travel preparation
briefings, but finally on September 24, 1942, approximately six
months after his basic training began in Missouri, Alec embarked
for parts unknown while Mary returned home alone to wait out
the war, both hoping against hope that it would only be a short
separation. Little did they know how long it really would be before
they were reunited.

*Alec doing a Sad Sack impression. Perhaps he just got his orders to report for
overseas duty.*

3

COMMUNICATION CHAOS AND OTHER CHALLENGES

EARLY DAYS, FALL 1942

After they said their goodbyes on that late-September day in New York, Mary and Alec weren't able to communicate regularly with each other for many weeks because of the vagaries of wartime communication, in spite of the fact that each of them was most likely writing and mailing a letter to the other nearly every day. In this age of instant online communication, I doubt that many of us would have patience with long silences from loved ones, especially during wartime. But patience was exactly what the soldiers and their families had to develop after the United States' entry into WWII, especially during those early months. As military scholar Ken Lawrence writes, "It was immediately evident [after Pearl Harbor] that rapid, reliable postal communication was not just a military necessity, but an essential element of national morale."[1] However, it wasn't always easy because, "According to the official report *Army Postal Service During World War II*, 'Tremendous demands for rapid transportation of essential equipment and supplies during the early days of the war consumed practically all available space aboard aircraft and as a result very little mail was transported overseas by air.'"[2] This prioritized demand for supplies and equipment also meant that little mail from home was delivered in a timely fashion, even after it finally arrived at its destination.

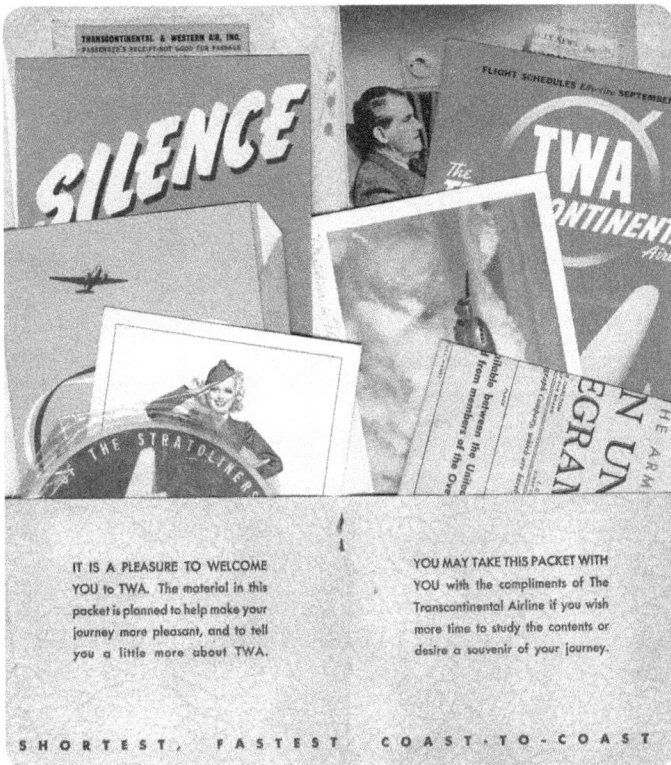

This was Mary's airline welcome packet when she followed Alec to New York before he was sent overseas.

Of the dozens of letters Alec wrote to Mary in his first months away from her, nearly all had some reference to his anxiety about not hearing from her and not knowing how or what she was doing. He knew Mary was an avid and faithful letter writer, so he was certain her letters to him simply had to be on their way somehow, and yet he worried that letters might somehow be going astray and that there might be better ways for them to communicate beyond regular airmail letters. This was a theme he returned to again and again in those early months. One of his earliest letters from abroad shows that he was thinking of how to communicate more quickly and efficiently from the beginning:

> If I were you I should look into the sending of V mail, as I understand that a great deal of time can be saved in sending letters that way.

As usual there are so many things that I would like to say and can't that letter writing is very difficult, so I will have to say only that I am feeling and have felt fine and I love you very much.

Take care of yourself and I will be expecting about a dozen letters, which you must have written by now. The pen [her parting gift to him] is working fine and it closes with I love you, which is meant to the utmost.

p.s. I think you are only supposed to write on one side of the paper so that it can be censored.

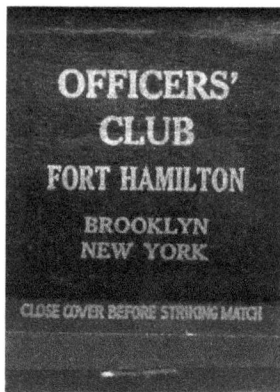

Matchbook cover from the Officers' Club at Fort Hamilton in Brooklyn, NY, where Alec reported before being sent overseas.

Prior to the development of V-Mail, or Victory Mail, by Eastman Kodak, one of the only ways to reach loved ones abroad was through airmail, which was often more expensive than regular mail and completely unsuited for any urgent messages. V-mail allowed for faster, less expensive correspondence. Letters were first censored and then transferred to microfilm before being shipped abroad. Once letters arrived at their destination, the negatives

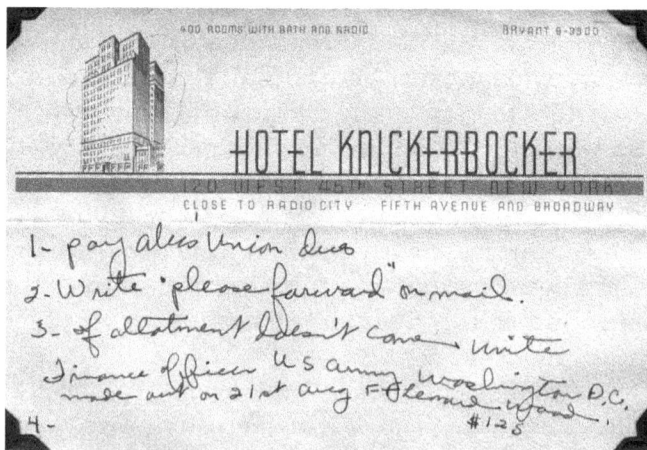

Mary made these notes on her hotel stationery of things that must be attended to after Alec left.

*Mary at her parents' farm in rural Oregon after her return home.
She's wearing a dress she purchased during her two weeks in New
York before Alec was finally sent overseas.*

would be blown up to normal size and printed before being delivered to individual soldiers. This meant saving valuable shipping space that was needed for necessary war materials. This use of microfilm saved the postal system thousands of tons of shipping space, fitting the equivalent of 37 mail bags' worth of letters into just one.[3] Eventually, Alec wrote that while it was efficient, he was not particularly fond of V-mail:

> I am close enough to things to really know how the mail goes.
> The V mail I believe is more certain but is just not personal
> enough. It's okay for writing short notes and especially good for
> notes to relations, but not near human or close enough for me
> to send to my dear wif*. You see, Mary, I must have something
> that gives me more personal contact with you, as you are my
> moving force, or I should say you are the force that moves me.
> (October 26, 1942)

He complains about the difficulties he anticipates in getting her letters, though he definitely does not want her to stop writing. He most likely knows by now where he will be headed next, and I

---

* Wif, an adopted Britishism, likely picked up during his stay in England, was his new pet name for Mary, possibly mirroring the more widely accepted nickname "Hub," which she used for him.

believe he was already a member of Eisenhower's support staff by this time, but he obviously can't tell her anything about it:

> Perhaps I better say that as far as I can find out I won't be able to get any letters that you mail for an indefinite period which might vary from a week to quite a few weeks, but even so I don't want you to stop writing as I will eventually get a permanent (APO) address at which I can receive mail. (October 12, 1942)

The APO, Army Post Office, address system was for troops in the Army and Air Force and, for obvious security reasons, did not use any actual geographic information, though the APO numbers did, in fact, correspond to certain geographic locations. Each APO number had a "postal concentration center" within the United States (for Alec's APO 512—used for both North Africa and Italy— the address was New York), where mail was switched from the domestic postal system to the military transport system at no extra cost to the sender. More importantly, mail sent to soldiers overseas cost the same as a regular domestic letter, though it was handled quite differently and sent via military transport once sorted at the concentration center.[4]

Another major challenge in their ability to communicate was censorship and the fact that once soldiers left basic training, they

This was the card Mary received after Alec arrived in England. The APO on this card was changed to 512 when he left England and remained the same after that for the duration of the war. The changing APOs could account for some of the early mail mix-ups Alec complained about.

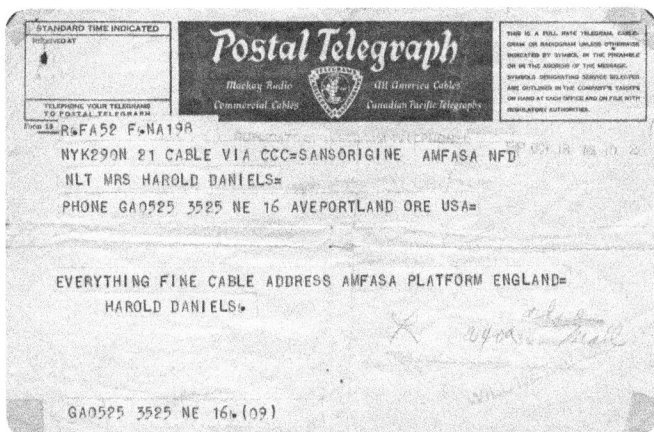

One of Alec's early cables home from England, giving Mary his cable address.

couldn't tell their loved ones much, if anything, about where they were going or what they were doing until such information became public and had been reported in the media. In another early letter, Alec wrote, "You see, so many things are not to be mentioned that it is very hard to say anything more than I love you." He was finally able to tell her in early October that he was "somewhere in England and feeling very well," but that he would be moving around a lot while he was there. He was never able to be explicit in his letters about exactly what he was doing in England, but for over two years, the British had been holding off the Germans on their own, and many of their major cities and military sites had been bombed during the Blitz from September 1940 to May 1941,[5] so there was undoubtedly plenty of work for an American utilities engineer to do in helping to rebuild important infrastructure for British Allies. At this point in time, the Allies were, with the utmost secrecy, preparing for what they called the TORCH invasion of Oran and Algiers in North Africa; though it's unlikely that a utilities engineer was involved in any way in battle planning. However, after only a few weeks in Britain, Alec was sent to North Africa in the second wave of soldiers involved in the occupation of Algiers.

Though most Americans know of the importance of D-Day and the Normandy invasion in 1944 as a decisive event for the War in Europe, much less is known about the invasion and occupation of North Africa in November of 1942. Before it turned its military

——ARMY——
U. S. EXAMINER No.

GPO 16—25701-1

*This is one of the stickers that was affixed to every letter
Mary received from Alec while he was away. It told her the
mail had been opened and approved by the Army censor.*

attention to Japan, the United States and its Allies needed an established location in Europe from which to fight the Nazis, at the
time perceived as the greater threat, and the Mediterranean region
seemed to be just the place from which they could mobilize major
military convoys. Given that Italy was allied with Germany, North
Africa's location on the southwestern coast of the Mediterranean
Sea seemed like an excellent option. The British were already engaged in fighting the Germans in Tunisia and seemed to hold
the advantage, at least temporarily, so instead of an invasion of
Europe, the Allies focused instead on North Africa. In support
of this plan, in late October of 1942, the largest war fleet ever
to set sail from American waters headed to North Africa. A decisive victory there under the command of General Eisenhower
on November 8-11, 1942, and the minimal resistance the Allies
encountered in Algiers, laid the groundwork for a successful occupation and establishment of Allied Force Headquarters (AFHQ)
there, to which Alec was assigned as a utilities engineer. He was
in or near combat zones throughout the war but was not a combat engineer.

It seemed his letters to Mary were mostly getting through in
those early days, but he didn't hear from her at all until they had
been apart for over six weeks, and it was a cable, not a letter he
received. He was still in England at this point in early November,
and the TORCH invasion was imminent, but the support troops
for the occupation of North Africa (including utilities engineers
like Alec) would not follow until after the invasion was successful,
thus not arriving until late in November, none of which he could
share with her, so he wrote in generalities about his movements:

> Well I received your first telegram today, just 18 days after
> it had arrived in England. It took that long for it to catch up

with me. Sure am glad to know you are home all right and hope to get some mail one of these days. . . . By the time you get this letter my address will probably have changed, as I move quite a bit, so I wouldn't send any more cables unless I send a new address or ask for one. I see you used my serial number so I guess you understand about how it should be sent as the postal directory lists my address by serial number. When I do cable my address I'll give you the cable address and also the postal address—care of postmaster New York will be understood. (November 7, 1942)

Finally, on November 20, after 55 lonely days with no word from her other than the single cable in October, he got the first of Mary's letters. But it wasn't the first one she actually wrote; in fact, it was fairly current and let him know she'd been getting at least some of his letters home:

The gods of good fortune have been smiling over me, and I received my first two letters this morning. And in record time, too, as a total of only eight days was required for delivery, the postmarks being the 12th and 13th of November. Surely you can realize what it means to me to hear of how you're getting along and from some of my other letters how fortunate such fast delivery is. (November 20, 1942)

In addition to the perpetual complaints about the mail service, he wrote to her in those early months about the things on his mind that he could share with her without fear of censorship, which included the various technologies that currently obsessed him (mostly radios and cameras, items he was fascinated with his whole life), rationing, military life (especially what soldiers did for entertainment and in their leisure time), the people he'd been meeting in England, his general health, what he wanted to do when he returned from the war, some general philosophizing about war, and most of all, how he felt about her and their marriage. As relative newlyweds, they celebrated their second wedding anniversary at Fort Leonard Wood and ultimately would celebrate their third, fourth, and fifth anniversaries a world apart from each other.

As yet, neither Alec nor any other Americans had a real concept about the possible duration of the war. In the fall of 1942,

Print the complete address in plain block letters in the panel below, and your return address in the space provided. Use typewriter, dark ink, or pencil. Write plainly. Very small writing is not suitable.

No.

MRS. H. A. DANIELS

3525 N.E. 56 AVE

PORTLAND   OREGON

[CENSOR'S STAMP]

1st Lt. HaroldA. Daniels
Eng. Det. Utilities

(Sender's name)

APO 512 c/o pm

(Sender's address)

New York, New York

April 10, 1943   -4

(Date)

Dearest, Well the deadlock finally broke and the mail is coming through in bunches. The day before yesterday, three; yesterday, three; and today five, so you can see that I am well off in that respect. In another respect as you know the cities of tunis and bizertia have been lost by the germains so that we are all better off in that respect. They had a victory parade here today as the French are very enthusiastic about the whole thing. As far as we go here why it is just the natural thing and we don't get the least excited about it. I can gather that there was more excitemnet in the states over it than there was among the soldiers. Of course the faster that we take things from the germans the faster it will be until I get to come back to you again. I finally received the bill for the work on the car, and from that I can tell that you practically had a new motor built. It needed it even if the block hadn't been cracked, as you can remember the time in Kansas when we ran it without oil and it began to squeek and I wondered what was wrong and soon found out when we stoped the filling station and there was no oil in the crate. After that it never did work as it should and used lots of oil and made lots of noise, so now if you have the woodwork in good order then we will be all set to go traveling. Now that Africa is all sewed up I wonder where we will be going next, and I am not the only one. The soldiers try to guess where the next front will be. Some say ____ and some say ____ and some even say ____. Now I wouldn't go so far as to say that we would go to ____ that just a little to far from Africa although it would be a nice trip. An speaking of trips reminds me that we are supposed to have a trip one of these days and were would you like to go with me on that trip. I was disappointed in one of your letters today you didn't send me any gum, and I am still waiting for an 8oz package. I have to say what we say to the men around here when they get a little mixe up in what they are doing. "Get on the Ball" One of the men received a magazine with with the cover and the edges all cut off so as to make it less than 8oz. and a bar of chocolate (large) would just clear the line. You should here us around here when the mail begins to come in or doesn't come in it doesn't make any difference. We say "Smeed" go check the mail. (Smeed is the mail clerk) and he goes and checks to see if there is any mail. We look over what he brings back and read it then right away it is Smeed go check the mail. The post office ask him today why he didn't bring over his bed and just sleep there all the time so that he could bring each letter back as it came in. You have $25 dollars still coming from the government on you allotment, as the $150 should have started with the check you received in January. the first part of January. Write The Disbursing Officer, 213 Washington St. New Wark New Jersey. and see if they won't straighten it out. Well I guess I will close now as it is time to leave.

Lots of love from your hub
Alec

V-MAIL

This is an example of Alec's humorous self-censoring in one of his V-mail letters home.

the song "Praise the Lord and Pass the Ammunition" was number two on the popular charts and reflected the sense of American optimism on the home front, and Alec's own youthful optimism had him regularly writing about coming home as soon as they got the situation handled, which he presumed would be soon. His early references to the war usually involved the words "this mess" or "this business," and he constantly told her things were going well enough that he should be home again in no time. He also shared with her his thoughts about the war, which seemed to be optimistic at this point about the outcome of this war in spite of his distaste for war in general. Shortly after he set off in September of 1942 he told her:

> Some day it will be over and we can look back on it as a great experience and think what a good time we had up until we had to part for a short while. I know I have enjoyed military life except the point of having to leave you, and think that you probably have, too. Anyway we have this damned old war on our hands and we will just have to make the best of it and trust that things are for the best. As far as I can see we couldn't have avoided the war anyway. . . . Personally I can't justify this whole business but at the same time I can't see any way it can be avoided. . . . Perhaps I am a pessimist but how can you change a world that has been having wars for as long as it has existed?

He also tried to explain to her why he didn't refuse the commission and stay at the Navy Yard in Bremerton, mostly because he didn't like the work and wanted to do something more important, challenging, and fulfilling. "I rather like military work, and if it wasn't for the uncertainty of the war, it would be a good job. So now you can see partially why I didn't resign and stay home with you. You see I don't want to leave you any more than you want me to leave. We are just a couple of gears in a machine, which are being separated by someone or some force unknown" (undated, probably late September 1942). After about a month of separation, he tried, once again, to explain in more detail his feelings about the war and his place in it.

> Anyway, my sweet, since I can't be near to you in person, I can write letters which sometimes help to pass away the troubled times and also make a great outlet for the thoughts of a puzzled individual. And I am a puzzled individual. Here I gave up a job that would have kept me near my wife, and traveled away; yet even though at present I would give anything to be near you, I can't say that I regret the move; and if that isn't a puzzling situation there just isn't any thought that is puzzling. You know men are a queer bunch, and your hub is the queerest of the lot! What he wants is to have his cake and eat it, too. As far as the "war" is concerned, I can't say that I can see the actual point

in it, nor can I see where it is going to lead to something better as good as things were; but I do think that if it weren't for the stand we have taken, it could lead to things much worse. You see we lived in a state of being very happy within ourselves and with what we had. So I don't know how you feel, but if something had changed my way of living, by which I mean the time I had to spend as I saw fit and in our own amusement, I would have lost something that would have taken the joy out of living. Now if you don't enjoy living, why live? So you can see that it is sort of a personal problem with me.

The enemy, or more properly the other side, stood for something which would have made what I enjoyed living for impossible, so it just narrowed down to a personal problem of what side of the fence I was going to stay on, the side that let someone else do all the work or the side that got in and helped a little. As far as my helping more here than where I was, I don't rightly know, but I do know that my importance, at least to myself, in the navy yard was very small, and I felt perhaps I could do better here. Then, too, even though I am a quiet

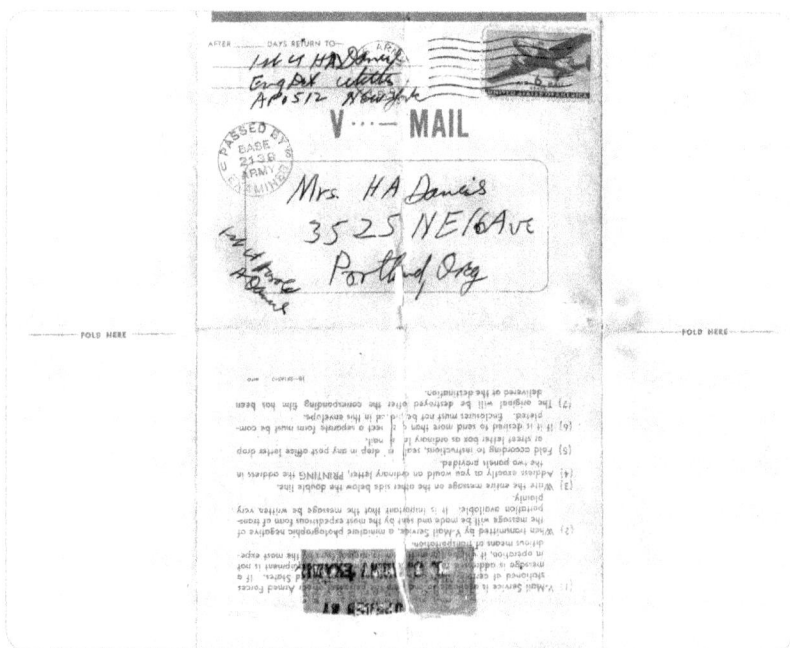

The exterior of that self-censored V-mail letter.

individual, I have certain ambitions for personal gain, not with respect to money, but just with respect to me as a person in doing important things, and this business just seemed to be a means for becoming more important. (October 26, 1942)

While Alec was trying to find meaning and purpose in his situation overseas, Mary was undoubtedly trying to discover her place on the home front as well. Once he left for Europe, she and Pete moved back home to NE Portland to live with her parents and her younger, unmarried sister for the duration of the war. As a result of America's entrance into the war, things were changing dramatically all over the United States.

Americans rose to the challenge of doing whatever was necessary to support the war effort. They bought billions of dollars' worth of bonds to help defray the cost of the war. They saved metals and fats to be recycled into military material and collected rubber until the nation successfully produced synthetic rubber, necessary because shipping lanes to obtain natural rubber were blocked. They planted 'victory gardens' to provide fruits and vegetables for personal use. 'Use it up, wear it out, make it do or do without' became the slogan of the day.[6]

Most significantly, as men entered the military, women entered the workforce in record numbers, doing the jobs that had once been taken mostly by the men around them. Mary was no exception. After two and a half years of being a housewife, she started work in the fall of 1942 as a sales clerk at a major local department store, Meier & Frank, in downtown Portland, most likely commuting to work via the streetcar or local bus system. Given her lifelong love of gardening, and the fact that her parents owned a small farm on the rural outskirts of the Portland metro area, Mary would have helped out with a family victory garden. Everyone was making his or her own contribution to the war effort.

4

EXPLORING A NEW PLACE, EXPLORING A NEW LIFE

ENGLAND, FALL 1942

Though anxiety regarding mail service and the lack of letters from Mary tended to dominate his early letters, Alec was also a soldier overseas for the first time and was quite busy with preparations for the active involvement of American soldiers in the war. While censorship prevented him from telling her anything about his location or his military work, he had been able to tell her that he was in England, though he never did identify specific locations other than one short trip to London rather late in his time on the island. In one of her short essays, Mary claimed he had been in both

Alec was confused at first by the British system of money and he wanted Mary to see one of their bills, so he sent her a shilling in one of his early letters.

Alec didn't have a camera with him in England, and he couldn't tell Mary exactly where he was, but he praised the English landscape and sent her a packet of postcards from Oxford, about 50 miles northwest of London.

England and Scotland during the war, but his letters don't really give much of a clue as to exactly where he might have been, other than to say he was in the countryside, which is rather plentiful in that island nation. American soldiers started arriving in England in January of 1942, and Eisenhower took command of the US forces in Europe in June of the same year. Alec arrived in England in October of 1942 and was, presumably, assigned to utilities engineering duties at various American military bases from Cornwall to Scotland. By the end of the war, over 1.5 million American servicemembers had either been stationed in or passed through Great Britain, and the National WWII Museum reports:

> Because many of [sic] servicemen had never been abroad before, the War Department sent with them a pamphlet called *Instructions for American Servicemen in Britain.* This pamphlet was designed to familiarize these servicemen with life in Britain-the history, culture, even the slang. The pamphlet also encouraged the men to get along with the British to help defeat Hitler. It is filled with great advice like "Don't be a show off," "NEVER criticize the King or Queen," and "The British don't know how to make a good cup of coffee. You don't know how to make a good cup of tea. It's an even swap." The pamphlet

concludes by telling the servicemen that while in Great Britain, their slogan should be "*It is always impolite to criticize your hosts; it is militarily stupid to criticize your allies.*"[1]

Because Alec moved around quite a bit, it's hard to know where he was when he encountered British civilians, and in his first letter mentioning his location, he was only able to say, "Well, here I am somewhere in England and am feeling very well. There isn't very much that I can say about this place except that the country and people are very nice" (October 8, 1942). In a letter the next day, he told her a bit more about his surroundings, comparing them to the temperate and green Pacific Northwest:

> This English country is much like our Willamette Valley and is very picturesque. The weather so far could be compared to that we have at Bremerton, so the sudden change from Waynesville has made me a bit chilly especially on the feet. And of course the fact that they have heat rationing here is new to me.
>
> The English money is a little hard to figure for making change, as the system of coins and their relationship to each other is about as bad as our foot and inches. (October 9, 1942)

He also had some difficulty understanding some of the British dialects he encountered, saying, "The people speak English, but many times they are hard to understand; yet it doesn't seem as though the country is foreign" (October 9, 1942). Mary must have encouraged him before he left to make friends with the people he would meet and work with because he wrote to her that he remembered her advice, but he didn't want to go to a pub with other guys in his unit just to meet young girls, in whom he had no interest; nor did he wish to drink beer, which he disliked. What he did tell her was this:

> There is one thing here that I do like very much; that is going to some of the out of the way pubs, which most of the soldiers stay away from, and engaging in conversation with the British about different things of the day. Last night it was on credit buying, which has been abolished here due to the war. I can't say that I am a great talker but they, the English, ask me many questions about things in America and seem to be very much interested in both the condition of things in America and my

opinions on subjects which affect the life of everyone here. (October 16, 1942)

It seemed that his outlook on talking to the English (i.e., not trying to pick up girls and not getting drunk) also won him a bit of notoriety in at least one of the pubs he visited:

I was told one evening by a woman in one of the pubs that I was a queer person, not at all like most of the American soldiers that come into those pubs. You see there are many girls here who have men in the army whom they haven't seen for several years. Now this is a drinking country, and beer is consumed here much in the manner we do cokes, and the presence of girls in the pubs is as common as mustard on our hot dogs. Well these girls go to the pubs to have their drinks and sit around to talk to the soldiers. Of course there are a few who have no particular sense of values in our outlook on things, but in the main the English girls one meets there are very sincere and show a remarkable ability to take things on the chin without showing their trouble on the surface. But when you start a talk you can get the real conditions that exist in their heart. Now it is possible that I talk more about their problems and try to get an insight into what the war is doing to them and the English way of living that made one say I was a queer person, as mostly the soldiers here that I know engage in a bunch of pitter patter. (October 26, 1942)

Without revealing his specific location, he described his surroundings, including a beautiful landscape with a flowing stream

While Alec was using his ration book for candy in England, Mary was likely using hers for just about everything at home, including meat, dairy products, dried fruits, jams and jellies, and many other food and non-food items.

and lots of trees, and he mentioned the "grass" on the roofs, which probably meant he was in a rural part of the country where there were thatched houses. He also noted that walking into town was usually an easy thing to do from his quarters. In another letter, he told her about some of the interesting differences he noticed between England and America:

> You know there are quite a few things that the British do that are different from the way we do things. For one thing they have a more sensible way of using a knife and fork together. An Englishman holds his fork in his left hand the same as we hold a knife and holds the knife in the right hand as we hold a fork and when eating do not change hands but use the left hand to put food to the mouth. If the food requires no knife then the fork is held, as we do, in the right hand. Another thing, which is queer, was a type of toilet they have here. You pull the chain, nothing happens; you let the chain go, and the toilet flushes. (October 23, 1942)

In addition to his observations about the English people, he shared with her what the guys in his unit did for entertainment when they were not on duty and not going to a pub.

Going to the movies was a regular activity for American GIs abroad, and I remember from my youth that both my parents loved going to the movies, though many were foreign films that had no appeal for a teenager like me. Alec told Mary about most of the movies he was able to see, and occasionally he would review the films for her. He explained that the free films were provided by "some service organization" (likely the Red Cross or USO), and the

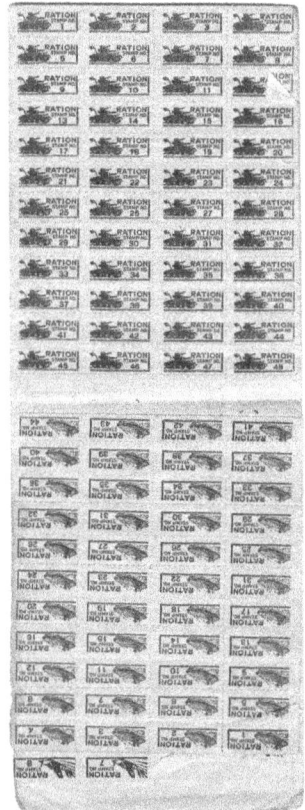

Mary put her unused ration coupons in her scrapbook after the war. They look similar to the S&H green stamps that were popular from the 1930s to the 1980s in the United States.

Gas was also rationed throughout the war, even after the Germans had surrendered.

films ranged from fairly current to several years old. He had already seen several of the offered movies and so skipped them even though they were free admission, but he thought *Babes in Arms*, a 1936 musical, was "good entertainment" in spite of "some dull musical sections." He seemed quite taken with *This Gun for Hire*, spring 1942, starring Robert Preston, Veronica Lake, and Alan Ladd, which he described as "quite different and very interesting." It was considered a film noir instead of a traditional western, which might have been what he meant by calling it "quite different," and it was the film that made Alan Ladd a breakout star for his role as an enigmatic hitman and "pretty boy killer."[2] Alec told Mary he was also hoping to see John Ford's recent hit, *How Green was my Valley*, a 1941 drama starring Walter Pidgeon, Roddy McDowell, and Maureen O'Hara. This film about working-class Welsh coal miners won five academy awards in 1941, including best picture and best director, but by Christmas of 1942, he hadn't written to her about having seen it, so perhaps he was unable to attend before being shipped to his new assignment. He mentions *My Favorite Blonde*, a 1942 comedy with a war theme, as something he'd seen before but was happy to watch again, and he and a buddy tried to get into *Pardon My Sarong*, a 1942 Abbott and Costello comedy, but it was so popular they had to see a different film, one he didn't even acknowledge in his disappointment. He sometimes described his movie-going experience in more detail for her:

> Last night I went to another cinema with the company commander and saw a couple of very good shows, not

The gas coupons looked slightly different from the general ration coupons, so there was no danger of mixing them up.

masterpieces but entertainment. Can't remember their names, but think you would be interested in English cinema. Smoking in the theater is so common that the large theater . . . is filled with smoke. The ushers use their flashlights to attract the patron's attention by shining in your face from across the theater and then show you the seat to take by spotting it, so that while you are watching the picture the usher's flashlight swings across your face for the seating of other people. Quite annoying I should say. (November 1, 1942)

Another leisure activity Alec mentioned frequently was the regular card playing on and off base. He occasionally character-ized his participation in the card games as being a "bad boy" be-cause he should have been writing to her, and he felt guilty about risking their money on cards, but he did seem to win often, at least in the games he wrote to her about. It seems the soldiers had quite a series going on during one trip away from the base:

I never did tell you about how the long succession of games came out. Well up until almost the last game I was about $5.00 behind, then I suddenly had a lucky streak, so that I ended the trip about $5.00 to the good. So as yet I haven't lost anything playing poker. Of course, I know that anything I might lose you could put away, but it's about the only thing money is good for here. We have a small allowance of candy we can buy, and then we can spend money on railroad fares and beer, but other than that there isn't anything to be gotten. (October 27, 2942)

He also mentioned trading his ration cards for candy, since he didn't like cigarettes or beer, which appealed to many other GIs. He also hoped to find some Coke syrup, because he didn't like the local soda pop and wanted to make his own with the soda water readily available to him.

There were also dinners and dances for off-duty servicemen, though these may not have been an option for all soldiers, and he wrote to her about one such event:

> This evening I am going to a dance at the officer's mess; don't know how it will be; they say that last week there wasn't anyone to dance with. Anyway it will be something to do to pass away the evening. I don't think I told you that I have to dress for dinner every evening and me with only one pair of pinks and those needing cleaning very badly. Cleaning here, especially dry cleaning, is quite a problem and hard to get done because of the shortage of cleaning fluid; so I have gone into doing my own washing. (October 24, 1942)

Pinks were the name given to the Army dress uniform wool trousers that were actually closer to a drab light brown in color. Pinks could also refer to the brown uniform shirt worn with those trousers, though Alec's reference to dry cleaning suggests that he's talking about his slacks in this instance.* Officers were responsible for purchasing and maintaining their own uniform clothing, and for all but the most affluent individuals, officers' uniforms were much like those of enlisted men, though often with somewhat better quality fabric and perhaps with a quality lining as well.[3] Though not required by military code, it was common practice to wear dress uniforms for events like dances and special dinners. After the event, Alec reported in more detail on the evening's festivities:

> Well to the dance and back I have been; and there I found Red Cross Girls (British) doing their bit for morale. But since I am very shy and bashful, well I just watched, ate a few sandwiches, with spam between the brown bread, almost like rye, which is all that is allowed here for health reasons, mind you, and home I trotted. . . .

---

* I have not been able to find a credible source on why they were called "pinks" instead of browns.

Alec had to dress for dinner in England and was responsible for keeping his uniform "pinks" in good condition, which was a challenge for him at first.

[T]he wallflower is a problem here, and I gather it is just as much so in peace, as there is a considerable number more females than males. Realizing that, you can understand that the American soldiers are not going to be without company. But don't worry about your hub. He's still as true as can be and will be till he gets you back again. (October 24, 1942)

Other amusements he mentioned include occasional free concerts, but he seemed to prefer listening to music on his radio. During his time in England, he acquired his own radio and recounted what he had been listening to:

I received my radio today and it works just swell; in fact it brings home just how close things really are. I can tune the set to get British, French, Spanish, German, and Italian stations with ease. It is interesting for me to listen to the German stations and see just what I can understand. Quite a bit of German, and with a little study I think it would be comparatively easy to understand all of it. Even the pronunciations are the same as I learned in school. The programs offered vary. The German stations have some good classical programs and some of the others have a popular program, but the music seems to be a little old fashioned. The news broadcasts are full of propaganda but good to listen to. (October 14, 1942)

Shortly after this, he wrote again about how interesting it was to listen to the radio where he could get so much variety in the stations:

I am sitting here listening to my radio, and just had a French station singing American songs in French; but one of the boys wanted to hear some German propaganda so I changed it. Last night a funny thing happened. I was listening to a British station broadcasting propaganda in German and then about an hour later I heard a German station denying everything the British had said, this time in English. It's fun for me to try and understand the German. Also wish I had taken French, Spanish, and a few other languages. (October 16, 1942)

However, Alec complained that he didn't really get any news except the war news and hoped Mary would be able to send him a local paper from home now and then. Some weeks later, he told her, "Right now the radio is going full blast with a dance orchestra

Once Alec was assigned a permanent APO, he submitted the allotment forms, so most of his wages would be sent to Mary in Portland.

and I really believe that by now I know more dance tunes than when we were together, as now my principle diversion is the radio, when before it used to be you" (November 11, 1942). It turned out that it was a German station, but he said, "at least the music is good." In fact, he seemed to really like the music he heard on the German radio stations, which prompted him to observe, "You know it is a shame things are the way they are. Here I am listening to a German broadcast, and the music is exceptionally good, better in fact than some other music on their radios. Yet even so, here we are having to rid the world of something or other, I don't quite know what" (undated fragment).

The camaraderie between the men who worked together was undoubtedly an important part of their service experience. In the early days of his time overseas, Alec seemed to be working and living mostly with the fellows with whom he first shipped out, but that started to change after a couple of weeks as soldiers started getting reassigned to different tasks and locations. Because he couldn't tell Mary any of the military or professional details, he tried to describe their personalities instead:

> Peterson and I have been separated as of yesterday so one of my particular friends has gone. Possibly I liked to go out with him more than some of the others, as he was rather quiet and his interests were more along the same lines as mine; but Saddoris is here now, and I think he will be just as satisfactory, as he also is quiet and doesn't care too much for the rah-rah night life, which is very boring to me most of the time. (October 17, 1942)

Only a week or so later, he explained that he was now separated from all the fellows he had shipped over with and feeling rather lonely, especially since he hadn't yet heard from her. "This evening I was looking at your pictures and wishing you were here to keep me company; for you must know that I have left the rest of the boys and am now quite alone. Of course, there will be new friends to make and lose, as is always the way in this business. Still you will remain my most dear friend and in addition you are my constant companion, both when I was with you and now as someone to think about and to write to" (October 23, 1942).

He also had a new address to give her, yet another location in England, and he was finally doing electrical work of some kind

In England, Alec started referring to the photos of Mary that he treasured. This one was likely taken outside their Bremerton house.

since he mentioned how much the British system of light distribution interested him. In spite of feeling quite alone, it turned out that the Army was a small world, and Alec had started running into people that they had known before the war, including a fellow in his new unit who was married to someone Mary knew in Oregon. He also mentioned that his friend Clyde, possibly someone he went to school with, was stationed nearby, and he was hoping to visit him soon.

Though Alec experienced some health challenges in the later months and years of his overseas adventures, at this point he was in excellent health and even gaining enough weight that he worried about popping the buttons on his uniform. Perhaps it was all the candy that he loved so much, or perhaps he was just eating really well:

> Sometimes the long evenings just get me down, and tonight would have been one if action wasn't taken; so I borrowed a bicycle from one of the boys and pedaled into town and feasted on a chicken dinner; then took in a show and pedaled back. Now you might wonder what would give me such a burst of energy for it must have been 15 miles round trip. Well, you see

today I had a qt. of fresh milk to drink, the first fresh milk I have tasted since we parted. One of the men got it for me, just where I don't know, as milk is only for children here; but then I am just a child at heart. Even the Army thinks so, for the knives, pocket-type, that we get say "official Boy Scout knife" on the blade. (November 19, 1942)

Some of this enthusiasm was bravado, pure and simple—Alec making light of the war in order to keep Mary from worrying too much—but it was also possible that he was having the adventure of a lifetime, at least until he found himself in a major combat zone.

5

KEEPING ROMANCE ALIVE AT A DISTANCE

FIRST MONTHS, FALL 1942

Being in a combat zone may have challenged Alec's sense of optimism, but it never cooled his ardor. He always started his letters with an endearment. At first, he alternated using "My dear little wif," "My sweet little wif," "My little sweet," "My sweet," "Sweetheart wif," or "Dearest Mary, my sweet," but eventually he settled on "Dearest Wif" for most of these early letters. Pet names like these are common between married and other committed couples. In fact, one study conducted in 1993 concluded that couples in their first five years of marriage without children reported using the most idioms.[1]

Early in their separation, his closings were sweet and low key: "Much love," "Lots of love and kisses," "Very special love from your loving hub," "Give my love to Pete and take lots of it for yourself," and "Remember I am thinking of you always." As time went on, though, his closings grew more elaborate and intense, including "Lots of love from your hub to his favorite and only wif," "All of my extra special love to an extra special wif, friend and companion," "Lots of love and many kisses from your most loving and devoted hub," "Love, kisses, hugs, and you know what from your hub," "Just lots and lots of love from your admiring and faithful old hub. Who thinks you are the best girl in the whole world," "Lots of love and kisses from your hub who remembers you as the best wif in the whole world, especially when it comes to love and kisses," and my personal favorite, "Very much love and love and

Alec used his many photos of Mary to keep him company while overseas. He said that in her wedding dress she had "the poise of a goddess."

love and love and love and more love," written more than 70 years before Lin-Manuel Miranda got such acclaim for his moving "Love is love is love is love . . ." acceptance speech at the Tony Awards ceremony in June of 2016.

In addition to these endearments, Alec also reassured Mary that separation would not change their relationship, saying, "Remember, Wif, I love you just as much as you love me and so will act accordingly" (October 21, 1942). Perhaps she had been expressing some nervousness about the temptations he would encounter when going abroad. It was, after all, the first period in their marriage when they were not going to be together every day, and Mary might have already been a bit envious that he was able to go to Europe but had to leave her behind. In any case, he felt the need to reassure her that she was his "only love" and that he would always be true, no matter what happened during their time apart. He may also have been worried about his own ability to express that love with words that would satisfy her.

> I do love you and want you to just feel it in your bones, as one might say, but don't seem to be able to express it in writing. Perhaps it is because I am tired, but in any event remember you're the only girl I ever loved; in fact you're the only girl who ever got even a nibble from me in the way of love. You see I am a self-centered person and taking people or leaving them alone just doesn't make any difference to me. But with you why there is a difference. Perhaps it is just that you were nice to me, but I don't think so. It is something deeper than that. It's what you might say, "we were in resonance" or in tune to make it a little more down to earth. So you see, wif, when I say I love you I really mean it just as much as you do when you say it to me. (November 8, 1942)

In our current era, couples who are living half a world apart can see and hear each other regularly. In 1942, the only options for connecting with loved ones at a distance were the written word and photographs. Alec clearly used his photos of Mary as substitutes, however unsatisfactory, for her daily presence in his life. Early in their separation he explained, "I took out your picture today and thought how nice you looked—just the way you are" (September 8, 1942). And he reiterated that idea the next day, "I looked at my wif's picture this morning and sure thought she was nice looking. From her picture I would just bet that she would be swell to live with; and she is" (September 9, 1942). And weeks later he was still at it, "Just kissed your picture. Good night" (October 24, 1942). Luckily, they were both camera aficionados and had taken many photos of each other in the early days of their marriage, so there were plenty at hand, and it was easy to presume more would be forthcoming just as soon as the mail got straightened out.

After being separated from her for over a month without receiving any letters from her, he asked for a new photo to admire: "Anyway honey (I don't use that word much for some reason), go out and get a new outfit and send me a picture of it, and remember

Alec mentioned that this image was one of his favorites because it captured something special about Mary that he had no words for.

your hub loves you more than he is able to say" (October 23, 1942). And even without a new photo, he regularly returned to using her photo as a kind of stand-in for what he really wanted, which was to have her nearby. "Well, my sweet, I just took a look at your picture, the one with the broad grin, and find I would like to get very close to that grin in person" (early November 1942). Those photos also became emblematic of aspects of their physical relationship that he missed very much. "I just sit and stare at your picture, my private picture of you, the one with the smile and your hair cut off at the top which is a shame, as I like your hair, especially running my hands through it which I would do among other things if you were here right now" (November 9, 1942). It's clear he was trying to explain what it was about the pictures that he especially liked and how they sustained him through this difficult separation. Unfortunately, we don't know what Mary wrote to him, but it's a good bet it was equally ardent, perhaps even more so.

> You know, wif, I look at your picture quite often and see a person whom I can't help but admire and love. There is the wedding picture where you have the poise of a goddess. Then there is the cut off hair picture with its smile of understanding and vivaciousness. Then you are with Pete and show the spirit and mischievousness of a nymph. Then lastly there is the

Junction City park picture, which shows your humorousness and understanding. So you see wif, I have pictures that remind me of how perfect you are for me, and I have my memories of the days when we were together and further the visions of when we will be together again. (November 10, 1942)

After the first excitement of his overseas adventure wore off, his letters started to reveal a new set of feelings. He was both self-effacing about his perceived lack of skill with language and cautious about expressing himself freely, knowing his letters could be read randomly by others because of censorship.

Perhaps it was part of his introverted personality, but he didn't seem to like talking about his own experience and felt like that might be a selfish thing for him to do, telling her, "It seems as though this is developing into an I letter, so I think I will stop for a while and start writing again later" (October 17, 1942). Frankly, I expect Mary might have found this kind of modesty frustrating, since she was probably interested in knowing everything possible, given the limitations of censorship, about how Alec was spending his days and nights away from her, not necessarily because she was suspicious but because she was genuinely curious about many different things throughout her life, some of which were unconventional for women to pursue in her generation. One of her greatest passions, for example, was reading and collecting books about Robert F. Scott's and Ernest Shackleton's various expeditions to Antarctica in the early twentieth century. She also once took a class on earthquakes and volcanoes in which she was the sole woman.

The fear of censors reading his most intimate thoughts was probably not Alec's biggest concern. However, his sense of feeling inadequate in how he expressed himself in writing didn't keep him from some occasional late-night musings, as he tried to explain his love for her:

Here it is a Monday evening and I am thinking of you, for that is who I think of the most. Now when I think about you, the first thing that comes to my mind is your sweetness. Once you told me you were stubborn, but seldom did your stubbornness overcome your sweetness. What next does your good for nothing hub think about you? Well, there is your generousness, which is there even to the extent that it provokes you when

Alec also mentioned Mary's vivacious smile. This picture was taken while they were at Fort Leonard Wood and would most certainly have gone overseas with him.

Alec also mentioned that he saw her sweetness and generosity in her photos, like this one taken at their Bremerton house before the war.

I take more advantage of it than I should. . . . Next I think of your attractiveness, and you are attractive, for I have a picture here that proves it. Next I think of your depth of character, for you know that is one of the more important things that I appreciate in you. (October 2, 1942)

In spite of regularly alluding to his sense of inadequacy as a writer, he continued to wax philosophical about being lonely and missing her. He also let his feelings about needing to be tough around other men come out as well:

You know it is strange how much you miss someone. You think before they have left, "well sure I'll miss them," but you don't actually realize until after they have gone just how much missing can be. When I left you there was a lump in my throat but as the rest of the boys were there, and there was the necessity of packing, why the actual effect of parting didn't come until much later when I was alone. Now things don't seem so bad as long as I am busy, but it is just as if half of life was

Mary would certainly have had plenty of pictures of Alec, too. It makes sense that many of those might be of him in uniform, but she might also have enjoyed images of him before the war tore them apart.

gone not to have you to meet me when work is done. (October 19, 1942)

In his next letter, he continued his explanation, but he couldn't resist adding a bit of humor to his deepest feelings, a characteristic habit:

> Remember sweetheart, I love you very much and will do nothing to make any change in that which exists between us, as I want to come back to you just as the day I left, except for the fact that I now eat everything except squash, as vegetables are a treat to be had only at regular meals. (October 20, 1942)

In one letter, much longer than his usual ones, Alec tried to explain his feelings in more depth. Though he was practically a teetotaler, his naked expression of feelings could have been mistaken for drunken and uncommon spontaneity. Perhaps it was the extreme situation they were in that loosened his inhibitions and helped him find the words and the confidence to share them:

> I wonder if you can understand how I feel about you. I mentioned being in the pubs with the girls here. It is an interesting side light on the way people of a foreign country— which doesn't feel foreign but is only foreign in the actions of the people—act and think. It is more like a college professor who has a profound interest in his students but is still glad to get home to his wife in the evening. So my wife, you remember your hub thinks of you at all times; compares you with others he meets, and sees the reasons why he loves you so and why he wants so much to be near enough to you to reach out and give you a big squeeze. . . .

> You know, wif, I think you have realized before that I wished to be sort of important, as you have done many things to make me feel that way. Perhaps you have been reading one of those books on how to be a good wife; but I wouldn't believe that, for there was always a genuine feeling that you had, which just seemed to say "gee, I am glad I am married." And that, you must know, made me feel good. And then, too, there is just something about you that draws me in closer. You see, not only are you of the opposite sex, but you have a depth of character

that just makes me feel like I have something better than anyone else can have when I have my wif.

Well, Mary, I sort of rambled along this evening, approximately two hours of it, but anyway if it is not all just as clear as it might be, remember . . . the pen doesn't write fast enough to get some fleeting thoughts down on paper until after the thought has progressed on. . . . So, my sweet, go to sleep with the thought on your mind that your hub thinks of you as his one and only sweetheart and his most precious possession. (October 26, 1942)

In the late 1930s when Mary and Alec first got married, ideas of marriage were what we would now call traditional. Though marriage for love was a new concept in the early twentieth century, Alec seemed to have an interesting combination of ideas about love and marriage at this point in his life. On the one hand, he saw Mary as his "possession," even going so far as to say in one letter that even though he wasn't sure why she chose him, he wasn't going to trouble himself about the reasons because "possession is nine points of the law," and she was his wife. On the other hand, he started to hint in some of these early letters that he'd be happy if she was the one to make the money to support them after the war. He attributed it to his "laziness," but the idea didn't seem to threaten his sense of himself as a man and was a rather progressive view of gender roles in the 1940s. Alec was happy to be married to a strong and ambitious woman, and he was genuinely proud of her identity as a writer and hoped for her to find great success in a writing career.

The longer they were separated, the more his letters included references to physical desires, albeit discretely:

You know, during the day I think of many things I want to tell you, but for the life of me I can't remember what I intended to say, but I do think of how much I would like to kiss her right now and just squeeze her until she squawked. But at that I wouldn't hurt her physically or in anything I might do except not resign, for you see, wif, you have a forward spot in my heart, a spot where nothing else can enter except a love for you. And when you love someone so much, you just don't want to do anything to hurt them in any way. (October 27, 1942)

Since Pete was an important part of their life together, this picture of Mary with Pete would also be among Alec's most treasured momentos.

"Squeeze" was most likely his code word for wanting to make love to her, "What I really want to do is give you one great big squeeze, and a thousand kisses and then a continuous squeeze until you yelled enough and perhaps then I wouldn't stop" (November 7, 1942). Reading between the lines, it even sounds as though they might have been talking about the physical things they missed during their separation:

> I am sorry the old war interfered with us the way it has, but I promise you I'll make up for it someday. Maybe we might even get married again if you wish but remember what you said we could do when I came back. After that we might think about marriage. Remember sweet, I am loving you always and just want to prove it is all. (probably late 1942)

Even though his words of love were ardent and heartfelt, he might also have been feeling some guilt because he didn't take the safe and easy way out when he was offered the option at the

Alec said he often missed being able to run his hands through Mary's hair, which in spite of all the work she did with pin-curls at night to make it curly, was straight, fine, and soft to the touch.

shipyards to avoid active military service. He even apologized for how his choice to serve made her feel bad, "every evening I spend some time writing to you and try to make it clear and understandable that you are my one and most precious wif and that I am sorry for the way my leaving has made it hard for you" (November 17, 1942). But even with his guilt at leaving, or perhaps because of it, he was definitely thinking of her in increasingly sensual terms, including adding more physical intimacies in his closing phrases, such as "Love, kisses, and a run of my hand through your hair" while trying to explain this mix of feelings to her:

> Well my wife, I have been thinking of you constantly and surely would like to run my hand through your hair right now. This is a hard business to adjust to. . . . When I get out and stroll around this country and see so many things, and when I am busy working on something interesting, why everything seems to be so fine, and I feel as though I wouldn't want to miss it for the world. But on the other hand when I get home alone, golly, I think of my wife and my home and things just get confused. For it's then that I wonder just what it's all about. Anyway, wif, don't worry about your old hub, for I am having a good time, which would be just perfect if you were only here, but of course that is impossible. . . .

Well, wif, consider yourself smothered in kisses and just loved
and loved, because I am going to make up to you for all this
trouble that I caused you by running off all by myself to see the
world, and when I do you are going to find out how smothering
in kisses really feels. Remember I love you, sweet, and will
think of you continually until we are together again; then I am
just going to grab you and hang on. (October 28, 1942)

Scholars of WWII generally agree that letters from home were
an important lifeline for soldiers fighting abroad, and there's
plenty of evidence to support this. In 2007, a PBS series on WWII
included many first-person accounts by servicemen and service-
women about how important letters from home had been to them
personally and to the war effort, especially for troop morale.[2] Alec
voiced similar thoughts on the matter, "You see, it's the wif back
home that keeps up his spirit and gives him something to think
and dream about, and things we did now come back to mind as
the most pleasant part of living" (November 19, 1942).

In addition to words of love, he shared with her the newfound
sense of confidence he'd been finding in his military challenges
and responsibilities:

As the days go on, and more things happen, there is a greater
feeling of capability that comes to your hub. Back at the time
when we first took off in the old station wagon for the wilds
of Missouri, why I wondered just how I would take to the new
problems. Well the problems weren't of much consequence
and seemed almost to solve themselves, but there was still
that feeling that perhaps I couldn't handle the job. Many are
the times when I have seen others whom I have thought unfit,
and in all I acted so as to appear as well prepared as possible.
Now I find that as time goes on, more and more I consistently
do the correct thing. By that I don't mean the right fork at the
right time, but the right dinner for the occasion, if you can
gather the similarity together. At present I realize probably as
well as you do just what I lack in both initiative and in training.
Probably the matter of training, though important, I don't think
is the most important. What I need more is the ability to make
decisions and carry them through with the feeling that they are
correct and yet with the openness to allow for correction. Now

I think I am getting into that state of mind, and in as much as I didn't and couldn't have this opportunity at the Navy Yard for the actual exercise of control and decisions, why I believe you can understand why to a certain extent I had to leave the yard, yet fully understanding that it probably meant leaving you, perhaps forever. . . . I do regret having left you but not at all the Navy Yard, and I am sure that we shall be together again after this mess is over. (November 20, 1942)

Even in the weeks just before his departure from England to North Africa, these early letters still showed a strong sense of optimism that he would be home soon, "Well with the more days that pass and the closer I get to seeing you again, and I surely want to do that because you are my sweetheart and companion and my lady love and everything I want" (early November 1942). Further, he reiterated his constancy and devotion, "Anyway sweet when we do get together again we can take up where we left off

Alec often referred to Mary's attractiveness and her playfulness, and this picture seems to capture both nicely.

and enjoy being together again as we did before only more so because we will realize what is missing if we were apart" (early November 1942). He even used specific reminiscences about their time as a young married couple before the war to keep the vision of their civilian life active in his imagination, which helped to keep the marriage strong and to keep his morale up as the war intensified and their separation lengthened:

> Can you remember what we used to do in the evenings? There would be a show with Pete patiently waiting in the car, then maybe an ice cream soda and then home with my wif, which was the best of all. There are many men here that miss their wives, and some wonder if their wife still loves them, due to the poor mail service; but here is your hub—no letters yet—and he doesn't wonder about whether his wif loves him, for he just knows she does, as he can tell by her actions that it is so. (early November 1942)

This sense of the solidity of their love and trust in each other is what sustained both of them for what turned into nearly three years of separation due to his assignments in North Africa and Italy before the war was over.

6

A NEW PHASE OF THE WAR, ARRIVING IN NORTH AFRICA

NOVEMBER-DECEMBER 1942

Most of us who weren't there don't really know much about the day-to-day reality of American soldiers serving overseas in WWII, especially for those not on the front lines. Returning GIs often didn't want to talk about their experiences, and families were glad to have them back and didn't press for details. Movies and big events—Pearl Harbor, the London Blitz, Iwo Jima, the Normandy Invasion, the Battle of the Bulge, the Holocaust, Hiroshima—live on in name, but what has been lost is what the war meant for an average soldier. Most of what we might know is probably based in battle narratives, but in the European Theater of Operations from 1942-45, only 39 percent of American troops were engaged in combat, what the military called the "teeth" of the operation. The rest of the military personnel were called the "tail": 16 percent were headquarters/administrative personnel, and the rest, a whopping 45 percent of all troops in Europe, were considered logistics and life-support soldiers.[1] Logistics involved direct support to the combat troops (such as supplies, service, maintenance, ordnance, ammunition support, transportation, medical), and life support was concerned with infrastructure and command assistance at headquarters, as well as general troop welfare and morale.[2] As a utilities engineer, Alec was in the life-support category, since his assignment was to keep things running smoothly at

Though Alec found Algiers very beautiful, he had to be careful that his photos didn't include anything of military significance. This view of Algiers Harbor gives a sense of the mountains that surrounded this port city.

This photo from Mary's scrapbook of Alec on a boat, presumably in Algiers Harbor, was taken by someone else, since Alec didn't have his camera in his first weeks in Algiers.

headquarters. Further, the war in the Mediterranean and Middle East—critical for eventual Allied success because of the shipping access it allowed them to control for bringing troops and supplies into southern Europe and the protection it afforded against Axis access to the Mideast oil fields—was one of the longest fought-over theaters during the war. Even so, it was not something that garnered as much media attention as the war in northern Europe or the war in the Pacific, though it's likely that Mary scrutinized the news eagerly for any happenings at her beloved husband's latest-known location.

Because of his responsibilities as company censor and his careful attention to the rules of censorship, Alec's letters do not reveal exactly when he moved from England to North Africa. However, Mary most likely knew that he was not a combat soldier and would not have expected him to be a direct part of Operation TORCH, the British and American amphibious invasions of Casablanca, Oran, and Algiers in North Africa, led by General Eisenhower in early November of 1942, especially since Alec was still writing letters from England at that time. Originally, the Allies had planned to focus on the Germans in Europe before turning their full attention to the Japanese in the Pacific. However, the British, who would have taken the brunt of the preparation and casualties from an earlier European invasion, successfully persuaded the Allies that opening the Mediterranean via North Africa first was essential to eventual success in Europe. They argued that the Axis powers were vulnerable to a surprise attack since they were focused on invading Russia at the time. The Russian Campaign, also known as the Eastern front, was one of the most lengthy and brutal of the war, beginning in June of 1941, extending until May of 1945, and involving a huge number of troops and equipment. This strategic decision to postpone the Allied invasion of Europe from the original plan of early spring of 1943 into the following year, actually helped the Allies in the long run, as they were able to build up more significant resources in advance of the eventual Normandy invasion.

In Operation TORCH (November 8-11, 1942), the Allies moved quickly and successfully against French North Africa. France itself had been occupied by Germany since May of 1940, and Algiers was considered crucial to the Allied cause and a perfect place for the Allies to start their push toward Tunisia, where Field Marshal Erwin Rommel, the brilliant tank commander known as

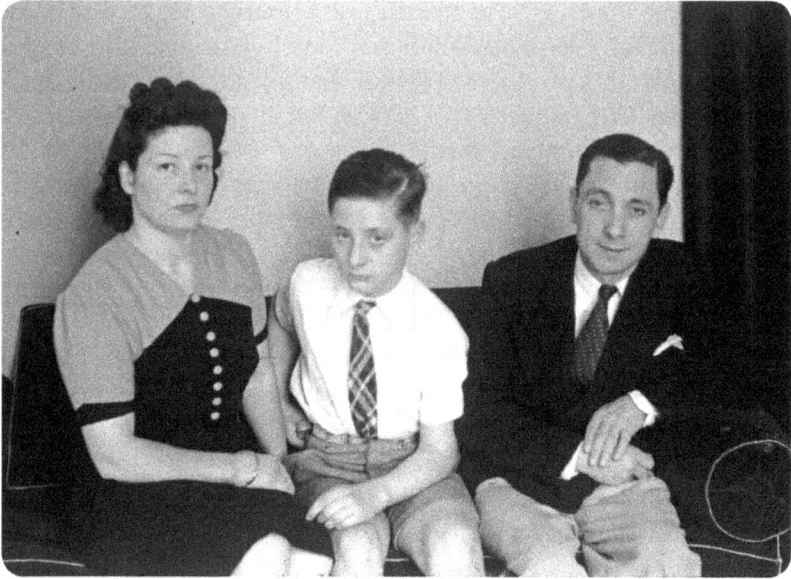

This was most likely the Melquiot family, Alec's French hosts before he got his own place.

the "Desert Fox," who had kept British troops at bay for nearly two years, waited for them. By late November of 1942, Eisenhower had moved his headquarters to Algiers, and on Thanksgiving (November 26, 1942), the first tank battle between American and German forces in Tunisia began. Originally envisioned as a lean wartime command center, the Allied Force Headquarters (AFHQ) in Algiers quickly grew into a sprawling, unwieldy operation. Author Rick Atkinson, in his account of these events, explains: "Within a fortnight [of being established] the headquarters would occupy nearly 400 offices scattered through eleven buildings. Three hundred officers now devoured as much meat as rationing allocated to 15,000 French civilians. . . . AFHQ would remain in Algiers for years, expanding into a 'huge chairborne force' of more than 1,000 officers and 15,000 enlisted troops occupying 2,000 pieces of real estate."[3]

Though it doesn't appear anywhere in Alec's letters, Mary's stories and the few anecdotes she shared later in her life made it clear that he went to North Africa with the second wave of soldiers, arriving in late November. As a utilities engineer, his responsibilities related to establishing and maintaining the vast enterprise that became AFHQ in Algiers. Mary knew that Alec had idolized his boss, and "keeping the lights on for Ike" was how she always referred to his wartime job. And it took a lot of people to keep those lights on. As Atkinson describes, "By December [of 1942], 180,000 American troops had arrived in northwest Africa. Yet fewer than 12,000 of them could be found at the Tunisian front, plus 20,000 British and 30,000 ill-equipped French."[4] When he was finally free to tell her his location, Alec sent Mary a letter, dated early December of 1942, with some of his first impressions of this new country. Presuming that she knew where Eisenhower's headquarters were, she would be able to figure out where Alec was:

> Of course you must know that I am in North Africa. . . . The trip here was uneventful, but the place here is something to talk about. It is what you might call very modern and also very beautiful—the town reminds me of Hollywood very much, and is far superior than anything that the English have. We have dates and oranges, all we can eat, and do I eat them. Last night I had ice cream for the first time since I left the U.S. and was that a treat. The people here, the French, are very nice to us and appreciate our being here, but of course it is hard to understand their language. You can understand my difficulties when I say I am temporarily in the same business as my mother [who was a bookkeeper and office manager] and have to work nights translating the French system of handling the materiel to the English system so that others here can understand what it is all about. Also I have quite a bit of control of the rationing, as the materiel is very scarce. I hope to get over this job soon so as to have more time to spend in viewing the country, but by then I suppose there will be something else to do. The work is extremely interesting and involves quite a bit of dealing with the French. I know I should have taken six or seven languages. (December 8, 1942)

This tendency of Americans and Britons to enjoy all they could eat of the fruits they had been unable to find in England created new challenges in managing supplies. "Oranges that had been fifteen cents a bushel in Algiers jumped to fifteen cents a dozen. Beer went from two cents a schooner to a dollar."[5] And the thing that affected Alec the most probably included the fact that the logistics pipeline was so inflexible and overtaxed that all

Alec in Algiers. I believe this was taken outside his residence with the Melquiots.

rail loadings at ports and supply depots actually had to be suspended for four days in mid-December. Further, inventories were hopelessly muddled, a problem compounded by the combining of British and American units in Algiers.[6] No wonder Alec was hoping to get back to engineering tasks as soon as possible.

There were other, more personal, complexities in the mingling of British, American, French, and Arab peoples during the time of the Allied occupation of Algiers. France had originally colonized Algeria in 1830, and the country didn't actually become independent until 1962, well after the war. After the Industrial Revolution, white French colonists had modernized Algeria's agricultural and commercial economy, but they mostly lived apart from the predominantly Muslim Algerian majority, enjoying social and economic privileges extended to few non-Europeans. The expatriate

Alec sent Mary several French postcards with romantic images and sayings while he was in Algiers. This poem says, roughly, "My dear, I am alone, but my thoughts are with you, my dear love. Soon I hope for the happiness of kissing you with all my heart."

French were the ones who welcomed their Western allies with open arms in 1942, and as an officer, Alec was given the privilege of being housed with a local French family, the Melquiots, when he first arrived. It was there that he encountered some of the complexities of a multicultural household firsthand:

> There is a British [officer] staying with us who gets home shortly after we do. And what does he do but walk in without the politeness that is characteristic of the French, take out

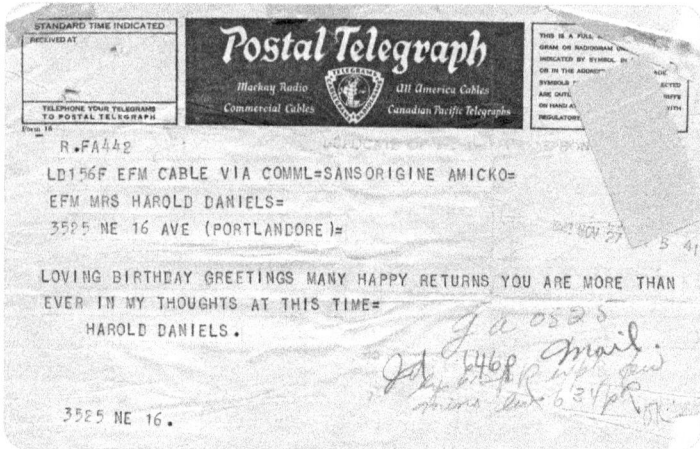

Mary's 27th birthday was on November 18th, 1942, and this cable with his birthday greetings was likely sent just before he left England on a boat for North Africa.

whatever he has that is good, and stand and eat it in front of everybody and especially in front of the Melquiots who can't get many good items such as candy, good coffee, etc. It is just an English characteristic to be aloof, I guess. Even the English girls mentioned to our men that they noticed and appreciated the politeness of the Americans in contrast to the rudeness or lack of politeness of the English male.

In another respect the French have it over on the English and that is cooking. It can be said that no matter how good the food, the English can spoil it, while no matter how bad the food the French can make it taste good. Last night I even had mutton that tasted swell, and that is saying something for mutton. Also I had sweet potatoes that were excellent.

Of course I am trying to learn French as I have to deal with them so much. I study the phrases whenever I get a chance, and practice the pronunciation with one of the Melquiots, but I don't learn too quickly and have only a French schoolbook, as English-French phrase books are not available. You could send me a cheap one if you could find it. (mid-December 1942)

Subsequent letters continued describing his stay with his host family:

Last evening when I was looking at your pictures, the French girl where I stay said I looked sad and invited me to stay for dinner. Before the dinner they said they wanted me to feel as though I was home having dinner with my people. As you know, they are rationed on food but even so the meal was very good. It started with soup made of mashed vegetables, then a type of white fish. The third course was cauliflower with a sort of a cheese sauce and topped with sausage, but it was so good that I had to have a second helping. The meal finished with a salad of a sort of lettuce material, while for a drink we had wine. I think I told you in one of my letters that they gave me coffee and toast in the morning and that their coffee is sweet and rather strong, but I just have to drink it as they would be offended if I didn't. There is another lieutenant there [possibly the aforementioned Brit] who leaves before they serve coffee in the morning, and I can tell that they feel he doesn't care for what they have to offer. . . .

Mary, you really don't know what you are missing by not being able to travel over the world with your hub. There are just so many things to see. I don't think I shall ever want to go back to a stable job again. When this is all over we shall just travel and travel and travel again. (December 15, 1942)

In spite of being closer to the actual fighting now, Alec's letters in these early months continued to be filled with the excitement of seeing new countries and meeting new people and with enthusiastic plans to travel after he got back home.

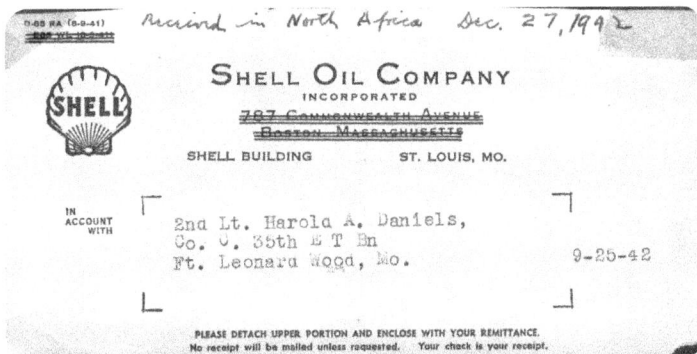

Though Alec didn't get very many personal letters from Mary his first weeks in Algiers, this bill from Shell Oil made it through to him with no trouble.

Alec was unhappy not having his favorite beverage, Coca-Cola, available in Algiers.

Though he could never share specific details, Alec did seem to be enjoying his work at the new AFHQ. In fact, at one point he even said, "the Army would be fun if it weren't for the war" (fragment, December 1942). He found the work interesting and challenging, and taxing as well, as it probably was for all the support soldiers:

> Just at present I feel rather sleepy and would appreciate a little horizontal bunk fatigue. It is probably that I dash around like mad so much that when things ease off then I get drowsy. Be that as it may, why there are many things about this work that are better than the navy yard. Of course the seven days a week are bad, and because of that I lose track of just what day it is, but even when I was home I could forget rather easy. Since being here, why I have drunk quite a bit of wine. We have it for two meals a day, but I don't drink that stuff but have a sweet wine at home. The whole reason is the excellent wine here only costs about 40 cents a quart. I really don't think I will be a confirmed drinker, though. I do drink a little coffee now and

then so as to use the cream, but if it comes to a choice I would still rather have a coke, as I haven't had one of those since I left the U.S. (December 20, 1942)

Soon after telling Mary about his exhausting schedule, Alec apparently received a few letters from her. Responding, he shared a few more details about his work, in necessarily vague terms:

Your letter questioned what I was doing, particularly what I was doing when I wrote you from England saying I liked to work outdoors. Well at that time I was doing construction work and taking hikes through the English countryside. At the present time my work is somewhat like when I was at Northwestern Electric, except that I have more authority and the work is quite a bit more varied and sometimes more complicated due to the French that gets mixed in it. Really that is about all that I can say about my work for censorship reasons, so you will just have to guess about what the rest of it might be. (December 22, 1942)

In his next letter, he tried to describe a day in his life, whimsically using blanks where information would have to be censored before mailing, had he actually included it:

If you really want to know what I have been doing today, why I shall tell you—that is I shall give you an idea without actually saying anything I shouldn't. Well in the first place I was awakened by the telephone at __ a.m., then a few telephone calls for __ to get __ and then to breakfast. Now I don't quite remember but I think the breakfast was powdered eggs and grapefruit juice, nothing very fancy if you get what I mean . . . bread with something (peanut butter) to spread on it. From breakfast to work. Get that __ for __, fix that for __, look at __ and decide what to do, then get someone to do it. Then to lunch, which also wasn't too good; then back to work for the afternoon. Then home to wash, as I haven't been able to get home and use soap for two days, but after walking home I find I had no key. So I had to go back and eat dinner dirty. After dinner: back home, listen to the news and a few radio programs and then a letter to you and off to bed. From day to day the same thing—get up, eat, work, eat, work, eat, sleep. So you think I must be a very important person; but you must know

Alec sent Mary a card wishing her a Happy New Year and closed it with, "It would be nice to visit this place together after the war."

I am just a wheel, which is not too important. Someday I'll give you a real talk about what I am doing in person. But for the present just guess and write what you think it might be. (December 23, 1942)

In the same letter, he tells her he's writing while on "dog watch," which, he explains, is the same duty as OD, or officer of the day, when they were in Missouri. OD duty rotated among officers and involved spending the night on base overseeing security, law enforcement, and even inspecting dining facilities, something that had been part of basic training for all commissioned officers.[7] Alec also shared that earlier the same day he had spent the entire afternoon in bed because of an upset stomach due to something he ate, calling it "quite a system for getting a day off."

In spite of now being nearer the battlefront in Tunisia, with General Eisenhower coming and going regularly, Alec felt he was not getting much in the way of reliable news about the war since most of what he heard on the radio was German propaganda. He'd heard via an American officer who recently arrived in Algiers directly from the States that folks back home were generally optimistic about the "whole business" at this point, but he still wanted Mary to send more news in her letters. He acknowledged that she might be doing this already since he had only a few letters from her and had heard through the grapevine that military mail was accumulating in Florida due to lack of space on transports heading overseas.

He also started to describe more about his new surroundings:

> North Africa is quite different from what one would suspect. One thing that is noticeable is the men who come in by plane with khakis on and shorts, expecting it to be very warm and of course not bringing any other clothing. So they just have to go around and shiver as the weather is just about like our fall with a bright sun between showers and a penetrating chill whenever you get in the shade. There is also very little means of heat and as the buildings are built almost entirely of concrete and tile, the interiors do not get any too much heat. It is, though, an ideal place to live in the winter months and the more I see of the world the more I think we should change our residence to fit the seasons. (December 22, 1942)

When Christmas arrived, the soldiers' celebrations were necessarily limited by the wartime conditions and their seven-day-a-week work schedule. Nevertheless, Alec described his Christmas dinner to her and expressed continued optimism, in spite of everything:

> Well tonight marks the passing of Christmas Day with us far apart. It is sad in that we are apart, but all is not so bad that there isn't some good. I think first I should say that since Christmas came on one of the seven days of the week, and as we work seven days a week, why we worked today. Up until noon there wasn't anything that would remind me of Christmas. . . . In the first place the men were not going to have any turkey for Christmas, as there wasn't enough to go around, but after scouting through the country from farm to farm we got three. In the meantime, though, some of the men thought they would do something about Christmas dinner and bought a total of nine chickens, one here and one there, etc. Now the men are living in a very nice school with an enclosed yard and a marvelous view of censorable material, so since

we had enough turkey, why they had to keep the chickens. If so many of them were not roosters we would keep them for eggs. Well, we had our dinner—turkey, beans, sweet potatoes and wine—and ate it on the porch of the school on tables that the men have made since they got here. The funny part of it, though, was the nine chickens walking around our dinner table and making chicken hell. The dinner was a great success and everyone forgot their trouble for the moment and had a grand old time. You see, Mary, a war isn't all that you would think it might be. You just have to be in one to understand how people live almost as they would if no war existed, except for short periods of extreme activity. (December 25, 1942)

While the men were celebrating the Christmas holiday as best they could, Eisenhower was complaining to the Allied chiefs about their recent failures, especially the losses at Longstop Hill, about 30 miles outside Tunis, and the temporary abandonment of the drive toward Tunis, which would be resumed in the spring of 1943. But on the positive side, in spite of strategic delays like this, the American troops were learning more about field craft and the ebb and flow of battle, knowledge that would serve them well over the long haul, as the war would continue for nearly three more years.[8] Though Alec told Mary only the chicken story of the

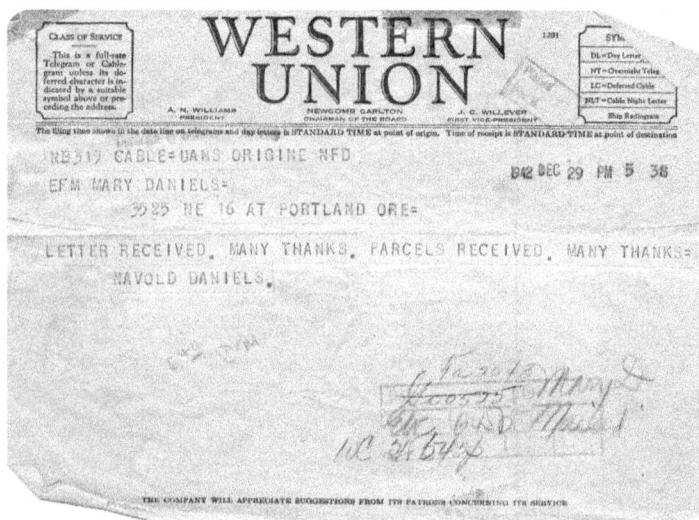

In spite of initial mail difficulties, Alec was able to tell Mary that her letter and Christmas packages had been received.

soldiers at AFHQ, Atkinson gives his readers a broader sense of what that first Christmas in Algiers in 1942 was like:

> Algiers on Christmas Eve was festive if not quite spiritual. The white houses spilling down the hills gleamed beneath a mild winter sun. Palm fronds stirred in the sea breeze. French mothers bustled from shop to shop in search of toys and sweets for their children. The price of Algerian champagne— Mousse d'Islam—doubled during the morning. Outside the city, soldiers decorated scrawny evergreens with grenades, mess kits, and ammunition bandoliers. Security had relaxed to the point that a sentry's challenge was answered not with the daily countersign but rather with 'It's us, you daft bugger!' Nipping from hidden casks of wine, troops washed their uniforms in gasoline and gave one another haircuts in preparation for midnight chapel services. A signalman in the 1st Division picked up a BBC broadcast of Bing Crosby singing 'White Christmas'; men from the Fighting First huddled around the radio and wept.[9]

On December 29th, Alec finally got his long-awaited Christmas present: a letter and parcel from Mary, and he sent her a cable the same day giving her his thanks and his enduring love as 1942 and their first three months of separation drew to a close.

7

SETTLING IN TO ALGIERS

JANUARY – APRIL 1943

As 1943 began, fighting between the Germans and the Allies continued in what has been described as a "desultory" fashion in the
Tunisian desert east of Algiers.[1] Personnel at AFHQ began getting
organized, finding regular routines, and documenting structural
relationships. This last, Eisenhower complained, was impossible to get on paper because the organization had become "too
complicated."[2] Meanwhile, in January, Churchill, Roosevelt, and
Eisenhower gathered in Casablanca for a conference to determine
their next moves against Germany. At the end of the conference,
Churchill called for the unconditional surrender of Germany,
Italy, and Japan, a call that clearly went unheeded, and Allied
planning for the invasion of Sicily began in earnest by the end of
January.[3]

In the midst of these larger endeavors, and in spite of historical evidence that things weren't going well for the Allies in North
Africa, Alec continued to write optimistically to Mary. Because
censorship rules had clamped down before Christmas to be sure
no one wrote home with news that would make the folks there
unhappy,[4] it's hard to know whether events he was hinting about
in early January really happened or were simply hoped for:

> The news is interesting now as things are developing rather
> fast and I am expecting an explosion when the conditions are
> right which will end this affair over here and let us all come

Alec's first residence had a magnificent view of the Mediterranean. The boy with him might be the Melquiot boy or simply a street Arab, interested in what this GI might be up to.

back home. It seems to me that the way the war is going now that we won't have long to wait now until it will be finished for this 25 years anyway. Personally I don't believe a word of this talk about no future war, as the living conditions over here are so low that the people have very little to lose in having a war. I think the people of the States will probably lose the most by it in the way of a lower standard of living. We will end up with a big debt whereas the Axis will just liquidate their debt. Financing a war by selling bonds seems to me to be fooling yourself anyway. The government borrows money from the people and then gives it back to the people for war materiel. After the war the government takes money away from the

One of the streets in Algiers that Alec walked, perhaps between his residence and his "shop" at AFHQ.

people in taxes and gives it back to the people to pay the bonds and the interest. It would seem a lot better to take it away in taxes in the first place and save the interest and stop giving the impression that we are getting something for nothing the way it is now. (January 7, 1943)

In taking his position on war bonds, Alec seems to have missed the point that one of their primary purposes, in addition to serving as a loan to the government to help finance the war, was to prevent inflation during a time when there was simultaneously full employment and rationing in the United States.[5] In the same letter, he told her about a recent experience in the mountains not far out of the city. Algiers is a port on the Mediterranean, surrounded by mountains on three sides. It's hard to know why he was sent into those mountains, because the front was a couple of hundred miles away at the time, but he experienced quite an adventure:

> A couple of days ago, Red, another lieutenant around here, and I went for a ride over to a town about 30 miles away, but because the main road was closed we had to make the trip over a twisting mountainous narrow detour of about 50 miles. This route took us right up into the snow country, and when we reached the town we decided that it would be better if we could find a better way to come back than going over the mountains at night, so we made some inquiries and started out on a good highway. The road was fine, and we had no complaints there, but we had neglected to ask the distance that way and it seemed as though we drove for miles and miles. Then, too, it was a well-used road and the traffic delayed us so that it was way after dinnertime and we were still traveling a long way from our destination when a rock went through the oil pan of the car and put it out of commission. That left us out on the road still some 50 miles from our bunks. I found a farmhouse and we got some of the Italians to help us push the car into the house (the people lived in one room above the stable). After that we flagged down a truck but there wasn't room for all of us on it as it was loaded, so the [enlisted men] took out first, and Red and I waited for another ride. The Italians asked us in then and gave us wine and nuts, which made our dinner, and about a half hour later we got a jeep driver to stop who was part of some air corps outfit. I personally think he thought he was in a plane the way he took that jeep bouncing over the road. Anyway we went with him about 25 miles and then transferred to a couple of trucks and finally made it home in about two hours. In all we had traveled about 150 miles to go between a couple of towns about 30 miles apart. Next time I'll ask some distances before taking a different way back. (January 7, 1943)

The Italians were technically allied with the Germans at this point, but the Germans didn't think much of their fighting abilities, even this early in the war. Perhaps such unwarlike attitudes were part of the reason why. On the other hand, there were plenty of Yank-friendly drivers along the road, so perhaps the Italian family they encountered was simply trying to stay safe in Allied territory.

Alec continued to write about his day-to-day responsibilities in veiled ways that could get past the censors, but one thing was clear: he was enjoying his new work. "I partially solved a very pressing problem today so will be able to rest a little better tonight though perhaps I should keep my fingers crossed. It wasn't that I didn't know what should be done, but that I got the work completed before something drastic happened. It's really too bad that I can't talk about my work because it interests me" (January 16, 1943). In another letter written in the same week, he shared a bit more about his new city:

> Today, or should I say "Adjour Hui" [aujourd'hui], I did just about the same as every day, but I did take some time to buy a few postcards which I will send home so that you will have some idea just how civilized this country really is. Why we have electric lights, radio, automobiles and even indoor plumbing, which is more than you could say about most of Waynesville. It seems to me that the standard of living here is more nearly equal to ours at home. Of course they haven't had much because of the war but there is still the indication that this was

Because he didn't have a camera in the early weeks in Algiers, Alec sent Mary numerous picture postcards of the city and country. Though he was probably never in the desert himself, this one would have been interesting to both of them.

at one time a prosperous place. For instance the garages of this country are equal to the best we have in the states and look quite similar, even down to the name, whereas in England there seemed to be few garages and no super service stations. . . . I'll tell more about this sometime after I get back . . ., if you are interested in such stuff. You see much of which I might like to say is censorable so it doesn't get said. (January 14, 1943)

Alec had dated the previous two letters as being written in December, even though the postmark and the day of the week he mentioned, plus the continuity with previous letters, revealed that he had been writing in January. This goes to show how tired and overextended he was from his seven-day work week. In his several books about WWII, Atkinson confirms that many officers often put wrong dates and even wrong months on their letters home, primarily due to exhaustion.

One of the things Alec could tell Mary about being in Algiers was the ongoing and frustrating language challenge he faced every day, and even those complaints could quickly be turned into a love letter by a lonely GI missing his beloved wife:

> You should have heard me today trying to talk to a Frenchman on the phone who spoke only a little English and me with my very little French. It was what the French call a Russian salad or a mixture of languages. Anyway I got over what I wanted to say and maybe someday I will really learn something that is something besides the fact that I love you. You see that's one thing I do know. I have forgotten what little I used to know about spelling; almost all that I knew about Engineering (the lights just went out and on again; I hope it doesn't mean I'll be up all night), but the one thing that I haven't forgotten is the girl I so enjoy living with. The girl who contributed so much to my happiness, the girl who traveled over the states with me and made even Waynesville feel like home, and after this war is over there is one thing that we are going to do and that's have a lot of time together, even if we have to do with less money to get it. (undated fragment)

It sounds like language wasn't his only problem in dealing with the French, though, and he complained about the tendency of the French to take their time, which made him feel like he wasn't getting

Though he never named the place because of censorship, Alec's mountain adventure with Red in January 1943 might have involved this place. The US Ninth Infantry passed through Duperre (northwest of Algiers, in the mountains) in February 1943, on their way from Morocco to the Algerian front.

much accomplished. A few days later, he grumbled, "Dealing with the French is quite a problem. It takes lots of time, lots of searching, and a few cigarettes and candy to oil the way. The French people just love to talk and argue so that they waste a great deal of my time when I have to contact them" (January 11-12, 1943). He also groused that things were hard to get in the first place: "I spent the afternoon today on a shopping tour for the government but didn't have too much success. There is a French saying that I hear

Alec in his jeep in Algiers.

many places when I ask for something— 'C'est difficile.' It means it is difficult, and that is the truth" (January 13, 1943).

A few weeks later, Alec mentioned that some of the French were learning more English and consuming Americans' time in new ways: "The Frenchmen that can speak a little English are now trying to get soldiers for conversation practice so that they may be able to pass the interpreter's examination when they get drafted. It is quite amusing for me to watch the life go by and see how much alike people are here as at home. They all want to win, but no one wants to get up to the fighting except a few who would normally be classed as crackpots" (February 11, 1943).

At this point in January, it's clear he had received more letters from her and that she had been complaining about a gender double standard, possibly in relation to the fact that women were not permitted to serve in the military at that time, so she was forbidden to join up to be near him:

> What you say about the double standard is quite true. In fact, too true. It is a shame the people have to consider that women must be different from men. It must be an inheritance we have from the Arabs. For even the Arab women think women are nothing and are disgusted when they have girl children. The Arab women have no rights at all, are purchased as wives and

An interesting site in or near Algiers that Alec did not identify for Mary, but it's clear that Egypt wasn't the only place in North Africa with pyramids.

told to scram when the man wants a divorce. The Arabs also have more than one wife if they can afford it. That has its good points and its bad ones. At times, why more than one wife might be enjoyable, as I do like women, but if I had more than one wife there would be something lacking between me and my wives. You see, just by my being your hub alone and you being my wif alone there is a close relationship that exists between us and I wouldn't want to change it for all the queens in the world, and there are some beauties here as I have seen when going through the town. There seem to be more beautiful women here than there were in England. I don't imagine I will be meeting any, though, as I have very little spare time in the day and every place closes after 7:30 at night. Then, too, there is the difference between the languages. (January 8, 1943)

Early in the war, many men, including members of Congress, the press, and the military establishment, had joked about the notion of women serving in the military, but as America increasingly recognized the demands of conducting a war on two fronts—Japan and Germany—leaders also faced an acute manpower shortage. So, in May 1942, the House and the Senate approved a bill creating the Women's Army Auxiliary Corps (WAAC). At first, though the women who joined considered themselves *in* the Army, technically they were civilians working *with* the Army. By spring of 1943, however, 60,000 women had volunteered, and finally, in July 1943, a new congressional bill transformed the WAAC into the Women's Army Corps (WAC), giving the women true military status.[6] In late January, Alec wrote:

> The WAACs have taken over here now and things are in a hubbub to get them fixed up. They seem to be a very conscientious bunch and very much enthusiastic about the work, and also a little acclimated to Army life. I understand some of them can and do swear as bad as any of the soldiers, but that's only the minority. As for any getting jealous, it's not necessary as they are by far a homely bunch and I never have enough spare time to do any chasing, which I don't care about doing anyway. All I want to do with my spare time is sleep and possibly go to a movie. (January 31, 1943)

In a special history of the Women's Army Corps, published by the Army's Center of Military History, the group of women Alec described in January of 1943, was identified as a unique unit:

> The 149th WAAC Post Headquarters Company, called by newspapers "the first American women's expeditionary force in history," was one of the most highly qualified WAAC groups ever to reach the field. Hand-picked and all-volunteer, almost all members were linguists as well as qualified specialists, and almost all eligible for officer candidate school. The company was shipped from the United States on a regular military transport, which encountered no enemy action. . . .

> The unit reported on 27 January 1943 to General Eisenhower's headquarters in Algiers, a location now considered safe, except for air attack, from the conflict still raging to the east. . . . Working hours were long; women were carried in trucks to the headquarters at an early hour, and home again for an early curfew. The nightly bombings, with brilliant displays of antiaircraft fire, made sleep difficult for the first weeks.

> Nevertheless, most women managed a satisfactory adjustment. . . . Morale was high, and women called themselves the luckiest in the Corps. . . .

The largest part of the company went to the Signal Corps and to the newly organized Central Postal Directory. Others were assigned, by twos and threes, to various headquarters offices: three to the Office of Psychological Warfare; three to the adjutant general's office; one as General Eisenhower's secretary and one as his driver; more than a half dozen to drive other officers. Ten more were assigned as cooks and bakers to keep food ready for workers on three shifts.[7]

Based on Alec's reaction to things Mary said in her letters, it seemed that she might have been thinking of becoming a WAAC in hopes of being closer to him. He tried to dissuade her, but not because he disapproved of women in the military:

> You have hinted so much about the WAACs that I must say it would probably be interesting to you if you could get to travel, but you would never get to see me, as that is forbidden. So

An officer, possibly Lt. Col. W. E. Northrop (one of Alec's "bosses"), with two members of the 149th Post Headquarters Company of WAACs in Algiers.

make up your own mind, as I am quite a ways away to do it for you. Many of the soldiers don't seem to like the fact that the WACs are over here. What I think is it is jealousness in finding that women can get into a war as well as men. I think lots of the soldiers feel that they are protecting their women and so want them to stay where they are safe. Personally I think it is a good idea to have them here, as they are just suited to some of the work that must be done. Anyway I think a woman's place is where she wants to be, not where someone puts her because of her sex. (undated, probably mid-March 1943)

This was an unusual point of view for a man of his time. In fact, a reporter in Washington, DC, printed the protest of a soldier to his girl, who wanted to join the Women's Army Corps: "'I won't have a girl of mine called a WAC.' When the girl defended the [idea] the soldier said firmly: 'All right, you can be a WAC, but you won't be mine.'"[8]

By mid-February, it had started to become obvious to the rest of the world that things were not going so well for the Allies in North Africa. Two successive and connected losses between February 14 and 20—at Faid Pass, near the village of Sidi Bou Zid, and then at nearby Kasserine Pass—brought the Allies their first significant defeat of the war and challenged American optimism

WAACs from the 149th taking a break for refreshments.

about quickly ending the war, though censorship concealed the full extent of Allied losses from the public for a while. However, it was only a matter of time before alarm grew widespread.[9] As it turns out, though some historians consider Kasserine to have been "the worst American drubbing of the war [in terms of yardage lost] . . . as grievous as the [ten day period had been]," it proved to be "a tactical, temporary setback, rather than a strategic defeat."[10] The Kasserine Campaign, as the battle came to be known, was the war's first major clash between American and German troops and a stunning blow to American optimism: "In just two days, the strength of the 1st Armored Division had been depleted by a total of 98 tanks, 57 halftracks, 29 artillery pieces and 500 men. Instantly swept away were 100 of its highly trained tank crews. These were the darkest days of the division's history."[11]

Alec's letter about how things were going was perceptive about the media's slant on the war:

> I suppose the newspaper reports have you quite worried now. Really I can't shed any light on the subject, as I don't know and if I did I wouldn't be able to mail it. . . . But really I don't think it is as bad as it sounds. You see, I have read some of your newspapers, and it seems to me that they have been conveying too much optimism, which makes a setback seem worse than it really is. Anyway it will work out alright, and I'll be home sooner than it appears on the surface, as I think things will sort of collapse all of a sudden. (February 19, 1943)

Though he claimed not to know much about how the war was progressing, he must have experienced the same aerial attacks that so disturbed the newly arrived WAACs a couple of weeks before this, and it's possible that some of the troops wounded at Kasserine might have been brought to hospitals in Algiers before being shipped home. Perhaps he was claiming ignorance in order to calm Mary's fears, but it's hard to know how much a soldier at AFHQ would have known at the time, especially since they had been directed not to talk about it with their loved ones. However, it was naïve of him to think an Allied victory in North Africa would bring him home right away. The Allies were ultimately able to turn the situation around, but not without some uncoordinated and ill-conceived strategies that would have seemed funny if the stakes weren't so deadly. For example, after the engagement at

Kasserine Pass, Rommel realized that even in victory, his forces had been seriously weakened and were terribly disorganized, so he withdrew. Unfortunately, the Allies were experiencing such confusion and lack of coordination in their own command structure, they didn't recognize the Germans' similar state and didn't try to pursue them. Rommel left North Africa for Italy in early March, and the Allies didn't even realize he was gone until much later and spent over a month "swatting at his ghost."[12] Though Eisenhower was emerging as a stronger leader than some had given him credit for initially, he was trying to keep his eye on Tunisia while also starting to plan for the Allied invasion of Sicily, called Operation HUSKY, tentatively scheduled for mid-June.

In Tunisia, the Germans were trying to keep the Americans and the British from physically connecting their respective divisions. Based on one of Alec's letters in February, it seemed that the Germans were trying to keep American and British forces from coming together in other ways as well:

> Right now I am listening to the radio and to the German propaganda broadcast. They are trying to drive a wedge between the U.S. and England and are quite clever at it when you consider what they bring up in the way of past history. The truth is Germany's past history is so bad that few people believe anything she says, and we know here of so many obvious lies that we just laugh to hear the stuff. I suppose the bad feature is that there are some people who would be taken in by such reports. (February 29, 1943)

He continued to share how hard he'd been working, both for the Army and on studying his French. The language, he complained, "just mangles one's throat" (March 1, 1943). He thanked Mary profusely for the English-French dictionary she recently had sent him, so it seems the mail was more reliable after his unit spent a few months in the same place. And he continued to share what stories he could about his engineering work, most recently with the loss or theft of a fuse:

> We had a little trouble with our lights here. Someone stole the fuse and I took a ladder and went to replace it with a new one. The manager of the place caught me and wanted to help the situation, but as I can't speak French I couldn't make him

understand that I knew what the trouble was and was going to fix it. So he delayed things by trying to find the trouble. Then a French family got in on the argument and before I hardly knew they started to walk off with the ladder. I couldn't let them take it, as I needed it to put in the fuse, so I just had to take the ladder and walk away with it and fix the fuses later in the evening when no one was around. I could understand enough French to know that the manager claimed that the light company took the fuse, which I am sure wasn't so, as what would the light company be doing taking fuses in the early hours of the morning? Also I understood that the people wanted to borrow the ladder until tomorrow when they would fix the fuses. I should explain that fuses are scarce in this country and can't be bought very easy. (undated fragment, probably early March 1943)

It's not clear how the building he referred to is connected to AFHQ, though he often mentioned a place he called "the shop" as one of his workplaces, but it was becoming increasingly obvious that Alec was often coordinating his work with locals who were involved with the Allies. And just as clearly, he didn't trust those locals and not just because of the language barrier.

In late March, and after a combat command change instigated by Eisenhower because he believed the inadequacies of his commanding officers were directly responsible for the Allied losses, the Americans were able to eventually re-take the hills and villages they had lost. They also scored a significant victory at the Battle of El Guettar, with Major General George Patton at the helm of the Second US Army Corps in what Omar Bradley, another storied American general and Patton's assistant corps commander at the time, called "the first solid, indisputable defeat we inflicted on the German army in the war."[13] By early April, American and British troops had finally met each other across the desert, in spite of the Axis efforts to keep them apart, and by early May, the final assault on Tunis had begun. Interestingly, there are no letters in the collection during the entire month of April 1943, which doesn't make much sense, since Mary seems to have saved every scrap of paper he sent her during the war. Perhaps he was kept too busy to write for several weeks, which undoubtedly would have driven her crazy, and yet there's no apology for the long silence, so the mystery remains.

Alec having lunch with two of the WAACs at AFHQ.

In early May, he once again referred to his progress in French as well as the progress of the war, the details he could talk about, that is:

> Of course you have read how the Tunis campaign is about over and will probably be finished by the time you get this letter. And then I suppose we will have to tackle Europe. I don't suppose that Europe will be a pushover, but it shouldn't take so long. If something big would just happen in Asia, why then we could be counting the days until the war was over. (May 3, 1943)

Tunisia finally fell to the Allies, and the Germans formally surrendered in Africa on May 13, 1943. There was a victory parade in Tunis on May 20, after which Patton and Bradley returned to Algiers to resume planning and training for the invasion of Sicily the following month.[14] Ten days earlier, the French had held a military parade in Algiers for the Feast Day of Jeanne d'Arc on Sunday, June 9, which Alec seemed to have mistaken for a victory parade, but the premature revelation didn't get his letter censored, so perhaps news about the Allied victory in Tunisia was already public. Once again, he did his own humorous self-censoring, excising certain words carefully with an Exacto blade:

> The cities of Tunis and Bizerta have been lost by the Germans, so we are all better off in that respect. They had a victory parade here today, as the French are very enthusiastic about the whole thing. As far as we go here, why it is just the natural thing and we don't get the least excited about it. I can gather that there was more excitement in the states over it than there was among the soldiers. Of course the faster that we take things from the Germans, the faster it will be until I get to come back to you again. . . . Now that Africa is all sewed up I wonder where we will be going next and I am not the only one. The soldiers try to guess where the next front will be. Some say [word cut out] and some say [word cut out] and some even say [word cut out]. Now I wouldn't go so far as to say that we would go to [word cut out]; that's just a little too far from Africa, although it would be a nice trip. And speaking of trips reminds me that we are supposed to have a trip one of these days, and where would you like to go with me on that trip? (April 9, 1943)

Though Alec may not have known it at the time, the success in Tunisia coincided with a change in the second battle of the Atlantic, a naval battle that had been going on since 1939, as the Germans tried to prevent England from receiving supplies from their Allies. Though the naval skirmishes continued until 1945, in the spring of 1943, there was a significant decline in U-boat and submarine attacks on Allied convoys, mostly because of improved electronic surveillance and the ability to crack the German codes that finally gave the Allies the upper hand in the North Atlantic.[15] After this and the decisive Allied land victory in North Africa, Alec maintained his optimism and his desire to show Mary the world after the war.

8

DAILY LIFE IN ALGIERS DURING THE TUNISIAN CAMPAIGN

MARCH – MAY 1943

While the Allies struggled with the Germans at the Tunisian front, life at AFHQ continued to unfold normally for the support troops, or so Alec wrote to Mary during the first few months of 1943. Alec was also learning about another new culture, something he could share with Mary in his letters, even though he couldn't show her in person. At least not until the war was over. In spite of his frustration with some of the French ways, Alec developed friendships with several French people during his year in North Africa. In fact, in February 1943, he started planning to rent an apartment with a friend and colleague that he described as "one swell Frenchman." But his friend, Joe, got unexpectedly transferred, so Alec had to look for other housing because he couldn't afford the apartment on his own:

> The apartment was quite expensive—you know, soak the poor solider—$60 a month in American money. You see since the change in the value of the money, why we get less than what the true exchange should be, I think. I believe the reason for it is to prevent the soldiers causing an inflation, which would be detrimental to the civilians, a condition which they have practically started already. (February 28, 1943)

This is one of the photos Alec shared with his French friends.

This is undoubtedly the photo that his French friends reacted to with their comment, "Still water runs deep."

Joe had helped Alec with his language challenges, but Joe didn't always give him the complete translation:

> Wif, you know you are still my sweetheart and I am always thinking of you. I just put my last set of batteries in the slide viewer yesterday to show the picture to some French people I know. They said I was a quiet person, and then said something in French when they saw the picture of me and you in a kiss. From what I could gather they went something like "still water runs deep," but Joe, who was here when they came to see me, didn't tell me exactly what it meant. Anyway they all laughed about it. (February 19, 1943)

Given their cultural penchant for romance, the French would certainly have appreciated that Alec had a romantic nature hidden beneath his quiet and businesslike exterior. In addition to spending time with Joe, Alec apparently socialized regularly with other French engineers and gained some insights into their ways with food, which interested him greatly, and their family situations. He described a meal at the home of one of his engineering colleagues, admitting he took seconds even on dishes he didn't like much because "the French mention it if you don't." He also noticed the order of dishes and other patterns in French dining, especially the custom of serving salad at the end of the meal. (None of these insights changed how meals were served in the Daniels household after the war.) Alec knew Mary was hungry for more details about his experiences, so he also shared comments about his host and the other dinner guests:

> Both of the engineers were from the same school in France. Mr. Chaufer-Dumez (Dumez is his wife's name and it is a custom for husbands to add their wife's name in the part of France where he came from) came to [here the name of town is cut from the page; presumably it's somewhere near Algiers] to set up his business with the idea of bringing his family (9 children) over as soon as the Germans would permit. The other engineer and his wife came over for a business visit and left their two children in France. Then the Americans came so that they can't return to France. They said that the people of France were starving and that the shortages I have noticed here were nothing compared to the shortages in France. (March 1943)

Alec and some of his French friends, including his French teacher and probably his friend, Joe, the engineer.

Though he didn't actually share his own feelings about the matter, Alec would have been sympathetic to the plight of these French families, especially their separation from their children. He also told Mary about his French teacher, who had become a good friend:

> My French teacher's fiancé was reported missing a month
> ago and she thought he was dead, but when I went down for
> my lesson Friday night she had just received a cable from
> Switzerland that he had been taken prisoner and released to
> the custody of a relative he had in France. She was so excited
> that she vibrated just like you did that day when I came to
> see you in Eugene and you, crazy kid, went walking along the
> tracks when you had such a bad cold you should have been in
> bed. I wonder if all women vibrate when they think about men
> they love. Perhaps you could enlighten me on that subject.
> Of course, I know you said get a homely teacher, but I didn't
> know any homely ones. This one works as an interpreter in
> a lot of the dealings that I have with the French is how it all
> came about, and I can assure you that all I do is study French.
> (March 1943)

It seemed Alec took a fair bit of ribbing from his American Army buddies about his glamorous-looking teacher. Occasional references in various letters made it clear that the other GIs thought

More of Alec's friends in Algiers, including his French teacher (center).

he was nuts to acknowledge her beauty to his wife. In fact, Alec even sent Mary a picture of the teacher with some of his other buddies, which he hoped would prove both to her and to any others that he truly had eyes for no one but his beloved. He also regularly reported on what his teacher said in response to Mary's comments about her, which is definitely not something a man who was hiding anything would likely do. Curiously, both women seemed to be a bit nervous about his openness, even though he probably thought he was reassuring when he updated Mary on how his lessons were going:

> Your new French book looks to me to be just the thing that I need as what I have to learn most is conversation. I told my French teacher what you said about me getting a lovely teacher, and she was a little concerned about whether you would approve of her. It's just like a woman, that is being vain, or is that what they say about men? I really don't know. Anyway I have now gotten to the point where I can ask directions in French and get an understandable answer. The process is simple. I say "Ou (est) la—?" and watch the policeman's finger, drive a ways and repeat, and eventually I arrive at my destination. Very simple the French language, isn't it? (March 20, 1943)

Alec's French teacher on the beach.

He also added a little romance to his French lesson references to show her exactly where his heart lay: "Let's hope I don't have time to learn perfect French but get to take lessons in perfect love from you. You see, wif, in that subject y

ou are an adept teacher, for your pupil just comes back for more and more learning. The preliminary course you gave me was very good, the graduation was excellent, but it's the postgraduate course that means so much. Wif, what I want is a DLL degree (doctor of legal love) from you" (March 1943). He eventually even enlisted Mary's help in finding a wedding gift for his teacher and her fiancé once he was able to return to Algiers:

> I was going to ask you to send me something that would be good for a wedding present, as my French teacher's fiancé is coming back, and they will probably be married soon. It seems that he escaped from France to Spain and will be back as soon as the necessary arrangements can be made for his release from Spain. Perhaps you wonder just how much French that I know. Well, it isn't very much but it is quite a help at times. One of the men heard me talking in French over the telephone and said he would give a hundred dollars just to be able to do that, but what he didn't know was that I was just talking in phrases and that the Frenchman was doing all the talking.

Maybe when I go to some other place I will have to learn their language. The trouble is that I don't study enough. It wouldn't take long to learn a language for talking if one would just spend a little time at it and not lie down and go to sleep every evening. (June 11, 1943)

This mention of constantly falling asleep when he should have been studying his French lessons was a regular theme for most of the spring of 1943. It's in reference to what he characterized as his laziness that he also started to hint at one of the medical problems that had been bothering him, a mystery ailment afflicting his eyes that made it hard to read when he was tired. His doctors didn't seem to be able to identify or help with the problem. He reminded her it had been going on for several years, even before his time in the Army, and he hoped someone would figure out what was wrong soon, so it was probably not a typical vision challenge, such as near- or far-sightedness. Eyestrain such as he described could be caused by stress or fatigue, so it's possible that his discontent at the shipyards, followed by the stresses of entering into active duty in the Army, and then being sent overseas, plus the fatigue of having seven-day-a-week duty were mostly to blame for his eye problems, but it's also possible that the eye problem was an early manifestation of rheumatoid arthritis, an immune-system disorder that would plague him in his later years.[1] He also told her that, because of his eye problem, he didn't read much anymore for pleasure, excepting her letters, of course. By now, the mail service was more or less regular, and he thought he might be mostly caught up with her letters, though probably with a few still missing.

By the third week in March, while the American troops at El Guettar were gaining their first solid victory since the initial invasion and occupation of Algiers in November, Alec wrote that he had found new housing—not the apartment he'd hoped to share with Joe, but a room in a house with a French family different from the one that hosted him when he first arrived:

My new location is in a room with a French family consisting of Ma and Pa and two sons, the youngest son being about 5 or 6. I now have a bed to sleep in and find it more comfortable than the cot I have been using since leaving the states. . . . The only bad part of the place is that I have lost the commanding view of the sea that I had from the balcony at the other house. One of its great advantages other than my personal comfort is that I am nearer to the men. The people are quite nice and I am sure I'll learn some French from them. (March 20, 1943)

In subsequent letters, it became clear that he shared a meal with this family at least once a week while he was renting a room in their house, so it's likely he was able to improve his French conversational skills while doing so. In fact, his landlord, who spoke no English, seemed to think he would be quite fluent in only a few months, so he must have been doing reasonably well, in spite of his tendency to downplay his abilities.

In the same week he moved, Alec was promoted from second lieutenant to first lieutenant. In his typical humble fashion, he didn't boast much about the promotion, saying only, "If you will look on the return address on the envelope you will notice a change, which I have been expecting for some time (that is a couple of months), only that there was some opposition to it. Someone thought that I was a little too easygoing but changed his mind finally" (March 25, 1943). Sure enough, his new title is part of his return address on this letter, but that's the only fanfare involved. Second lieutenant was the normal entry-level rank for a commissioned officer, which Alec had been because of his ROTC experience in college, and usually meant leading a platoon-sized group of 16-44 soldiers. He certainly did so at

This may be the view from Alec's second housing situation after he lost the "commanding view of the sea" he had with his first housing assignment.

HEADQUARTERS
ENGINEER DET (UTILITIES) HQ COMD
APO 512, US Army

3 May 1943

SUBJECT: Mail

TO   : CO, ENGINEER DETACHMENT UTILITIES HQ COMD AF

It is requested that permission be granted to have a birthday present mailed to me.

HAROLD A. DANIELS
HAROLD A. DANIELS
1st Lt., CE
Engr. Det. Util, Hq Comd

1s. Ind

Hq. Engineer Detachment Utilities. Hq Comd AF, APO 512, US Army, 3 May 1943.

TO: POSTMASTER, PORTLAND, OREGON.

Approved.

Carl O. Shytle
CARL O. SHYTLE
Major, CE, Comdg

Planning ahead for Alec's July birthday in Algiers, his first away from Mary since their marriage.

Fort Leonard Wood, though the size of his unit wasn't clear once he went overseas. A first lieutenant gets a pay raise—and often, though not always, could command a much larger group, such as a company-sized unit of up to 250 soldiers. Or, a first lieutenant might receive an assignment with more significant responsibilities.[2] Alec never distinctly said how many men he was responsible for, but the size and scope of AFHQ suggest that he most likely had many engineers and other support troops working for him, and they had multiple utilities areas to take care of. The promotion to first lieutenant was a standard promotion when a junior officer had reached 18 months of service and had been doing a satisfactory job.[3] That Alec was promoted after only 12 months of active duty could mean that he was doing an outstanding job, or it could mean that wartime circumstances accelerated the usual timelines for many junior officers.

While Alec seemed to be doing well and enjoying his job, Mary apparently was not entirely happy with her job as a retail clerk. Though the war brought many women into the labor force who might not otherwise have been working, he knew this kind of work was not something she aspired to do as a career. He was aware she had a dream of being a professional writer one day, but he also had another suggestion for her to consider:

> I have noticed from some of your letters that you are not
> quite satisfied with your job because it doesn't seem to lead
> to anything. I have thought about that, too, and think that if
> you like something that is all that matters, but when you write
> of having taken the radio apart and soldered and unsoldered
> wire, I think that you have missed your calling. You should
> have taken a course in radio fixing or some other allied subject,
> then you could work with your hub, or I should have taken
> leatherwork and I could then work with you. Anyway I was
> thinking it would be fun if we could work together on things
> when I get back to you, whether it's what you know how to do
> or whether it is what I know how to do. (March 25, 1943)

Though this idea never did become a professional reality, Mary was always engaged in complex craft projects and was never afraid to tackle fix-it jobs around the house on her own. By May of 1943, it seemed that she had been complaining to Alec that she was not getting enough appreciation from him regarding her work abilities. He reiterated the refrain that ran through many of his letters about how he had been hoping she would eventually find a profession that would allow her to support him, but that, too, never happened:

> So you think I should appreciate the way you are bringing in
> the money from your job? You know darn well that when I
> married you I had in mind that you would support me some
> day, so you see I knew before you did how easy it would be
> for you to take hold of a job and make it pay money. There is
> one trouble I find with work and that is that it takes too much
> time. Over here it doesn't bother me, as it is interesting and
> you aren't here for me to have anything else to do, but at PSNY
> [Puget Sound Navy Yard] I used to get disgusted, as it took so
> much time and much of it was so boring, and when the night
> work came on, why it was getting to be too much. Ft. Leonard
> Wood was better, as it was outside and different, but this set
> up is better yet, except for the separation. Perhaps the powers

will get started on Europe soon and we can then get a chance
to get back together without too much delay. (May 12, 1943)

By late May, Mary had found a new job that she liked better,
and what few hints there are in his responses suggested that
she was continuing to work at Meier & Frank, but in a different
department. As usual, there wasn't much he could tell her about
his own new job since the promotion in rank, so he generalized
with humor and quickly changed the subject to something more
pleasurable:

> Well how is that new job coming along? I am anxious to find
> out all about it and what you do. I suppose that you will
> counter with the fact that I don't tell you what I do. Really
> all that I do is chase around and see people and things and
> tell someone else what is wanted. What I am is a middleman
> between the person who does the work and the person who
> wants the work done. Now does that explain my job to you
> clearly? If not, there isn't much more that I can tell you about
> it until I get back there, and then it won't be important at all,
> for there would be better things to do than just talk. You know,
> like making love and lying around with each other and taking
> things easy and let the rest of the world go by. (May 28, 1943)

During the spring of 1943, as the Allies continued to drive
back the Germans in Tunisia, Alec again started to become philosophical about the nature of marriage, especially as they passed
their third wedding anniversary separated by war and with no
idea when they might be reunited. He also reminisced about an
incident during their courtship when their relationship seemed to
have taken a more serious, possibly physical turn:

> Sometimes, wif, I imagine you have wondered about what I
> thought about that Sunday evening we had at Eugene after
> the Military Ball. It was rather strange in a way for actually
> until that time I had always been rather bashful, and at the
> same time I was sure that it was something quite new to you.
> In fact I was so certain of what kind of a person you were that
> I was quite sure you must have liked me very much. After I
> had known you longer, I really found out about you. I found
> that you were very much the person I suspected you to be and

Postcard image of Notre Dame d'Afrique, a Roman
Catholic basilica built in the late nineteenth century on a
cliff overlooking the Bay of Algiers on the north side of the
city and easily reached by cable car from the city center.

more, and that you were working under a conflict between what
you thought you should do and what you wanted to do (you
can correct me if I am wrong). It always seemed as though you
wanted to let me do as I pleased, but yet you couldn't let go of all
the values that you had learned to believe in. Anyway, I think it
was quite an ideal courtship, what with its emotional excitement
resulting in our being drawn much closer together than we
might have. It really gave us more of a chance to understand
each other and to see that we were meant for each other.

Many times here I hear about other men's wives. Of course sometimes the trouble is with the men, but also it is with their wives. Each time when I hear one of them talking about being married and wishing they weren't, I think that they really have never been married at all, but have just lived together. If they had ever been married as we have they never would want to part. It is true what you said about marriage being built block by block as the two people live together and become more dependent on each other. One of the things that make a permanent marriage is getting to know your partner so well that no one else can possibly take your spouse's place and still maintain the relationship. Perhaps I can make it more clear if I give you an example. Here we have lived together for 2 years + and during that time I have come to know the many things you stand for: that is, basic principles such as your kindness, understanding and loyalty, and it is as though your mind and heart were an open book, which only I am permitted to read, and the reading is so enjoyable that I want to keep it all for myself and only let the rest of the world admire my wife from the surface, but never from the interior, for that spot is reserved for me. (April 1943)

Around Alec, it seemed that several of his buddies were experiencing troubles in their marriages, which he reported regularly to Mary, especially one of his friends who had gotten drunk in

Another postcard image. It's likely Alec saw scenes like these most days in Algiers.

England, gotten a local girl pregnant, and then somehow acciden-tally informed his wife of the problem. He told her that this guy didn't drink often, but every time he did, he got into trouble of some kind. Then Alec made light of the whole situation by joking about his own sparse drinking habits, saying, "Some people just can't hold a little alcohol. Your hub is one of them: just a little and he falls asleep. I don't even get noisy" (fragment, probably early March 1943). In this same letter, he also reminded her of their own wedding:

> There I was standing in front of the preacher, who was shaking like a leaf, and I turned my head backward over my shoulder and what did I see approaching me but a queen all rigged out in white. In plainest words, you knocked me for a loop when you came walking up, and I actually gulped to myself because you looked so beautiful. (fragment, probably early March 1943)

I'd venture to say that this kind of shared memory is what kept the marriage rock solid, and those memories sustained him through what would turn out to be another two or more years of separation.

9

THE SICILIAN CAMPAIGN FOR THE ALLIES IN ALGIERS

JUNE – NOVEMBER 1943

Though the Allies could claim a victory and the war was mostly over in North Africa, Alec's responsibilities in Algiers were far from finished. It was now time to start planning for another big move, this time to Italy, though it's not entirely clear when Alec knew for sure what would be next for him. In mid-May of 1943, he wrote to Mary:

> Now that the Africa war is over, why they should let all of us veterans go home for at least a month, but they won't. I will enclose my campaign medal for being in Africa. It signifies that I was present here while the fighting was going on and so doesn't mean anything, as everybody got one. I think they give one out every time one takes a boat ride. Now that the summer has arrived you should really be here. It is such a nice country and it would be a good place to live after the war, but I want to take a look at South America with you first before I make up your mind to make up mine. (May 14, 1943)

Atkinson wrote that in this period in time after the success of the Tunisian Campaign, many of the involved American troops shared a conviction that, now that they had done their bit, they would be able to go home, or at the least get some home leave.[1]

Alec with his buddies in Algiers, possibly Lt. Kelly (center) and someone else in his utilities unit.

However unrealistic this hope might have been, the Americans were also developing a new attitude toward the war. At first, there had been a shared sense that this had been someone else's war, but now that there had been significant American casualties—over 70,000 between the Oran invasion and the Tunisian Campaign—the attitudes of the troops were shifting, and they had a stake of their own in the outcome of the war. Still "incorrigibly optimistic" in spite of the loss of life, Atkinson asserted, "every man was really fighting for the right to go home."[2]

At this same time, Churchill visited the US for a two-week Allied conference on war strategy, which resulted in the decision to launch an immediate attack on Sicily (Operation HUSKY) in June of 1943. Additionally, they postponed the cross-channel attack of the European continent until spring of 1944 and instructed Eisenhower "to plan whatever operations following the conquest of Sicily seemed 'best calculated to eliminate Italy from the war and to contain the maximum number of German forces,'" which they had determined could only help the future invasion.[3] The Allies used "ultra" code breakers to intercept Axis communications and used various feints and deceptions to keep the Axis from knowing about the impending Sicilian invasion. Sicily is a rugged, rocky island in the Mediterranean, part of the kingdom of Italy since 1861, but separated from the toe of the boot of the Italian mainland by the Straits of Messina. The island is only 90 miles from the northern coast of Africa, making it a natural bridge between Africa and Europe. The strategic significance of Sicily was that, under Allied control, they could not only re-open the sea lanes to the eastern Mediterranean, but it would also give them a base from which to launch further offensives in the region.[4]

As spring turned to summer, combat troops were given recuperation time to prepare for the next campaign, and even more severe censorship on letters home was the order of the day. Those soldiers who had believed they would be sent home resented being requisitioned by Patton for the invasion, but Eisenhower delivered inspiring words to the troops: "We are fighting for liberty and the dignity of the human soul."[5] Alec wrote to Mary in early June that he was now wearing khakis with no tie but suspected it wouldn't last because of the "diehards" who wouldn't let their men go without ties, no matter the weather. He was likely referring to Patton, who reportedly said he would fine any soldier he encountered in Algiers without a helmet or a tie, so many soldiers kept their ties folded and tucked into their belts in case of a chance encounter with the general.[6]

While it's hard to be sure just how much Alec knew at this point about the coming invasion, he was clearly starting to get restless in Algiers:

> Things here are starting to get boring and I am beginning to wish that they would start something soon so that there would be some more excitement. As far as the battle in Tunis, I don't think I ever did get excited even when it was over. I guess that it seemed too much of a sure thing. The town here is not as exciting as it used to be, either. It is just too busy now, I guess. Too much of this having to wait in line for whatever there is to do. I am inclined to think that your rumor on repugnance is a little bit exaggerated. I would say that it should be about 5% but I really wouldn't know. Anyway, it doesn't make a heck of a lot of difference in the long run. (June 7, 1943)

There's no way to know for sure what Mary's reference to rumors of "repugnance" might have meant, but Atkinson suggests that at this point in the war there were bandits in Algiers, and soldiers in the city often traveled at night with pistols drawn against

Alec was getting bored in Algiers as the active fighting moved to Sicily, but all he could do was wait.

the possibility of attack. Further, and in spite of a ban issued by the military, prostitutes were said to be the highest wage-earners in the city, so perhaps word of these unsavory developments was getting to folks back home in spite of the increased censorship.[7] In late June, Alec's letters increasingly showed his impatience with the slow pace of the war and complained about the censorship, "It's another day and the war still keeps going on and I'm still thinking of you. . . . The censor doesn't like me to guess where the invasion is. Well I should have sent the newspaper clipping that I have here instead of just mentioning the place that it mentioned. Or perhaps they don't want you to know anything about an invasion, but I thought that the newspapers were yelling for one" (June 18, 1943). A couple of days later, he wrote, "Every morning I look in the paper to see if we have begun to fight in Europe, but every morning I am disappointed. I wish they would hurry up so that we could get back together again" (June 20, 1943). He also made an interesting observation about how he might talk about the war once he got home, an observation that turned out to be eerily prescient, though possibly for entirely different reasons:

> You know there are three lieutenants including myself to do the work that I was doing before, so I am not near as busy, but I think I would rather have more to do. We kid each other about the work. Something electrical comes up that can't be fixed

so I kid the supply lieutenant and tell him to get on the ball. The phone rings and one of us says, "So and so wants some water," and so it goes. We've decided when we get back to be the silent type who won't say anything about the war as it was too horrible what you heard about from the last war. Of course, the reason is that we won't know enough about the war to say anything. Anyway, I guess they will always need lots of people behind the fighting just like they need lots of people at home. (June 20, 1943)

By early July, Algiers was even hotter and full of soldiers waiting for their next directives and signaling the coming invasion to each other with a flash of the index finger. At this point, there were 4,000 officers at AFHQ, plus nearly 8,000 aides, cooks, clerks, and other personnel, for a total support workforce of nearly 12,000.[8] American ships left Oran and Algiers for Malta, and the British fleet assembled off the Egyptian coast. Malta, an island nation in the Mediterranean Sea, had been part of the British Empire since 1814, and it was the home of the British Mediterranean Fleet. Eisenhower had his last meeting with Patton in Algiers before flying to Malta, while a dummy AFHQ in Oran began broadcasting radio traffic to screen his movements.[9] There were significant gaps in letters from Alec to Mary during these summer months, so perhaps he got so busy with the preparation to move AFHQ to

Probably the Bastille Day parade Alec saw in Algiers.

Italy after the invasion that he was unable to write regularly. Or perhaps because of the invasion and continued fighting in Sicily, mail got delayed or lost.

The HUSKY invasion began on July 10, and because there was little resistance from the Italians at first, the Allies started this campaign with a strong foothold in Sicily.[10] Unfortunately, Allied good fortune didn't last very long. The day after the invasion, German counterattacks began against the Americans, and on this day, there was also one of the worst friendly fire episodes in modern warfare, with over 400 American casualties and 23 planes destroyed, 37 badly damaged.[11] Eisenhower didn't find out about it until late the next day, and the Allies were able to keep it out of the news for a long time. The following day, British general Montgomery took an unexpected and unilateral action by ordering his troops to cut across Patton's front and into the American sector, which not only hindered the struggle but prevented the Americans from severing the main escape route for Axis forces leaving Sicily, thus crushing any hope of a quick Allied triumph in Italy. Montgomery's action also stoked the enmity among the Allies for the rest of the war.[12] Though Alec never specifically mentioned any of this, in some letters he clearly had a negative reaction to having to report to a British commander when Eisenhower left AFHQ for London to plan the Normandy invasion. However, it's possible it was simply the individuals involved and issues of personal loyalty to Ike that affected him rather than the greater national tensions. The battle for Sicily was one of the largest combined operations of WWII, involving an Allied armada of 2,590 vessels. Over the course of thirty-eight days, half a million Allied soldiers, sailors, and airmen grappled with their German and Italian counterparts for control of what the Army called, "this rocky outwork of Hitler's 'Fortress Europe.'" When the struggle was finished, Sicily had become the first piece of the Axis homeland to fall to Allied forces.[13]

While Alec was prohibited from writing to Mary about how the invasion was going in Italy until the news was public, he shared an interesting personal anecdote about his day-to-day routine before the battle. This letter illuminated his situation and especially his relationships with his superior officers:

> One of my bosses, a very important one, sent me out to check
> something and by a strange coincidence I found exactly the

condition he mentioned but entirely with the wrong people. Well I reported to him and he immediately recognized that I had been to the wrong place; the funny part, though, was that he thanked me for my trouble rather than boiling over with steam. It sort of took me by surprise. There is one thing you can say about him, even though he gets rather angry at times, he knows his job and gets it done without any ifs, ands, or buts. (July 19, 1943)

An officer at Alec's rank would probably not have much direct interaction with Eisenhower himself, though Ike was reported to have a temper that he had to learn to control. It could perhaps have been Ike's chief of staff, Walter Bedell Smith, another man with a notorious temper and no-nonsense attitude. Or it could have been that the commanders at the top assigned to mid-level supervisory roles men who were a lot like they were.

By mid-July, either the censorship had been loosened or the invasion was in the news because Alec wrote to Mary:

For two days now the Army has been invading Sicily. . . . The only news that we get that says anything is the report from the States, and I suppose that is like your newspapers and distorted all to hell. Anyway, Sicily is a start towards the end of the war and that is something as far as we are concerned. (July 12, 1943)

On July 14, 1943, he wrote, "Today is Bastille Day over here, and so not much of anything is happening, at least as far as I am concerned. It might be a big day for the French, but I can't really say as to that. . . . There was some sort of a parade this morning, but I am not particularly interested in parades, so I don't know just what it was. The only parade that I am going to be interested in is the parade into your arms." He also suggested that "the news from Sicily seems good, so it shouldn't be too long before we can get together again. I hope I have more to do than I did today, as it gets rather trying to just sit around and wait for something to happen. Of course, when it does happen, why I then go around in a flurry of real sweat until the trouble is over" (July 14, 1943). Once again, he tried to explain his job without telling her exactly what he was working on:

So you are still wondering what I am doing. All you have to do is think of a water company, a light company, a construction company, and a repair company, and add them all together, and take a very small piece of the total and you have got my job. I can't really say that it is engineering, though part of it is, particularly my part, but it does involve a lot of fooling around the way I used to like to do in Bremerton when I had the time and the material. Savez bien, maintenant, ma chérie? Perhaps when it's all over and I am boring you with long tales of what I did way back when, you will completely understand the whole affair. (July 19, 1943)

As the fighting raged on in Sicily, a rapid succession of events made it clear that the campaign would not be the slam-dunk the Americans were hoping for. On July 18, Hitler visited Italy in person, and Mussolini told him that Italy should not be sacrificed in order to delay a direct assault on Germany. The Allies bombed Rome on July 19, and Allied doctors found the first cases of malaria in the Allied troops in Sicily on July 23. The Luftwaffe commander, Albert Kesselring, who would soon become the supreme commander of all German forces in Italy, advised Berlin that

Though there's no photo of Mary in the tight blue sweater Alec sent her, he must have enjoyed this one of her in a pink sweater, tight or not.

the occupation of western Sicily was complete on July 24, and Mussolini was deposed by his own Fascist Council on July 25.[14]

While all this was happening in Italy, Allied planning for Operation OVERLORD continued, with a target of spring 1944 for the invasion of western Europe. In early August, the Italians, believing that they had backed the losing side, started making secret diplomatic overtures to the Allies. As fighting continued, American soldiers learned that in addition to being a stickler about proper uniform etiquette, Patton didn't believe that malaria and shell shock were real, publicly calling afflicted soldiers cowards in two separate slapping incidents on August 3 and 10, for which he was eventually censured by Eisenhower. On August 11, 1943, the Germans finally began evacuating troops, and the campaign for Sicily effectively ended on August 17, with the fall of Messina.[15]

Alec continued to write encouraging words to Mary about how the battle was going in Sicily. Presumably, he could say these things without fear of censorship because the public media were by now covering the battle. However, if he had any inside information about the Allies' next move, he certainly couldn't tell her that he would soon be on his way to a new location, though he may have been preparing for that change. In early August, he responded to one of her letters complaining about the Sicilian campaign:

> So you have been impatient about getting this war started so that it will be over sooner, but by now you must know that it is well on its way and everything is popping quite fast, and the faster that it pops, the sooner I can pop back to you. It looks rather bad for the Italians now: if they quit the war the Germans will give them hell, and if they don't we will. The radio tonight said we had started bombing Italy again and also that we have started in on another country, Romania [Romania, a key German ally, suffered an air attack on the oil refineries in Ploesti on August 1, 1943]. Hitler can withdraw back into Germany soon, but I wouldn't want to be a German in Germany, as it seems as though they are getting an awful pounding. London looked quite bad in spots when I saw it, but if the reports in the papers are true, why German cities are taking a greater pounding. (August 2, 1943)

Unidentified people (likely friends of Alec's) overlooking the Bay in Algiers. The gun seems to be a disabled ack-ack (anti-aircraft) gun.

The fighting continued in Italy through the month of August, as did Alec's references to the war in general, alternating between positive and negative. "The fall of Italy seems to have given us an easier entrance into Europe, but even so the Germans seem to have taken over part of the country and the news mentions fighting. It isn't over yet" (August 10, 1943). The next day he transformed his thoughts about the war into thoughts about their future together, trying in this way to maintain his optimism in the face of current challenges:

> So all the commentators think it's going to be a long war, but there are a lot of people over here who think differently, and I am banking on the differently thinking people as I want to get home just as soon as possible to see my wif and get my arms around her and play roughhouse in the morning before we get up. It would be fun to live for a short while after we got back together in a good hotel and just have only ourselves to think about and push the button and have things brought to us. We could make love and more love and just open the door for the food to be passed in and then shoo the bellhops away. Anyway, anything that we do together will be fun, so we don't have to plan a thing but just do what we want on the spur of the

moment. I was looking at the latest picture that I have of you last night, and I think you have added some weight, which is more becoming to you. You know there is one place where you can add weight and I will not mind about it, and that's where the blue sweater I sent you would show you to best advantage. Of course, there is also another place to put on weight, but that will have to wait until I can get there to do something about it. (August 11, 1943)

Though he often talks about their future plans for possible traveling, this reference to "gaining weight" in another place is one of the few references to their hopes of having a family someday. In mid-August, he wrote with continuing cheer, "I don't remember the date, but it's one more day nearer to my coming home. Sicily is just about finished and all that is left is to start the final battle." As he brought this same letter to a close, he waxed more philosophical about war and his ideas about strategies of war:

I was just listening to the German propaganda station and find if you believe the Germans, and I don't, that Russia is losing the war, as the Germans are fighting a new kind of defensive offensive in which they cause the Russians to waste men and materiel. And the Germans are fighting a good battle against the Americans in Sicily, but it isn't a fair fight because they are outnumbered. Who ever heard of a fair fight? If both sides were even why fight? Just flip a coin, as it would be the lucky one who would win anyway. The trouble with countries is that they don't let each other know just how strong they are. If Germany had known that Russia was so tough she would never have attacked. If Germany had known that the U.S. could fight Germany she would have never declared war on us. If Japan had known she couldn't beat us with a raid on Pearl Harbor she wouldn't have started after us. I saw a newsreel of Pantelleria [an island off the coast of Sicily that the Allies took over early in the campaign] after its fall, and the city was completely destroyed. I can imagine that all of the Italian cities will look the same whenever a fight is put up. You would think they would get wise and stop fighting in their own country. Germany never will fight in Germany because by that time she will realize the end is coming and crawling out would be the smart thing to do. (August 1943)

Actually, only a month before this letter was written, the Russians and Germans had engaged in the Battle of Kursk, the largest tank battle in military history, involving 6,000 tanks, 5,000 aircraft, and more than two million men. There were over 350,000 dead on both sides when all was said and done, and facing the threat of an Italian collapse, Hitler withdrew his troops in Russia, ceding power in the east to the Soviets, so Alec was right not to believe the propaganda.[16]

A few days later, Alec remarked that the lights were back on in Algiers, which felt odd to him after so long with regular blackouts in both England and North Africa:

> This town looks like a Christmas tree now and seems quite queer for me after not having seen a lighted city for almost a year. I guess they figure the German Air Force is passé, which the news would seem to indicate, though they still put up some fight. It's hard to visualize what the airs raids over Europe must be like, as I have never seen a good one and the only part I know much about is the display the Ack Ack [a large anti-aircraft gun] makes at night. . . . The closest I have been to an exploding bomb was three blocks, and that was a mistake because they couldn't possibly have seen me in the dark, so they must have been aiming at something else. . . . Each day brings a new report of the end, and when it starts over here why it should be the final blow for Europe. There is no way of knowing whether they will keep us over here after it is over, but I suppose that depends on the policing necessary and the whim of Congress. You should just cast Congress a hint that your husband wants to be with you. (August 21, 1943)

He couldn't have known then that the battle for Italy would ultimately be long and drawn out, and that the European invasion wouldn't take place until the following spring. It seems as though he saw each battle as the beginning of the end of the war, rather than one piece of a larger strategy, but this point of view allowed him to keep his upbeat perspective for quite some time, at least in his letters to Mary. In late August, the Allies carried out a bombing raid on Berlin that made the news in North Africa, which also fed Alec's optimism about the outcome of the war: "I hear by the news that Berlin was bombed quite badly. That's the way it should be. It will make the Germans weaken quicker. The

As work slowed down, Alec had more time for sightseeing and photography. This is his photo of La Grande Poste (main post office) in the center of Algiers. He never mentioned whether the Army used regular postal facilities to deal with mail for the GIs, but there are definitely plenty of folks in uniform hanging around these steps.

Germans tried the same thing on England, but it just made the English more determined to fight, but I don't think the Germans will want to fight when things look too black" (undated fragment).

Negotiations continued with the Italian diplomats through late August and into early September, but even after the Italians signed a capitulation agreement on September 3, it became clear that the Italian army would not be able to defend Rome against German occupation.[17] Allies invaded the coast of mainland Italy at Salerno on September 9, not expecting much fighting because of the Italian capitulation. However, they encountered fierce German resistance, and the fighting went on for another ten days before the Germans withdrew, destroying and booby-trapping all infrastructure they possibly could as they retreated.[18]

This destruction set the stage for Alec and his crew to come in to start rebuilding. On September 8, 1943, he wrote to Mary, "Italy is out of the war, so now I'll be needing that Italian book that I asked for," which suggests he knew exactly where he was going next. He also described some soldiers' response to the Italian capitulation:

What do you think will happen now with Italy out of the war? That should make it much shorter I would say, and I should soon be back with you in the States. Let's hope Germany bursts just as quick. When the news was announced tonight, one of our men who can speak Italian said, "Italian lessons, 50 francs each, right this way," which gave us a laugh. I suppose that you are higher than a kite tonight, maybe so high as an airplane, with the good news. Our men let out a few big yells and then went right back to their poker game, so the effect here didn't last too long, though probably tomorrow will be an easy day as people won't be thinking about things they want done but about what's happening in Europe. What are you thinking about? I am thinking of you. (September 8, 1943)

Obviously, the Germans didn't give up, and fighting continued in Italy another year and a half after the Italian capitulation. In late September, the autumn rains began, and it became clear that the Allies had misjudged the harsh Italian climate with its mud and cold, which made fighting more complicated and unpleasant. But in the first few days of October 1943, Allied troops finally rolled into Naples to much local acclaim, only to find that the city had been "mutilated" by the Germans: "no running water, aqueducts and sewer lines wrecked, telephone and electrical service destroyed, bridges and railroad tunnels destroyed, many industrial plants gutted or wired for demolition, cultural atrocities everywhere, and the port destroyed."[19] As thousands of Allied troops poured into Naples throughout October, reconstruction began on the roads, railways, and harbor, and it was clear that there would be plenty of work for Alec and his crew of utilities engineers when they arrived in November of 1943.

10

LAST DAYS IN ALGIERS

JUNE – NOVEMBER 1943

While Allied combat troops were busy trying to gain a toehold in Italy, life was unfolding in relatively normal fashion for the support troops remaining in North Africa. Though Alec might have known he would likely be sent to Italy once the Allies had secured Naples, he continued to write to Mary with his impressions of the country in and around Algiers without mentioning any possible change for him. One of the incidents he shared concerned a boy and a donkey:

> Life here goes on from day to day without much excitement. There is a great deal of things of interest to see and quite a bit of humorous incidents, which help to make things more enjoyable and to shorten the apparent time. One day I saw a little Arab kid with a donkey out in the middle of a busy street. The kid was in front of the donkey just pulling for all he was worth, but the donkey just refused to move. It was just the type of incident that one associates with a donkey.

Alec told Mary how much he enjoyed the chance to swim regularly in the Mediterranean and wished she could join him where "the water is warm and the beach shallow so that you can swim right through the breakers, which are very small, and there is no undertow" (June 1, 1943). This was a far cry from swimming in the Pacific Ocean, which would have been his only other ocean swimming experience, colder and more dangerous and

Alec loved swimming in the Mediterranean, though he never mentioned surfing to Mary.

The beaches in Algiers were very different from the rugged Pacific Coast.

unpredictable. He sang the praises of the local fruits—melons, peaches, and plums—though they needed to be peeled for safety, and even then, they sometimes gave him minor gastric distress. He was happy, though, not to have experienced dysentery, which plagued some of the other soldiers in his unit. Though others complained about the heat, the local weather didn't seem to be as big a challenge to him as the heat and humidity they had experienced during basic training in Missouri the previous summer. In the absence of work-related anecdotes he could share with her, he occasionally gave Mary some details about his day-to-day life at AFHQ.

> I am sitting out in the front yard this evening again as it is so nice and cool out here while in the house the humidity and the flies make me rather uncomfortable. Humidity is rather funny: outside here it is slightly chilly while in the house one perspires. The people here talk a lot about their heat. "Il est fait chaud" is their expression. But actually it isn't as warm as Missouri and the nights are comfortable.

> Here we are not supposed to put ice in any drinks, as it is not considered clean. Well, one of our men was making up some lemonade for himself, and just as he dropped a big piece of ice into the pitcher the medic came around the corner and caught and gave him hell. You should have heard him afterwards say how all he could do was just stand there and make no excuses, as he had been caught red handed. He is such a conscientious person about the food for the men being clean that it made him feel rather bad about it.

> The Frenchman here has just brought me a glass of nectar,* which is my favorite alcoholic drink, as it is sweet and has a good flavor and also will make one very drunk if drunk in any quantity. Today I tried a cigarette just for a change of some sort, and you should have heard Majors Smyth and Kelly tell me how they would have to get a stretcher and words to that effect. Anyway, I can't see why anyone would want to smoke

---

* I've not been able to find any information about this drink, but it could possibly have been any fruit liqueur or perhaps something like a Bellini, which is peach nectar with prosecco (though for the French it would, most likely, have been a crémant or a champagne instead of prosecco).

the darn things. They don't taste good and the smoke gets in my eyes.

The fleas have been bothering me again, but I keep forgetting to bring the spray home. You know me and my memory. The government owes me $40 for some stuff I bought, and I keep forgetting to turn in a voucher for it. Anyway, money doesn't mean much to me now as I have plenty for everything I need. I do get gypped on my laundry, though. The prices here are about twice what they would be in the States but I think some of that is the artificial rate of exchange on the dollar to franc. My laundry runs about $10.00 a month, PX $4.00, meals $24.00, and the rest I don't know. Anyway, I am in the money now, but what's the good? I have no one to have fun with and just lie around and enjoy living with. (July 31, 1943)

According to an online forum thread for WWII combat engineers called "What Was Your WWII Pay?" the soldiers on that forum remember that officers in the Army at Alec's rank would have been making about $2,000 a year (the equivalent of about $22,755 in 2016), plus a 10 percent bonus for overseas duty, with 10 percent of the total sent home to wives or family members as an "allotment."[1] Because Alec didn't drink heavily or smoke, he would have been able to send even more of his pay home to Mary, once he had covered his own expenses. He mentioned sending money orders home in a number of his letters.

Alec continued to enjoy exploring the countryside in and around Algiers, which was probably part of his utilities work, though he was never able to say so directly:

This afternoon I took quite a long ride in the country and was very favorably impressed. This country here has the climate of southern California but combines the good features of eastern Oregon with the greenery of the Willamette Valley. Actually it is a prettier country than California, as it isn't so dry. The people here think it gets hot and have been complaining already (the French, I mean), but it hasn't yet been as warm as what we had most of the time at Waynesville. Now the French go to lunch at noon and get back at three because of the heat, but I wouldn't like that, as they make the time up by starting to work earlier in the morning and working later in the evening. Before the war they used to take the whole afternoon off, but not now. "C'est la guerre." (June 11, 1943)

One bit of excitement for the troops in Algiers was a visit in mid-June by King George VI of England to North Africa, where he made stops in Morocco, Algiers, Tunis, and Malta. Though the preparations were highly secret, once the king arrived, the media covered the visit extensively, so the world could follow His Majesty's tour, but it turned out that some parts of his visit were unexpected:

> I imagine that you have seen that the king of England visited this country. One of our men was doing some plumbing and someone behind him said, "It's warm here today," and the plumber looked up and it was the king, and it surprised him so that he couldn't answer. And that reminds me of something else that happened to one of our men. He was doing some work and a big shot asked him how long he had been in the Army. He said one year, and the big shot said, "I have been in it 42 years," and our man said, "I hope I don't have to stay in that long." (June 18, 1943)

Though most of Alec's interactions outside of those with other soldiers were with the French in Algiers, he did talk occasionally about the Arabs, but while he was definitely critical of their "filth," he rarely commented on the poverty they must certainly have been experiencing. In fact, his letters implied that he actually avoided looking too closely at Arab living situations at all, if he could. It was rather curious that he was interested in South American culture but not that of Islamic North Africa, but in that regard, he was probably typical of his generation. He reported to Mary about an interaction he had heard of between a soldier and an Arab family that seemed to exemplify the kinds of challenges westerners experienced:

> It seems that this soldier boy came from one of those small towns, something like Waynesville, and is what you would call a typical hillbilly. Well one day an Arab woman asked him if he would bring some old engine oil over and spread it around the Arab woman's baby crib to keep the ants from getting on the baby. This soldier boy, being an obliging soul, went over

and found that the Arab house had no "John" and that the Arab woman was using the yard and not covering it up. So he proceeded to give her a lecture about it, and as he couldn't speak her language he had to illustrate with actions. He showed her how she should dig a little hole and then cover it up afterwards. He then got some Arab kids and some shovels and had them clean the yard, and then told the Arab woman that he was coming back in a week to check and see that she was covering her piles up. So you can see that even though places like Waynesville had no toilets, some of the people had better ideas. (July 12, 1943)

Neither Alec nor the soldier probably knew anything at all about Islamic toilet etiquette, nor did the Arabs living in poverty in Algiers have indoor toilets, so defecating in the yard might have been their only alternative, though there were cultural strictures about exactly where to defecate, which hand to use, and how to wash afterward. Though covering the piles would certainly have been more hygienic, it's likely that the woman and her family never used the designated toilet area for anything else.

It was likely that the Allied soldiers interacted with Arab kids more often than they did with Arab adults. Alec told Mary about

Alec loved the fresh produce available to the GIs in Algiers, which was probably purchased in street markets like this one.

watching some of his soldiers outside "throwing tin cans back and forth to the Arab kid and having a great time of it" (July 11, 1943). In the same letter, he also told her that their office "is now situated so that the Arab kids can get to it, so I get a shoe shine every morning and now look like a sheik, your particular brand of sheik" (July 11, 1943). And in spite of not liking the squalor in which the Arabs lived, he did admire their craftsmanship and bought Mary an Arab veil. He said he was going to take a photo of himself in the veil and confessed that his French friends were interested in seeing that photo. Further, he requested that she take a picture of herself in it and send it to him, but unfortunately, no such photos surfaced in the images that survived after the war. He told her that a buddy of his had tried to send home a German helmet, but the censor had returned it because he didn't have written permission from the commanding officer, though Alec didn't think the veil was going to be a problem to send home.

In addition to his opinions about the Arabs, he continued to share with Mary the differences he had noticed between the Americans and the French, especially when it came to their attitudes about women and family:

> You know the longer you have among a people, the more you find out things about them that a first impression doesn't reveal. I don't think I mentioned it, but I had noticed the great number of babies here, so one day I asked a Frenchman about it. He said he had noticed it, too, and that after the Armistice [November 11, 1918] they passed a law giving money to people for having more children and making birth control illegal. Another thing, French women over here have no rights before the law or at least hardly any. If a woman leaves her husband for any reason before she applies for divorce or separation, she can't have it, even if he beats her. A few years ago they provided a law, though, that it was no longer necessary for women to obey their husbands. Even with this, why the French are visibly more affectionate than Americans. (July 1, 1943)

A few weeks after this letter, he got on that same soapbox and waxed philosophical about marriage, including some harsh critiques of French law and the rights, or lack thereof, of French women, ending with a strong denunciation of certain elements of Catholicism, the primary religion in France for centuries:

I wonder if I told you about the French law that a husband
can get a divorce if his wife thinks of another man while the
wife can't get one until the husband brings home his mistress
to his wife's house. It's a strange world we live in, or is it? The
people don't pay too much attention to getting married but
just live with a person whom they love. It's said that there
was practically no prostitution, perhaps because the system
makes it unnecessary. Really the only reason for having a
marriage ceremony is to protect the children and see that they
are brought up right, and I don't think it does that in many of
the cases. Maybe I just feel that you are my property because
you want to be and so I am not worrying about some law that
keeps you mine. You know people do a lot of self-torturing
by standing by standards that they realize are not true but
won't admit it. A country makes resounding speeches about
how they are making this the last war. I wonder if people who
make those statements really believe in them when in the
same breath they want to make part of their own people their
slaves, and what are you going to do about a church that cries
peace and brotherly love but condones poverty, disease, and
class discrimination if it will increase the power of the church?
Personally I think it's a hopeless situation and the only thing
anyone can do is admit the situation and adjust his life
accordingly. (August 30, 1943)

The event that seems to have provoked most of these musings
was the marriage of his French teacher, whose fiancé had finally
returned from Spain. When the wedding took place in the summer
of 1943, he sent Mary a detailed commentary about the ceremony:

Well you can finally relax now for my French teacher got
married yesterday. It was a funny sort of a ceremony for me,
as it was Catholic. There were a lot of young boys running
around and kneeling, a lot of ringing of bells, a lot of throwing
of holy water, and then the people were up and then they
were down on their knees, then he was up and she was down,
half of the audience was up and then half of it was on their
knees. I could understand the marriage words even though
they were in French, but I couldn't understand what the Latin
was, or I could hardly hear it. The audience seemed to know
what was going on, as they knew just when to get up and

down. All during the ceremony the organ played and when it hit a strong chord why then that was a signal for something to happen. Really though I did know what was going on, but just seems to be so queer as a form of religion that's all. They first had a straight Catholic wedding and then it was followed by communion and the jumping up and down depended on whether they were taking communion or not. The bride wore a white dress just exactly like yours and a white veil and looked like she had just conquered the world. In fact it seems to me that type of marriage ceremony is a woman's function for there were about a hundred people there and only about ten men. After the wedding everyone took turns kissing the bride in the French manner of rubbing cheeks, which must be a godsend to the bride over our way of kissing. Following the wedding there was a reception in the bridegroom's father's apartment for the relatives and a few of the friends, and they served seven different kinds of cakes, some chocolate, and some bubbling wine. The priest was there and told the trouble he had getting the material for her dress. You see she couldn't get any and so he used his influence, but he didn't understand about women's clothing and the people were suspicious as to why he should be buying organdy cloth. I think I now know why the Catholic Church has such a hold on their people. It's the ceremony and the fact that the individual has a part to take in the ceremony, but it seems sort of pagan to me, what with the waving of holy water and the continual motions over the altar. . . .

I don't like the formalities of society. It is nice to be polite, which I am not, but formal acting seems to me to make people just cogs, and as for me I want to be different and do things that others don't do, such as the way we dash off on the spur of the moment for a long trip or live in a place like Waynesville where most people we know wouldn't think of living. Maybe that's why I want to go to South America after we get together again. I just want to always be doing something new and different and never settling down to routine such as working too long at any one job. (August 1943)

A few weeks after the wedding, he wrote that his teacher and her new husband were planning to move to Oran and eventually wanted to settle in Madagascar, so to visit them, "we are going to

This postcard shows a scene that Alec would probably have seen regularly on his trips outside the city.

have lots of traveling to do after the war is over. I like to travel, though, and that's what I would like to do after the war, if you don't mind" (October 1, 1943).

In connection with his reports on his teacher's wedding, Alec again shared his thoughts about marriage with Mary and connected them to his thoughts about a woman's place in wartime. These are similar to things he wrote to her when the WACs first arrived in Algiers earlier in the spring, and it's fascinating to read his progressive ideas, especially for a young man in the early 1940s:

> Personally, I don't see what a marriage ceremony has to do with
> two people except making it legal. It was possibly originally
> made to protect the raising of children and later on to protect
> the wife, but now the only thing I can see it is for is to protect
> the children and possibly the wife when it is not possible for
> her to make a living other than being married. I don't think it
> should be something that is used to protect a woman who is
> not a good wife, and I think divorce should be made easy when
> no children are involved, possibly with just an application
> and a cooling off period before it was to become final. Where
> children are involved, I would say that no divorce should be
> allowed unless some arrangement was made for taking care
> of the kids. I get into arguments over here with the other men

about the WACs. They are all for keeping them back in the states, nice and safe from anything, which mainly amounts to keeping them away from the vultures (soldiers) over here. Their idea is that a woman's place is in the home; but I don't quite think that is true. I think a woman's place is where she wants to be, and if she wants to be in the front lines of a war, that's the place she should be. I know the place I like you, and that is in my arms and that's where you are going to be one of these days. (August 6, 1943)

In spite of his seemingly feminist point of view, he used traditional romantic phrases to refer to her, such as "my sweet," "my love," "my pet," "my one and only," "my lovebird," and other such possessive endearments. He also referred to her as his "one and only girl" and "his only sweetheart" and used the language of "belonging together" and belonging "to each other." In the midst of these declarations, he often hoped that she would agree or that she wouldn't mind that he loved her so much. He also suggested that it was her independence and difference from more traditional women that drew him to her in the first place:

Wif, you know I like you, and one of the things I like about you is how you can do things other girls can't. How many other girls do you know of would take a radio apart when it doesn't work to see if they could fix it? I get to see lots of times just how helpless they are when something comes up that they haven't learned before, and it makes me think, well my wif would have done something. It might not have been just the exact thing to do, but it would help the situation. Of course, I also love you, but that's for your lovemaking and for no other reason. You just wrapped your arms around me in some unknown way, twisted your finger, said some magic word, and you had me caught. Well, so I did chase after you, but there was something about you that just made me want to catch you and have you catch me. (July 19, 1943)

He also imagined what their reunion would be like when he got home after the war:

Sometimes I wonder just what we will do when we meet for the first time. It will be a strange sort of a meeting I'll bet, but we will act the same as we used to do only more so, for we will know what it means to be away from each other for a while. I wonder what Pete [their dog] thinks of it. Do you suppose that he will remember me when I get back, or has he transferred all his affection to you? Of course, Pete is a very affectionate person and always has room for someone else in his heart, so he will get to know me soon if he has forgotten. I think, though, that he is going to be a little jealous of me for taking up so much of your time, for you darn well won't have time for anything but making love in various forms. (June 5, 1943)

This postcard shows the kind of neighborhood it's likely Alec's buddy encountered visiting the Arab woman with the "toilet" problems.

He occasionally returned to his self-critical commentary, and as he got more and more exhausted, he seemed to blame that, too, on his "laziness" and lack of ambition:

> That has always been one of the things that I don't like about me. I never have enough push to make myself do what I want to do. It is even the same with the taking of pictures. I would like to take lots of pictures, but I just don't have the push so I practically never take any. Maybe I need some C vitamins but I imagine that what I need is to have been brought up liking work, though I don't know how anybody could ever have taught me to like work. I don't even like work that I like, if I have to do it so long. You see I am just a dabbler and after the initial dabble, why I want to rest and think of something else to do. . . . That's why I say that we must have a long vacation after the war, as it will take a super vacation like only hobos get to make up for the time we have lost. Really I can't say that all of my time has been lost, as I am getting a lot of enjoyment out of my travels, and I can remember how I used to look at the map of Africa and think how I never would get to see that part of the world. It is funny how things can change so suddenly. Maybe the war will change suddenly and we will all be coming home. And maybe I will change suddenly and get up and build the fire, but I doubt it. (June 11, 1943)

The business of building the fire appeared to be an ongoing joke between them, perhaps based on a disagreement when they were first married over whose job it might have been to get out of bed first thing in the morning to stoke the wood stove, and perhaps he believed that women could also be the ones to start the morning fires, which seemed to needle her a bit. He referred to it every now and then throughout his letters, usually as part of a reference to his laziness. He even asked her once, "What kind of love do you like best? The kind where I would look at you from a distance and sigh and build the fire in the morning, or the closer kind with poetry and fine words but no fire, or the real close kind with lots of heat but still no fire?" (August 31, 1943).

At this point in the correspondence, he started complaining again about the irregular mail delivery, but he did admit that supplies for the campaign in Sicily were likely taking up all the room and would get priority when it came to overseas transports.

He reiterated her complaints about his letters being too short, and agreed that she was right, but insisted that it "just seems that I never was made with too many words" (June 2, 1943). He told her he often thought of things to write to her during the day, but when he returned to his room and finally had time to write the letter, he had forgotten most of them. He often used the phrase that his "mind was a blank" or that he had "run out of words." He also turned his lack of ideas about what to write into romantic declarations: "Now that I have said all that I know my mind is a complete blank, and when I mean complete, I mean complete. It just seems as though I am an accomplished person in looking off into space and not seeing or hearing a thing but just dreaming about nothing. Of course, sometimes—in fact most of the time, I am dreaming about coming back to see you and to hold onto you" (June 5, 1943).

He mentioned that he had finally received the camera and film she had sent him, though he didn't always have the time or energy to take lots of photos, in spite of his interest in doing so. He continued to play poker with his buddies from time to time, but it seemed that the soldiers were getting quite a bit of entertainment provided by the Red Cross. He talked occasionally about the movies he'd seen but gave few of them much in the way of specific attention, so he seems to have tired of the more detailed movie reviews he tended to write in prior months when he was in England, saving that effort for only the most outstanding films. One film that particularly caught his attention was a romantic musical comedy from 1941, Deanna Durbin in *Nice Girl*, saying,

> It's the first one that I have seen in a long time that really kept
> me interested all the time. Of course, they had to bring in a
> little flag waving, but it wasn't spread too thickly. I guess it's
> necessary to add ceremony and pomp just to keep most of the
> people interested. The Catholic Church does that and seems to
> have the strongest following of them all. Anyway, I don't like it
> so much. It seems to me that when you have something that
> is good you don't have to go spouting about all time to create
> enthusiasm, but that you should just feel that it is good. I
> could be wrong, though, and probably I am. (July 19, 1943)

In fact, he didn't even name most of the movies he'd gone to see with his buddies, though he did say that there were movies

An unidentified soldier is swarmed by the Arab kids that seemed to follow the American GIs around much of the time.

every night and that he went to every show possible without seeing anything twice, a habit he reminded her they shared while living in Bremerton. Then he wondered, "Do you suppose we will be such movie fiends when we get together again, or will we be only love fiends? Now all we can do is make love by letters and think of tomorrow and remember yesterday" (August 18, 1943).

Alec kept Mary regularly updated on his ongoing health challenges, which included problems with his eyes and his teeth as well as his regular references to feeling sleepy all the time. He talked laughingly about his "choppers" and problems with toothaches and fillings that were falling out and needed to be replaced. He was only in his mid-twenties, but his sweet tooth, and possibly substandard dental care in his childhood, had already given him some false teeth, even before the stresses of the war. He mentioned that he looked like an old man when he took them out and that his speech wasn't good when trying to talk without them.* The eye problem seemed to be chronic, something he had apparently been complaining about since they lived in Bremerton, and his main frustration was that each new doctor he saw wanted

---

* I have vivid memories from my childhood of him dropping a full upper denture and flipping it up over his lip instead of behind it to make silly faces for me that were both funny and a little scary.

to start over to discover for themselves that certain treatments, even ones he'd already had from other physicians, weren't going to work for him. Further, the eye problems seemed to exacerbate the issue of falling asleep when he should have been studying his French, since closing his eyes often helped relieve the eyestrain and burning sensations he had been experiencing. As far as his constant joking about being lazy and needing lots of sleep, he made a reference to something he said his men jokingly called "Danielsitis" when referring to anyone who was flat on his back for any health reason, saying he was well known for that same pose. So perhaps it was a joke of sorts, but it's also possible his exhaustion was real and exacerbated by his rheumatoid arthritis, which was not diagnosed until well after the war. He also complained of getting colds with some regularity, in spite of the warmer weather, but they might have been allergies.*

In the midst of all the personal details Alec shared with Mary are some political suggestions and his musings about inflation and the cost of war:

> I have been reading some of the things the government
> (senators) are going to do for the soldiers when they get back
> home. Okay, I don't want them to do anything for me then; all
> I want is for them to prevent inflation now so I won't have to
> work when I get back. This stuff about training us to take our
> place in the world of space sounds like they must think we are
> some new species which has to be civilized before we are let out
> of the cages. (March 22, 1943)

He continued this same line of thinking in a later letter, complaining about the government focus on work instead of on living well:

> And that brings up the stuff we have been reading about what
> the congress is going to do for the returning soldiers. First we
> are to be trained to take our place in a civilian world where
> one has to look out for himself and doesn't have the guiding
> influence of the Army, and then we are not to be let out of the

---

* Neither of my parents thought much about the possibility of allergies, and when I was diagnosed as an adult with both asthma and seasonal allergies, I asked Mom if I had shown signs of allergies when I was a child. She said that I had no allergies that she knew of, but that I did get "summer colds" fairly frequently.

Army until we have a job waiting for us someplace. It seems that people always are thinking of work rather than of how to enjoy living. Every idea you hear of what to do with the soldiers is some way of putting them back to work, a sort of charity idea of "we don't really need you, but we will make room." Anyway I am wondering if any of these congressmen ever thought that some of us might not want to go back to work. (June 20, 1943)

In the fall of 1943, as the Allies prepared to move their head-quarters from North Africa to Italy, following the progress of the

If Alec ever took a picture of himself in the Arab veil he sent to Mary, she didn't keep it, so this is the closest any of his photos comes to showing Arab garb. It's not clear what this fellow's relationship was with the Allies, but he posed for this photo, so it was probably a good one.

combat soldiers and the slow retreat of the Nazis, the first major gap in Alec's correspondence occurred. After regular letters throughout the summer, there were only two letters in September, both before the middle of the month, only one letter in October, on the first of the month, and no letters in early November, either. Even though the entrance of Allied troops into Naples on October 1 would have been given lots of media coverage, the Nazi troops were not retreating as fast as the Allies had hoped, and they still occupied Rome. Perhaps the gap was due to an increased workload as the Allies prepared to move their support operations to another country, or perhaps many letters went astray as the military mail service tried to keep up with thousands of soldiers on the move. Regardless of the cause for this long silence, Mary can't have been happy about it, especially since the fighting in Italy was so fierce. The next she heard from Alec was November 19, 1943, when he wrote the first of his letters from Italy.

11

THE ALLIES GET ESTABLISHED IN ITALY

OCTOBER – DECEMBER 1943

According to historians, the Italian campaign during WWII, lasting nearly two full years from July 10, 1943, to May 2, 1945, "produced some of the most bitter, costly fighting of the war."[1] Alec didn't have to fight, but he supported the troops who did, and to accomplish this the Allies moved their primary European operations from North Africa to Italy as soon after the Sicilian campaign as possible. In a landscape complicated in the 1930s by various colonial conflicts in northern Africa, especially the struggle over the control of the Suez Canal, unrest in the Balkans, and the Spanish Civil War, Italy had become formally allied with Germany in October of 1936 by signing a treaty of mutual interest. However, Italy didn't actually enter the fighting against the Allies until nearly six months after Germany invaded Poland in the fall of 1939, which began WWII. On June 10, 1940, Italy formally declared war on France and Britain, but historians believe Mussolini didn't think the fighting would last long for his army. He was correct about that, but for all the wrong reasons. The Italian army, on paper one of the world's largest, was in fact, inexperienced at warcraft, lacking in training, and seriously under-equipped from the start. In late June of 1940, Italy invaded southern France and ultimately occupied the southeastern territory near the Italian border after France had surrendered to the Axis powers.

This occupation continued until September of 1943 and had the unintended consequence of actually providing a haven

This is likely from Alec's early days in Naples.

for French Jews fleeing the Nazis because Mussolini refused to round up and deport Jews in the occupied territory in France under Italian control. In fact, according to one account,

> Despite its alliance with Germany, the Fascist regime
> responded equivocally to German demands first to concentrate
> and then to deport Jews residing in Italian occupation zones
> in Yugoslavia, Greece, and France to killing centers in the
> German-occupied Poland. Italian military authorities generally
> refused to participate in mass murder of Jews or to permit
> deportations from Italy or Italian-occupied territory; and the
> Fascist leadership was both unable and unwilling to force the

issue. Italian-occupied areas were therefore relatively safe for Jews.[2]

Italy continued to fight in North Africa and the Mediterranean, as well as to aid in the German invasion of Russia, beginning in 1941. The Italian army took heavy losses in the Russian campaign, and by the summer of 1943, they had withdrawn the remnants of the troops back to Italy, where they provided scant resistance to the Allied invasion of Sicily in July 1943. It was the Nazis themselves who did most of the fighting in Italy and provided the strongest resistance once the Allies entered the country.

German troops had been a presence in Italy since the two countries had become allies against Britain and France in 1940, and when they were defeated, they didn't simply walk away. They booby-trapped or destroyed everything they could in the way of infrastructure on their way out of any city or town in which they had been established. This tactic meant that, even when the Allies were victorious, there was little left for them when they arrived. Allied troops entered Naples in early October of 1943 and had to begin reconstruction of the roads and railways immediately to bring the city back to life. In his book about the Italian campaign, Rick Atkinson asserts, "It soon became evident that Italy would

A view of rooftops and the harbor in Naples, possibly the view from Alec's lodgings with an Italian family.

be a battle of engineers," and "ingenuity became the order of the day, every day."[3] In the first few days in Naples, the Allies discovered several time bombs that forced the evacuation of certain sections of the city for fear the restoration of the electrical power grid might trigger explosions. Naples didn't have potable water until mid-October, and the sewers would not be fixed until mid-December. The battered docks in Naples harbor limited resupply efforts both for restoring infrastructure and for the fighting that continued in the mountains between Naples and Rome.[4] To top it all off, the Allies were totally unprepared for the kind of winter they would experience in Italy. Their initial optimism about a quick victory in Italy evaporated, even as Italy formally declared war on Germany on October 13, 1943, and turned from an opponent into another ally. They also began to fully understand that the Germans would not simply yield and leave the area after losing Naples. In fact, once Italy surrendered to the Allies, Hitler responded with Operation Axis, deploying 16 new divisions in Italy to prevent the Allies from establishing new air bases. Further, he instructed Field Marshal Albert Kesselring "to make the Allies pay dearly for every inch of their advance" through Italy.[5] As a result, what was called the Winter Line—three fortified battle lines south of Rome—which the Allies had expected to breach quickly, became a major challenge.

Of course, Alec could tell Mary none of this, and he wasn't part of the initial Allied entrance into the city, but his long-awaited first letter to her from Italy, sent about six weeks after the fall of Naples, does hint at his situation a little bit, especially some of the damage to Naples' infrastructure:

> Right now I am in bed, as it is chilly and we have no heat. I am afraid it's going to be a cold winter compared to the last one I had, and I am very much in need of you to keep me warm at night. After a year, why I am still lost in a bed without you and get chilly and wake up looking for you. (November 19, 1943)

In this same letter, he told her about looking for one of the men in his unit who had been hospitalized for an eye infection, but because they had moved the hospital just a day or two before, he had been having some trouble locating him, which illustrated a bit of the confusion the soldiers were dealing with. He also told her that he was "in charge of the outfit now." He was once again listening to German radio, and he mentioned that the music was fairly good, but that the propaganda they were broadcasting was "ineffective." As an example, he explained that he'd heard that the cruiser *Wisconsin* had been sunk, but he knew that there was no active cruiser named for a state. In fact, the cruiser *Wisconsin* was under construction and had been since 1941 but wasn't actually put into service until reporting for duty in the Pacific fleet on October 2, 1944. Broadcast propaganda Alec had heard on the boat on his way to Italy suggested that "the 4-Fs were giving all of our girls hot love, and here we were over here while our girls were at home all nice and ready to be pleasured" (November 20, 1943), so clearly the Nazis were trying to affect troop morale as well as to provide misinformation. Right away, he started to complain about locals cheating the soldiers:

> The people here are playing us for suckers, as in Africa. A workman gets 30 to 50 lira a day (50¢) and his wife charges 300 lira for a small washing. We furnish the soap and they want a whole bar of soap with each bundle. It's partly the government's fault for paying the soldiers more than $10 or $15 a month overseas. The rest should be held for us in the States until we get back. (November 20, 1943)

These days powdered or liquid laundry is standard, but during WWII, laundry soap came in bars the size of today's hand soap, and one bar might have been used for several loads. It wasn't until 1946 that all-purpose powdered laundry detergent came into regular usage.[6]

It's clear from his responses to Mary when her letters finally found him in Italy that he knew she was unhappy with what she had been hearing in the news about the Italian campaign, which probably added to her fear that he would have to stay overseas even longer. However, he tried to reassure her that, if necessary, he would tell his commanding officer to "blow it out his B[arracks] Bag," an expression used during WWII by soldiers at the front, meaning "Shut Up!" or "Go to Hell!"[7] He explained it was "an expression we use here when we would like to tell someone where to head in and don't dare" (November 22, 1943). He thought that defiant action just might assure him a trip home for reclassification. Of course, good soldier that he was, he never actually did it.

Alec complained that he could never get warm during his first autumn in Italy.

It seemed he was expecting some kind of restructuring of responsibilities and even a change in his relationship with his unit, now that he had been moved to Italy. Based on the little information he was able to share in his letters to Mary and the few pieces of correspondence from the Army that she kept in her scrapbook after the war, his next moves were ambiguous. What he told her first was:

> There have been some changes here, and I am sort of out on a limb and don't know just what I am supposed to do. Perhaps it will be the same as always but I guess it won't be with the Engineering Detachment. I'll probably find out tomorrow but maybe not for a week or so, as we are a long way from Africa. Anyway it's nothing to bother about as far as I am concerned, but I don't think it will be good for the men. (November 22, 1943)

In his next letter, he had a clearer idea about the impending change and told her that his work "will be the same as ever, but with more men, so I guess it won't be so bad" (November 24, 1943). Given that there was a huge need for infrastructure repair after the Germans retreated, we can certainly guess what the workload might have been for the utilities engineers.

The Nazis left Naples infrastructure in shambles when they retreated. Here Alec is checking a pipe, probably part of the local water or sewer system that had been purposefully decimated by the German Army.

He also made it plain that after only a couple of weeks in the country, he didn't like the Italians much, telling Mary on the night before Thanksgiving:

> [W]hat have we got to be thankful for? For one thing we will have turkey tomorrow and lots of it. For another, that most of us in the U.S. don't live like most of the Italians. I was in an Italian home today, one of the better ones, and the woman remarked in Italian, "Off with Mussolini's head" and ran her hand across her throat, so they don't all like Mussolini here. True, there are the ones here that liked him when he was in power, liked Hitler in his reign, and like us now, and there are the rats of Italians that take things from their countrymen and then say that the Americans have ordered it. It's a hell of a country to be a citizen of. I liked North Africa, even with its Arabs, but they can take this place with its history and stuff it up their hat. (November 24, 1943)

After Thanksgiving, he was decidedly less optimistic about his new situation than he had been only the previous week:

Things don't look so rosy for me now since the change. You see, we were taken over by a larger bunch, and they are now doing their best to ditch me so that there will be another 1st lieutenant opening for them. They are doing the same with Fennel [a peer officer in his unit who came with him from North Africa]; because his eyes are bothering him they are using it as a basis for a transfer, but as yet they haven't found any way to get me out, but just give them time. So, Mary, if I go back to a 2nd lieutenant it will be on my own request to get away from the outfit and not because of anything that I have done or haven't. Of course I will have to wait until things are straightened out so as to be sure of my status. (November 27, 1943)

At the end of this same letter, he joked that he had decided to quit the Army and join the Navy so he could take the first boat home to be with her. Then in a more serious vein, he confessed:

[I]t's going to be fun when things begin to pop here, and I always get more interested in things when they are going rather badly. I even liked the excitement when something went wrong with the lighting system and I had to rush around like mad. Incidentally I hear that they are having trouble with the lights since I left [North Africa] and that they were out all one night. Such stuff won't go very well over here as it's a much more complicated setup. (November 27, 1943)

A couple of weeks later, he was able to tell her, "I am still doing the same work as before with the same group but just under a different arrangement. I am in charge of the electrical section just as before, so things are better than I expected at first" (December 12, 1943). As usual, he couldn't give her any specifics about what he really was doing, but his letters even before this revelation were full of references to playing around with generators and motors and to having to write his letters by flashlight whenever the electrical power went out, which seemed to have been happening with some frequency, so he was doing more engineering than inventory management during his early months in Italy. He was also continuing to interact with various local folks and enjoying getting to know a new country, which continued to intrigue him, even if he didn't like most Italians as much as he had liked the French:

> Today I spoke to a woman who had one baby in a buggy and another well on the way, and she said the Germans took $1500, her jewels and her husband. I didn't ask how much her husband was worth. . . . I suppose that comes with a war. It's the men that make war and the women who do the suffering through them. (November 27, 1943)

The Army continued the practice of having its junior officers stay with local families, and Alec continued his commentary on local food while he did so:

> This noon I had dinner with the Italian woman where I have my room. We had raviolis, which tasted about like what we get in cans, except that I would rather that they were cooked a little more. And we had chicken, of which I ate a great deal. That meal tasted much closer to our cooking than the French dinners ever did. (November 28, 1943)

He said it was a nice place to stay, but he didn't think he'd be allowed to keep it for long:

> I can see that I will probably be outranked out of it and have to live in a barracks, but I don't really care except that it makes it so I have to take care of getting my own laundry done, which is nicely solved now by the family I am living with just collecting it off the floor and putting it in the drawer clean. You should have seen the stack of dirty clothing that I had when I was living in the barracks before and never got around to get it washed. I need you to keep me on the right path so that I will get the necessary baths and change my clothes before they start to stink. You always did keep me in a damn good style, a lot better than I deserved. (December 12, 1943)

A couple of weeks later, he told her, "I am going to change my apartment and move in with some other officers. This place is too lonesome all alone and is so nice that I will eventually be moved out for some big shot to move in, so I will try and jump the gun" (December 23, 1943).

He also had a few things to say about the cold weather and complained that Italy was a "disease-ridden country" where cuts took a long time to heal. He mentioned that he had just met an Italian who had scratched his thumb on a barbed wire fence and had to have it amputated because of infection. He also shared his observations of the way many of the locals were living:

> I see the women in this country, all old by the time they are thirty, and I am glad that it's not that way at home. I guess they are just so poor that work and bearing kids makes its mark on them. There are so many with no teeth and scrawny looking. I guess it's a lack of care when they are bearing kids. If you go into a workman's house here, you are likely to find cows and chickens and kids all over the place. (December 3, 1943)

He complained of having a cold that wouldn't go away and that exacerbated his eye problems as well. After several weeks, the cold had turned into laryngitis, which resulted in his doctor telling him to stay home from work until things got better, threatening that if he didn't, he'd be sent to the hospital to heal. Alec admitted to enjoying the ability to sleep in for a change but was sorry to have missed quite an event at headquarters in mid-December because of being home in bed:

> I really missed some fun by being in bed today. It seems that seven big shots got in an elevator and the elevator was only made for four, and when they pushed the button for up, the elevator went down half a floor and stuck. Fennel said the phone rang 20 times in two minutes and the Guard said, "make way for the electrician" and a bunch of Italians were dashing to help, and a bunch of GIs were doing what they could. We have been having our troubles around here. The thing is they are so darn funny that we just laugh about them and just let someone bawl us out about them. One day the bunch was kidding me about a light fixture that fell down. They said they knew where I could get another, in the opera house. It's one of those immense glass affairs about 12 feet in diameter and 20 feet high. They said that's what I needed so that when it fell down, the people under it wouldn't be able to bawl me out. (December 17, 1943)

This is likely Alec and another utilities engineer, checking out the pipes of the local water or sewer system in Naples.

After his laryngitis episode, Alec's primary mention of the cold was in reference to his feet, "I would like to be home getting nice and warm in bed with my favorite little heater beside me. The biggest trouble I have is with my feet. They just won't stay warm during the day. I guess it's the wet climate here that makes them that way. I want to get them next to you so that they will get burned a little because you are a very hot woman" (December 24, 1943). Cold feet usually mean something is wrong with the circulation, and it's entirely possible that the cold feet Alec complained about were secondary effects of having as-yet-undiagnosed rheumatoid arthritis, but it was easier to blame the cold and damp weather they experienced in Italy that winter.

In early December, the fighting in Italy took a turn for the worse, including the costliest sneak attack since Pearl Harbor, a

Locals get involved in the work to restore infrastructure to Naples, though it's hard to tell which men are working and which are simply looking on.

Luftwaffe attack on the harbor at the Adriatic port of Bari. The harbor at Bari, though on the opposite side of the country from Naples, was the main supply port for the Eighth Army and head-quarters for the Allied Air Force. The attack on December 2 killed over 1,000 Allied servicemen, many due to the accidental release of a secret cargo of mustard gas sitting unloaded in one of the ships destroyed in the raid. The news of this raid was heavily censored at AFHQ, and the gas wasn't actually acknowledged un-til after the war was over.[8] Though the Allies at AFHQ in Algiers had initially been quite positive about their expectations for suc-cess in breaching and overrunning the Winter Line, in reality, the fighting there went on for many weeks and eventually stalled before the end of December.[9]

On the two-year anniversary of Pearl Harbor, Alec noted that he and Mary had now been separated for fourteen months, though he certainly hoped the end of that separation was near and reiterated how close to her he felt, in spite of the distance that separated them:

> [W]hen I am writing to you it's the only tangible contact that
> I have, but there is an intangible contact that is always with
> me. It's the feeling that you are there for me and that you are
> such a fine person to belong to. Sometimes I might think of

doing things that I shouldn't, but when I think of you, why any thought of such things just passes away. You're just such a swell person for me that I want to be as good as possible for you. (December 7, 1943)

He also told her he was not sure what he would do with some of the items she wrote that she and others would be sending to him, presumably Christmas presents, which gave an interesting insight into his day-to-day reality:

I'll be darned if I know what I will do with the shirts you said were coming. I'll have to get rid of something so that I can carry them. Let me list the stuff that goes with me when I travel now:

Another view of the local work crew, presumably repairing damage the Nazis left behind.

one barracks bag—completely full and heavy; one cot; one suitcase; one radio; one mess set bag; one gas mask; one pistol and canteen; and one tin helmet. I have been thinking of going through the whole works and sending home everything that I can't use or need, including the six pairs of pajamas that I have left from last Christmas, because it makes me mad every time I have so much trouble moving all the stuff. I almost bought a pair of binoculars the other day but later changed my mind. The price seemed right but I guess I just didn't want them bad enough. If it had been an Exacta [*sic;* "Ekakta," the camera he already asked her to send to him] it would have been different. I would have bought it in a minute, or a ticket home to you in less than a second. (December 7, 1943)

It seemed her letters were now only three weeks behind, and he was eager to hear from her that she had finally mailed the Ekakta camera to him, though he had also given her instructions to test it out for him before she packed it up for mailing. He admitted, however, that when she mentioned turning knobs, he got "anxious all over" (December 15, 1943). She had apparently also complained to him about her in-laws teasing her over his beautiful French teacher, to which he replied with characteristic candor:

The kids in the barracks used to make remarks about her when I went down to her house also. It seems that everybody has to have a bit of the prude in their outlook on such things. I think I'll write my folks and tell them to quit kidding you, or should I tell them that I know who my wif is and why I want her above anyone else, so much so that I wouldn't do anything which might make her think I was untrue? Mary, I couldn't say that I haven't thought of being untrue to you, but that's as far as it will ever go and that doesn't have a thing to do with love but is just a passion. For while at times I might wonder how it would be to have someone since you are so far away, deep down I don't want anyone but you and I want you very much. You can let the people talk about your wild hub because secretly the laugh is on them, as you can be sure that you are my only girl. When the bunch around here gets joking about the 4Fs at home with our wives and allotments, why I just smile and say sure, but I know it's not so and that's something that a lot of the soldiers can't say.

Really though, I don't think I'll tell my folks anything, as that is
something between you and me and we know how things are,
and it doesn't make very much difference what others think as
long as we have each other. It's the thought that we are so sure
of each other that goes a long way to make our marriage as
perfect as it has been. If you were to tell most people how well
we got along together they wouldn't believe it because to them
it isn't possible. (December 20, 1943)

In mid-December while still on doctor-ordered bed rest, Alec
started to comment on larger events of the war:

This afternoon I heard the radio report that Ike might be sent
to London, so that indicates that there is some planning afoot
to get started with a big campaign. . . . If so that means that
we will be getting this war over soon so that going home will
be in order. Tonight another one of our men was selected to go
home for a visit. He was wounded in Tunis so I don't imagine
he will be sent overseas again. They ought to send me home
just for my benefit, but I don't expect it until it's over, as there
are so many over here that really have done something to
deserves a trip home. Sometimes it annoys my guts a little to
see some of the back slapping that goes on and I don't see why
persons who just do their job and do it right should be given
a medal for it when they sleep every night between sheets and
the most dangerous thing is crossing the street in heavy traffic,
but I suppose it helps morale somewhat somewhere. I saw
in the paper where your friend, Patton, was turned down for
permanent rank of Major General and so now I can say I told
you so, but you probably didn't understand. I saw him once
a long time ago. He sure wears a nicely tailored uniform and
highly polished riding boots. (December 17, 1943)

The refusal to promote Patton was possibly related to the slapping incident during the Sicilian campaign. In addition to being
reprimanded by Eisenhower and required to apologize to the soldiers, he was not given the command of Operation OVERLORD,
the Normandy Invasion, as many had expected, because Ike believed that Omar Bradley, though less experienced, would be a
steadier influence than the fiery Patton. However, this information was not publicized, which gave the Allies an opportunity to

create something they called Operation FORTITUDE. Because the Germans, who respected Patton above other American commanders, presumed he would be involved in any major invasion, taking Patton out of the limelight helped the Allies mask the actual location of the invasion by feeding the German high command regular false intelligence that led them to believe Patton was preparing to command an invasion at Pas de Calais, a location significantly to the north and east of the real invasion location in Normandy.[10] It's not likely a soldier at Alec's rank would have had any detailed information about Operation OVERLORD or Operation FORTITUDE, but he clearly had a sense that something big was in the offing.

As Christmastime approached, his letters complained about this being their second Christmas apart, but he didn't have much to say about what the soldiers might be doing for the holidays in Italy. However, Atkinson suggests that Christmas in Naples in 1943 was quite jolly for most of the soldiers, despite a near epidemic of typhus, which led many of the soldiers to greet each other with a cheery "Merry Typhus."[11] By this time, the Fifth Army had moved its headquarters to the palace in Caserta, 25 miles outside of Naples, and it's likely that Alec was working there as well as in the city. The Allies were now predicting victory over the Nazis by the fall of 1944, and as 1943 drew to a close, both Eisenhower and Montgomery left Italy for London to begin preparation for Operation OVERLORD, scheduled for June of 1944. On New Year's Eve of 1943, Ike sent a message to all his soldiers in Europe: "Until we meet again in the heart of the enemy's continental stronghold, I send Godspeed."[12]

Alec took a lot of ribbing from his buddies because he asked Mary to test his new camera system before sending it overseas to him, but she was an accomplished amateur photographer in her own right.

12

BACK AND FORTH; NAPLES TO ALGIERS AND BACK

JANUARY – JUNE 1944

Atkinson noted in *The Day of Battle* that Naples was among the world's busiest ports during the Italian campaign because of the amount of materiel required to keep the Allied troops supplied for battle with the Germans. It was 50 miles from Cassino and 90 miles from Anzio, both of which would become significant in the Allied combat strategy in the first few months of 1944, and Americans had complete control of the city in spite of the ongoing fighting in the mountains between Naples and Rome. The city was teeming with Allied soldiers, and for most of them, it was a place to indulge themselves between battles, though there were occasional air raids, bombings, and lootings. Entertainment abounded, including movies nearly every night and the reopening of the San Carlos opera house. Prostitution flourished and VD patients, both soldiers and prostitutes, took up over 15 percent of the available hospital beds. Typhus continued to rage in January and February, probably because most civilians were reported to have had head lice, which spread typhus, and which was treated by the Allies with DDT spray on the scalp. The locals were poor and relied on the Allies to prevent starvation, but in spite of all the American MPs on duty in the city, two-thirds of the Naples economy was said to derive from transactions in stolen Allied supplies, including gas, oil, food, clothing, and other items.[1] No wonder Alec was frustrated about the locals he encountered.

In early January of 1944, the Allied command decided on Operation SHINGLE, an amphibious assault near the end of the month at Anzio, a coastal town on the Mediterranean about three hours northwest of Naples and an hour south of Rome. The goal of this operation "was to land sufficient forces to outflank the Germans along the Winter Line and set up an assault on Rome itself."[2] In the weeks that followed that decision, ongoing fighting on the Winter Line, especially the Allied assault at the Rapido River, 50 miles north of Naples, was focused on keeping the Germans

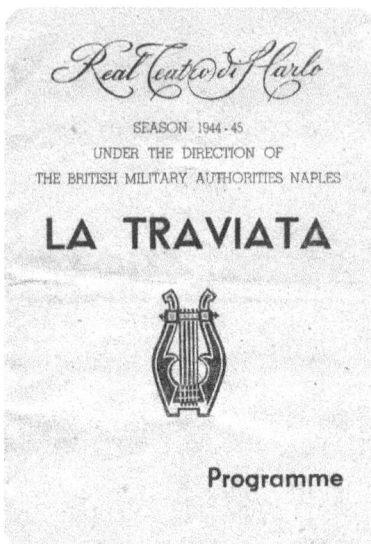

Real Teatro di Carlo

SEASON 1944-45
UNDER THE DIRECTION OF
THE BRITISH MILITARY AUTHORITIES NAPLES

LA TRAVIATA

Programme

Alec took advantage of the available entertainment in Naples to see some Italian opera.

diverted from the beachhead at Anzio. The diversion was successful, in that the Germans sent lots of reinforcements to the Rapido River, but the Allies were so disorganized there, and the German

While fighting raged in nearby Anzio and Cassino, GIs in Naples still played poker. Alec (left) sent this photo to Mary for her scrapbook.

The Allies were using Caserta Palace, near Naples, for their new headquarters.

resistance so fierce, that the casualties were high. In fact, it was considered "one of the worst drubbings of the war [with losses] comparable to those suffered six months later at Omaha Beach, except that that storied assault succeeded."[3] Operation SHINGLE went off on schedule on January 22, and the Allies achieved the hoped-for complete surprise and encountered negligible resistance to the initial landing at Anzio Beach. However, large German forces from northern Italy, France, Germany, and the Balkans soon were headed for the beachhead, and because the Allies did not press their advantage immediately, the Germans began a significant counter-attack less than 48 hours later, and by January 30, the Allies were outnumbered, and fierce fighting, referred to as the Battle of Anzio, continued there for several months.

While the Allies fought at Anzio, French and American troops also mounted an attack at Cassino, in the mountains near the Gustav Line—a staunch defensive line built by the Germans that spanned from the Tyrrhenian Sea to the Adriatic Sea[4]—about an hour north of Naples. The attack began on January 25 and culminated in the destruction on February 14-15 of the Monte Cassino Abbey, a cultural treasure and early home of St. Benedict, because Allies thought German paratroopers were hiding there.[5] February was the bloodiest month in the Mediterranean to date with 1,900 Allied dead, and by the end of the month, it was clear that the German strength seemed to be their ability to regroup, in spite of being outmatched in the air and outgunned on the ground.[6] Unfortunately, the Allies continued to squabble amongst themselves, which dangerously slowed battlefield decision-making,

The palace grounds looked a bit the worse for wear as the Allies took over Caserta after the Nazis abandoned Naples.

and they continued to underestimate the German resolve to hold Italy as long as possible.[7]

While this intense fighting was going on nearby, Alec continued to write to Mary as if Naples were just another assignment, using a matter-of-fact tone in his letters and focusing on mundane daily details. He told her about moving his lodgings, that he had recently been to a stage show, featuring GIs, including one fairly well-known soldier, whose name he couldn't remember but who supposedly also composed popular songs, and that there were movies to see nearly every night. He also told her that poker games had resumed, and he continued his modest winning streak. He even sent her a photo of one of the games, taken with his new Ekakta. He continued his grumbling about the people back home who believed that soldiers should have jobs before being discharged and complained, "Damned if I agree; for I just want to loaf around with you and make that my job. You can have me as your chauffeur to make the records look right. I sure could go for chauffeuring you around right now, or anytime" (January 15, 1944). He started talking more about wanting a family and needing to go home to do something about that: "You are my little sweetheart and I think something ought to be done about that brat* problem. They should give me leave to fix that up because I think you need me. That's something that will have to be taken

---

* In military culture, the term "brat" is not used as a pejorative but instead connotes affection and respect. Though today it refers to children of career military personnel, Alec was using the term to refer to their future children.

care of soon after we get together" (January 15, 1944). When tell-ing her that the only job he wanted after the war was making love to her, he referenced a recent movie he had seen, a romantic comedy called *Princess O'Rourke*, with Olivia de Havilland and Robert Cummings, about a European princess in exile in America during the war who falls in love with an American commoner. Her family is hoping for an heir, but she believes they will not allow the lovers to marry because of the difference in their social standing. Some hijinks ensue, including the involvement of the president and a Supreme Court judge, and eventually, the couple is allowed to marry and live happily ever after.[8] Alec enjoyed the movie, especially a particular joke he shared with Mary:

> I like the joke where the man asked what his function was as a consort and was told "producing children" and he replied, "that's not an all-day job." It could be for me with you though, and not with anyone else. There are a great number of things that I would like to do with you. I would like to make love, have a coke or an ice cream soda, or just relax with you by my side. (January 20, 1944)

Along the same lines, he responded to one of her letters with some opinions about the news that her older sister, Geraldine, was pregnant with her third child, while he and Mary hadn't yet been able to make even one baby:

> Your letter said that Gerry thought that she was pregnant again, which if true is sort of knocking them out on a production line. I thought your statement about the closeness between brats affecting the last one rather queer. I would think it would be Gerry that it would affect the most and then only if she weren't taken care of properly. I think you will note those women who have large families and at the same time sufficient money to finance them seen to be physically just as healthy as women who don't have so many brats. In Italy the poor women all seemed older than their age because of so many children, but I think the real reason was lack of proper care and too much hard work taking care of the brats. (April 22, 1944)

He mentioned that a group of her letters had finally found him, including a package with a light meter to go with his new

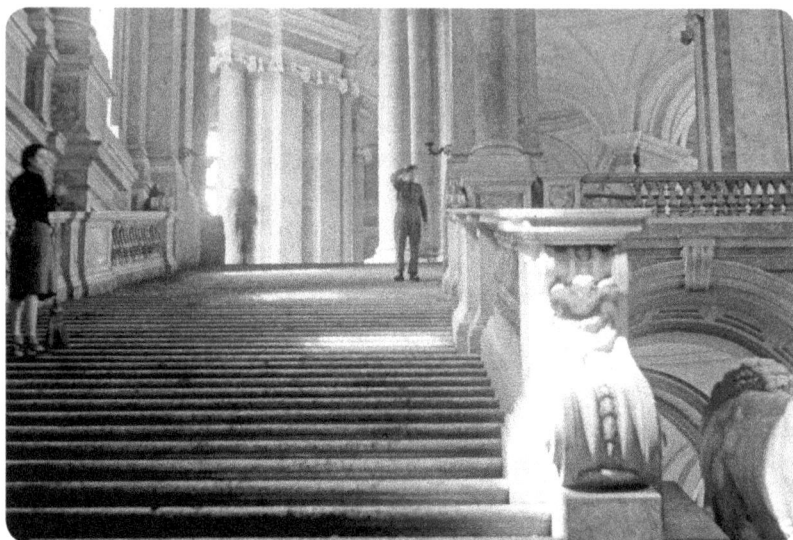

This is the main staircase in Caserta, where the Allies eventually set up AFHQ for the duration of the war.

camera, and he sent her some money orders to offset the cost of the camera, telling her they were "pretty rich, and so are a lot of other people so we aren't any better off for it" (January 20, 1944). He attributed having lots of extra money to the fact that he didn't drink or smoke and only gambled small amounts at the regular poker games. He also explained that he hadn't bothered learning Italian because he didn't like the people and the many dialects made it a rather "hopeless" course of study.

One of the few times he directly mentioned the war itself during this period, the reflection was brought on by seeing one of the free movies provided for soldiers by the Red Cross. This particular film was *A Guy Named Joe,* starring Spencer Tracy as the angel of a dead fighter pilot assigned to guard over a living pilot who happens now to be dating his former girlfriend.[9] Alec liked the film, though he didn't find it one of Tracy's best, but the theme of heroism against all odds provided him with much to think about:

> I like the theme expressed in it but that is probably because I think we only live once and should therefore live as happily as possible, even if new standards have to be made and old mores broken to do it. With a philosophy like that it seems it's very hard to understand what is to be gained by cutting one's life

Alec was fascinated by the artwork in the palace and tried to capture it with his camera. This is one wall in the Hall of Mars.

This is the ceiling in the Hall of Alexander the Great.

short by being a hero. I have wondered why, if the Germans are as atheistic as the papers say, what gives them that extra push to fight it out to the death when death would only mean that they have lost everything. It can't be that they are fanatics like the Japs, for they will surrender when things are hopeless, but with a chance of success they will risk the loss of everything. (March 2, 1944)

The letters from the first two months of 1944 are also full of references to coming home soon, so he clearly continued to share the prevailing American optimism about beating the Germans easily. Unfortunately, that proved not to be the case, but he never admitted it to her, even if he became more pessimistic himself. He told her how much he was enjoying his new camera, even though he often didn't have time to use it as much as he wanted, and now and then he was able to send her some interesting photos:

Yesterday I took some shots of some of the paintings I have mentioned before. I used some flash bulbs on one of the pictures and it took me a long time to get set up and take them. I think the Italians thought that I was a little nuts fooling around on the floor trying to get a shot that would give an idea of the size of the rooms. They are so big that the camera will only catch a small part of them. (February 21, 1944)

This letter suggests that he had already mentioned paintings to her in earlier letters, but there are significant gaps among the dates of the Italian letters, so probably a number of them are missing. The fact that he was working in or near large rooms full of paintings likely meant that he was working at the palace in Caserta, 23 miles north of Naples, in early 1944. The palace, designed in the mid-eighteenth century for King Charles VII of Naples, but not fully completed for nearly 50 years, is the largest royal residence in the world, with 1,200 rooms on five floors, total-ing over 2.5 million square feet in size and boasting gardens and grounds stretching 120 hectares, or almost 300 acres.[10] Caserta served as the headquarters for the Supreme Allied Commander Mediterranean, Sir Henry Maitland Wilson, who had taken over the command from Eisenhower, who had in turn been made the Supreme Commander Allied Expeditionary Forces (SCAEF) in Europe, and the palace would eventually become home to AFHQ, which at this point in time was still in Algiers. Caserta was also the site of the signing of the unconditional surrender of the Germans in Italy in 1945.

Near the end of February, Alec replied to one of Mary's recent letters, obviously feeling sentimental:

> Your letter assured me that you are still in love, even after 17 months [apart], and I can tell you it goes double for me, and then some. I ask you, where could I ever find anyone who would be as good for me as you or with whom I could have as much fun? There just isn't anyone who could possibly take your place because you are a super special deluxe custom-built job, which matches my wants and desires, and there just isn't any other model like that in existence. Mary, I think I am an extremely lucky person to have married you. It was the best thing that could have happened to me. (February 21, 1944)

He called her his "sweetheart," and his "happiness maker," and said that what they had between them was "a bit of heaven." On their wedding anniversary in early March, he wrote:

> Mary, do you realize that it's been four years since we were married? I hope you had a good one because that is all you will get for our anniversary other than that I promise to do better on the next one. It's been a long time that we have been married but it seems that we have been separated longer. It's always that an enjoyable time passes quickly while an unenjoyable time seems like ages. There is only one consideration in the whole affair and that is that this year is ours and after that we can forget our separation and revel in the enjoyment of just being together. (March 2, 1944)

After the anniversary wishes, there was once again a big gap, though some of the photos definitely survived, but it's hard to know exactly what he might have been doing during those weeks.

While the fighting continued in Anzio and Cassino, hope in Rome for liberation was starting to fade by mid-to-late March of 1944. Rome's food supply depended on southern Italy, so the Romans began to starve, leading to ever-increasing prices and even bread riots.[11] Violence surrounded the Allies in Italy, and even the mountains participated, when on March 21, 1944, after

The eruption of Vesuvius from a street corner in Naples.

four days of rumbling, roaring, and shaking that one *New York Times* war correspondent likened to artillery fire, Mt. Vesuvius, 14 miles to east of Naples, erupted with a smoke and lava plume that burst up to 3,000 feet above the mountain and fell back in golf ball sized stones near the crater.[12] Thick smoke obscured the entire Bay of Naples, lava flowed 40 feet deep on the western slopes of the mountain, and secondary eruptions persisted for another week, destroying 800 homes in several villages near the base of the mountain and even affecting the local weather. It snowed in Naples on March 26, and ash did a great deal of damage to trucks, airplanes, and train lines, and some rooftops collapsed under its weight.[13] Though there are no letters where Alec mentions the eruption, he clearly witnessed it, since he took photos of the mountain from a rooftop in Naples and sent those photos to Mary. It was a minor volcanic event compared to the first-century eruption that buried Pompeii—there were only 28 deaths in 1944, compared to over a thousand in AD 79—but when Mary observed the 1980 eruption of Mt. St. Helens from her home in western Oregon, she noted the similarities in the photographic images of both mountains.

Another view of the Vesuvius eruption from the hills near Naples, perhaps from a rooftop or balcony.

After a nearly six-week gap in the letters, Alec wrote again in April, and this time he was back in Algiers. He never clearly explained in the letters that remain why he had to return to North Africa in the spring of 1944, but the move of AFHQ from Algiers to Caserta would have involved a large number of support troops, those non-combat military personnel who provided direct support to the combat troops in Europe. It's likely Alec's travel back and forth between the two locations was somehow associated with planning and infrastructure support for the big move, which happened in July of 1944. He did mention lots of changes going on but that he hadn't been doing much heavy work since returning to Algiers, and he was frustrated with the administrative red tape he was encountering back at headquarters:

> I was so mad at my new outfit today that I almost blew a valve but didn't. They are just not on the ball. Kelly and I have designed a shoulder insignia for the bunch. It's a black ball on a white background encircled in red with a figure right in the middle of the ball. The white stands for the reams of paperwork and the red for all the tape they tie it with. Oh well, it will all come out in the wash and at least I don't have to work too hard

Alec with his beloved Ekakta camera in Algiers once again.

and have lots of time to do what I want and a lot of equipment to play with. (May 4, 1944)

Lt. Kelly turned up in Alec's letters regularly throughout most of 1943 and appeared to have taken over his engineering unit in Algiers when Alec first went to Italy. It seemed they were work colleagues and movie buddies. Alec gave Mary an update on several of his other buddies as well, at least one of whom had stayed at the palace when he had returned to Algiers, others having been transferred to other places. His former commanding officer had been sent "north," probably to England to continue working with Eisenhower, and there was a new major in charge of the utilities engineers in Algiers:

Maybe in another month they will have things straightened out but it really makes no difference. Here there is a lot of work for the men to do but not much for me as everything is all set and the work is mainly repair. Italy would have been a good setup but that whole deal fell through so that leaves me here. I can't say that I care about staying here, as I like to be someplace where there is a lot of new work going on to make it more interesting, but then I would rather be with you than to be anywhere else, so if I have to put in some time here why I can do a little reading and see if I can remember any of the stuff I was supposed to have learned in school. I don't imagine anyone would want to have me after the war with what I know now, so it will probably require a lot of studying on my part before I will be of any value to anyone. (April 19, 1944)

He also responded to her usual complaints:

So you are disgusted with the war because there are no signs as to when I'll be coming home. Kelly and I have a little private bet on what's going to happen, but I can't let it out, as we are not supposed to even guess at what could happen if such and such were true. You are still a civilian and can indulge in such stuff. You know civilians are lucky people and are allowed to use their heads and can almost do what they wish. We aren't bothered too much by that military stuff, but sometimes the petty things like fines for buttons undone or making an error in the trip ticket on a vehicle gets a little annoying. For a while we were plagued with close order drill [the formal movements and formations used in marching, parades, and ceremonies], but the confusion has put that into the background for a while. Our new big boss [British Field Marshal Wilson—popularly known as Jumbo for his size—who replaced Eisenhower when he left for London] is much more of a stickler for that military rigmarole than the old one was. (April 19, 1944)

In one of her letters Mary had, apparently, threatened to take up smoking to calm her nerves about the lack of progress in the fighting with still no definitive idea of when he might be coming home, and he let her know his feelings about that possibility:

Your letter mentioned you were thinking of smoking so I suppose I'll have a little smudge pot when I get home. Mary, you have the wrong idea when you think I don't want you to smoke. What I don't want is for you to smoke when I am around. I haven't got anything against smoking except that

Alec's buddy, Lt. J. T. Kelly, took over his unit when Alec was first sent to Naples, so they worked together again when Alec returned to Algiers for a short time in the spring of 1944.

> I don't like smoke or the secondhand smell of it when I am around, so if you have to quiet your nerves, why puff away. (May 1, 1944)

In the same letter, Alec came closest to explaining his current situation to her:

> It's hard to say just what the score is here, and I don't particularly like the setup or the staying in one place, but there isn't much I can do about it. Kelly has the utilities bunch though I do quite a bit of work with them and still hang around the same old office. I am sort of a glorified stooge because I understand the electrical part of the work and no one else does, so the new regime keeps me here for that purpose and gives me a high-sounding title, "Communications and Electrical Officer." It all came about because Kelly was running the outfit while I was in Italy and also because I was assigned to a different bunch then and because I don't bother to sling the bull with the big shots. I told you once that Shytle [his former major, who most likely went to London with Ike] leaving left me without any political connections and that accounts for a lot of my problems. It doesn't bother me, though, because if I stay here why I'll have time to take pictures and do things I want, and if

I go someplace else there will probably be more of the kind of work I want to do. I didn't say much about it before because I didn't know just what was going on, and when I mentioned a change in Italy why you bothered me with letters about it for too long. (May 1, 1944)

He told Mary that he had recently received a letter from Major Shytle, who had now become a Lt. Colonel: "He said he would use me if I could get up there somehow, and I sure would like to go, but there is a lot of red tape to cut to do something like that, so it is almost impossible" (May 13, 1944).

During what seemed to be a relatively quiet time for the support troops at headquarters in North Africa in the spring of 1944, while the fighting in Italy dragged on, Alec's letters were filled with thoughts about what he wanted to do after the war was over. He was particularly drawn to the possibility of space exploration:

> Every time I think of doing anything after the war, why I realize how little I know to do. There is one thing I would like to do beside loaf someday and that's build something to go to the moon, but I don't think I am smart enough for that and I know darn well I haven't learned enough in school for it. I don't really think anyone has discovered the force to do it yet, so it might be a long way off, possibly after our time, but I think it will be done some day and I sure would like to be in on it. (May 2, 1944)

With more free time on his hands, Alec filled his letters with elaborate declarations of his love for Mary in all its manifestations. In the middle of telling her how much he enjoyed toying with various pieces of equipment, he confessed:

> There is a major plaything that I lack, though, and that's you. I wonder if you realize that you were and will be my most complicated plaything, even more than a bunch of wires all wound over a desk and that you give me more pleasure than my Exacta [*sic*] does. You should know that I love you because I went so long without the Exacta [*sic*] just to have you. I miss a lot of the things between us by being away from you, but mostly I miss your companionship. There are other things I like to do but the thing that I enjoyed most was just being with you and having you to talk to and for my steady girl. (May 4, 1944)

He also used another movie he'd seen recently as a way to explain his feelings for her:

> I went to see "Jane Eyre" and in the last part of the picture when Orson Welles took hold of Jane and ran his hands up around her face, it made me think of you and wish that I were running my hands over your face (no remark from you about their staying around the face only are necessary—you know how I am). If I were in your arms now, I would search all over your shape with my hands and eyes. I'd let my hands run through your hair, and I'd look into your eyes, and I would place my head close to yours so that I could feel your heart beat, and I'd give you a kiss which would just go on and on and eventually I would be wrapped all around you and feel so good inside to have such a perfect woman for my wife, for my companion, and for my happiness. (May 7, 1944)

After reiterating a few of his thoughts about marriage and about why theirs was so perfect, he wrote, "You have a way of looking at me that makes me feel very important, even though I know I am not. I guess we all want someone to appreciate us and that is why it can be so much fun to be married, for we can appreciate each other and also have the fun of playing together" (May 24, 1944). As usual, he waxed philosophical as well as romantic: "being happy married is a lot more than a license. I know we have something between us, which no piece of paper could change" (June 20, 1944). In fact, he admitted that there was only one thing about their marriage he didn't like, "and that is your liking artichokes and I don't. We are quite well matched in everything else" (April 21, 1944).

In the spring of 1944, while Alec waited in Algiers to know what might be next for him, ongoing fighting in Italy resulted in extensive Allied casualties; and desertion, self-inflicted wounds, "combat exhaustion," and discharge for "personality disturbances" became problematic for both British and American troops.[14] By mid-May, however, Alec started to believe that "the Italian situation" was looking better than it had for the past couple of months, so he was even more hopeful that he would be able to come home before year's end.

In May 1944, the Allies began planning for Operation DIADEM, a large offensive to break the Gustav Line and take Rome, as well as to eliminate as many Germans as possible before the Normandy

Alec's Major, Carl Shytle, in Algiers before he was sent to London to work with Ike on the Normandy invasion.

invasion, scheduled for early June. Their strategy included some deceptive radio chatter designed to make the Germans think another amphibious assault in Italy would be coming soon. When the Allies finally did enter Rome on June 4, their success was almost immediately overshadowed in the media by the dramatic D-Day invasion on a 50-mile stretch of the French coast at Normandy on June 6, which Alec referred to in a June 9 letter as "a big rumpus elsewhere." In the last letter clearly sent from Algiers before he returned to Italy, he shared his frustration at the continuation of the war: "You know, Mary, this is supposed to be a civilized world, at least parts of it, and we spend time in blowing each other to pieces and then turn around and set standards of conduct which are based on what we think we ought to be rather than what we are" (June 20, 1944). Finally, in July of 1944, AFHQ was officially moved from Algiers to Caserta, and Alec went with it, back to the country he so disliked, and where he remained for the rest of the war.

13

RETURN TO NAPLES AND CASERTA

JULY – SEPTEMBER 1944

Though he complained of being bored with his wartime work routines, Alec's return to Italy in July of 1944 was anything but routine. While he was never able to share the details of his work in his letters, it's likely that he and other members of the Utilities Engineering Detachment were involved in the monumental endeavor of moving of AFHQ from Algiers to the palace at Caserta, where he had previously taken some photos on his earlier trip to nearby Naples. AFHQ remained at Caserta for the duration of the war. And if the headquarters move wasn't enough excitement, Alec unexpectedly found himself in a place where he couldn't work at all. After a month-long gap in letters, which most likely included travel time between North Africa and Italy, Alec wrote to Mary on Red Cross letterhead that he had been hospitalized in Naples for what he described at the time as "a light fever" and said that several other guys in his unit had it, too, so they were having difficulty getting their work done, especially since Alec seemed to be their primary electrical expert:

> Karas [his current major] is having a heck of a time with all the work, and someone buzzes down every day to find out what they should do about the electrical problems, which seem to cause everyone a lot of trouble. I give them my best advice and relax, and Karas wants to know if I'll be out soon, which I will, darn it all, as this job is a madhouse, and I'll have to get back and get in my working on it. (July 19, 1944)

Back in Italy, Alec tried to retain his optimism about the progress of the war, but it wasn't easy.

He ended up spending eight days in the hospital and another few trying to get back to normal once he returned to his own quarters. In another letter later in the month, he identified the problem that had been plaguing him and the other soldiers as sandfly fever, and he reported that, eventually, even his commanding officer went "down with it."

According to a book about the experiences of military nurses of WWII, sandfly fever was one of several common medical problems during the Italian campaign.[1] It's a "viral disease characterized by fever, malaise, eye pain, and headache."[2] The US Army Office of Medical History documented that "Sandfly fever, also known as Phlebotomus fever and pappataci fever, attained importance in Allied and Axis forces in the Mediterranean Theater of Operations, U.S. Army, in World War II by incapacitating large numbers of men for periods of 7 to 14 days, or longer."[3] Though not well understood when it first appeared in North Africa in 1943, F.U.O., or fever of unknown origin, had been troubling troops for many months before being correctly diagnosed. By the time Alec was hospitalized, Army doctors had become much more familiar with the disease, though some still resisted the diagnosis because there was no standardized medical test for this particular virus, and many of the men who were hospitalized with the fever had never actually seen the sandfly that bit them.

Alec had a relapse a month after his hospitalization, at which point he described his experiences with the disease to Mary in more detail:

> I had a bad night last night as I had a touch of that fever
> again. It's caused by the bite of a sand fly and makes you
> feel completely exhausted, so much so that you can hardly
> move and you get a high fever. I guess I have built up a sort
> of a resistance to it now, though, because I get right over it
> in a night where the first time it took 14 days before I could
> walk around without being all tired out. Anyway, the fever will
> explain why I didn't write to you last night. I just couldn't. I
> was so exhausted I could hardly get to sleep and my legs ached
> as though they had been walked for miles, but this evening
> I feel fine even though the weather is very warm and I am as
> damp as a Missouri evening. (August 13, 1944)

At the same time Alec was reporting to Mary about his hospitalization, she was sending him news about her new job. Though this job was never identified specifically, the way her retail job had been before this, she was likely working in the Port of Portland shipyards in some capacity.* Alec made a couple of letter references that seem to point to this new job being quite different from waiting on customers in Meier & Frank and even mentioned the port once. There was something he identified as her "Engr Det TO" and said it wouldn't tell her much about him because it wasn't "near big enough. There are a bunch of officers that I work with besides those I have mentioned, so you can see there must be a

---

* My brother, Toby, and I each recalled her saying that she had worked in the shipyards during the war and that she had found the work "interesting," which for her was high praise, indeed, but we were never given any more detail than that.

```
SPTAH                      ARMY SERVICE FORCES
Form No. 1155      Portland Sub-Port of Embarkation
5 Apr 45               CERTIFICATE OF AWARD

This certifies that ___MARY DANIELS___
has satisfactorily completed the prescribed course
in _Job Instructor Training_ offered by the
Training Section, Civilian Personnel Branch, from
_5 June 45_ to _8 June 45_ Appropriate notation of
such accomplishment has been made on _Tng_ record.

_____        _____
Civilian Training                 Chief, Civ. Pers. Branch
Administrator
```

This is the only clue to Mary's job at the Port of Portland during the war.

lot more work than your little TO would indicate" (July 24, 1944). It's not clear what TO might mean; perhaps transport order.

Alec suggested in response to one of her complaints, "I don't imagine I do any more than the lieutenant you have at the Port" (August 8, 1944), which implied that she was involved with military personnel in whatever this new job entailed. It appeared that Mary was trying to understand his work in the Army by getting as close to something similar as she could since he had previously talked her out of joining the WAACs, now known as the WACs. And perhaps his encouraging words about her abilities to do things other girls didn't or wouldn't do, like taking apart a radio or being interested in the cameras in the same way he was, had given her the idea to try a completely new kind of work, something that wasn't ordinarily considered work for a woman. The only other clue about this job, though it doesn't appear in any later letters, is a card in her scrapbook identified as being issued by the "Army Services Forces/Portland Sub-Port of Embarkation" and saying that on June 5-8, 1945, Mary Daniels "satisfactorily completed the prescribed course in Job Instructor Training offered by the Training Section, Civilian Personnel Branch." So she continued in this job at the port until the end of the war, perhaps even rising through the ranks in some fashion.

There's only minimal statistical information about women war workers, those women who would not have been working in peacetime, but there are a few general things we know. Richard

Lingermann, in his 1970 book about the American home front during WWII, reported that they were more likely to be married (56 percent), and husbands of one-fifth of those married women were away, presumably overseas in the services. A majority of the women workers were between 20 and 44 years old (Mary was 28 in the summer of 1944), but a sizeable minority were older married women, either childless or with grown children. Another sizeable minority (nearly a third) was young girls under twenty who had dropped out of school to work.[4] Lingermann described them this way:

> The flesh and blood females who womaned the machines and rivet guns and welding torches were all sizes, shapes, ages, and social backgrounds. Some worked under hardships equal in every way to those undergone by men; they showed themselves capable of equaling or bettering the performance of men, and they added both sex and idealism, distraction and enthusiasm to the smoke and grit and flame and sweat of the great factories. They also replaced men in hundreds of job classifications never previously open to them. They even preempted some jobs for themselves permanently because they could do them better. The surprise was not that they could do such jobs but the fact that anyone was surprised they could perform so well.[5]

Clearly, Alec was not surprised that Mary was doing well and enjoying her work at the shipyards, whatever that might have entailed, but he didn't want her to get too attached to her new job:

> I am glad to hear that you got settled in the new job but hope that you won't be settled too long because I want very much to unsettle you and possibly to excite you a little bit emotionally because I feel very emotional towards you. In fact, you are my little powerhouse and create storms of energy for me to do something even involving a little work of a sort. The work I like (and it's work only because it takes energy) is making love to you and it's one of those pleasures that seem to have happened so long ago that all I can do is look at your picture and remember how nice you are. I can write and read your letters of love but that can only be a stopgap to hold in back until such a time that I can get back to you in person. And that's the thing that keeps up my spirits now because I know that we have our

time coming and will be together some time to make our love and have our fun and live our life. (July 19, 1944)

Though Alec clearly admired what he perceived as Mary's strength, courage, and determination, her eldest sister said that during the war years, no one could ever talk to Mary about the war without her bursting into tears, so they avoided the topic as much as possible, especially while Alec was away. Mary was not alone in her distress. In the introduction to their 1995 oral history project about women on the home front during WWII, Sharon Strom and Linda Wood suggest:

> Although many knew the war had opened new opportunities to them and their loved ones, it also brought abiding sorrow and a sense that the world had entered a new phase of its history. [One of their interviewees] described the effect of the war in dramatic terms, "I think for girls and women, and perhaps boys and men, of my generation the war forced them to grow up prematurely. It made them far more serious about the bare realities of life: life, death, values. It robbed them, in a sense, of some childhood."[6]

While Alec was recuperating, and Mary was getting to know her new job, the Allies were starting to take the upper hand in the war in Europe. On July 20, the French troops began their withdrawal from the Italian front to get ready for the invasion of southern France. On the first of August, Patton's US Third Army was activated; on the ninth, the US Fifth Armored Division took Le Mans, and Eisenhower set up a headquarters in France; on the fifteenth, Allies launched Operation DRAGOON, a combined assault on the south coast of France from Toulon to Nice, which Adolf Hitler described as "the worst day of [his] life." On August 16, Hitler ordered the withdrawal of all German forces in southern France, and on the seventeenth, the remnants of the Vichy French regime in the French capital took flight for Germany as the Resistance came out into the open and took strong points throughout the city. Patton reached the Seine at Nantes in northern France on the nineteenth and made the first crossing 30 miles northwest of Paris, and Germans were granted a truce in Paris to withdraw troops. However, they staged a fierce comeback in Paris on August 24, and finally, on the twenty-fifth, the

Alec grew increasingly frustrated with the pace of the war and with what he saw as the frivolous requests he was getting for help.

German garrison surrendered as De Gaulle entered Paris. On the twenty-eighth, Germans in Marseilles surrendered to the French, and by August 31, many other French cities had been liberated by US, Canadian, and British troops. In the Mediterranean, German forces evacuated from Florence on August 4, and on the sixteenth Hitler ordered a withdrawal from Greece. On August 27, the British renewed the offensive on Italy's eastern coast but were slowed by rain and mud. Also on the twenty-seventh, the British attacked toward the Gothic Line—a German defensive line in the north of Italy that formed the last defensive line for the German retreat during the Italian Campaign—at Pesaro, and on August 31, the US Fifth Army successfully completed a 150-mile northward march from Rome by crossing the Arno.

One of the things that slowed down Alec's recuperation and return to otherwise normal health was what he called a "summer cold," which was probably yet another viral infection, which wouldn't be surprising given that his immune system was already compromised by the sandfly fever. Alec was having a miserable summer, and in early August he struggled with exhaustion and headaches every night for another week, but he was also heartened by the reports in the newspapers of the Allied progress in early August. Perhaps being ill for so long caused his temper to fray, but he seemed rather proud to tell her that he actually had gotten mad recently and "surprised everyone" in the mess when he got tired of waiting so long for his meal, so when the waiter reappeared to ask him to resubmit his order after a 40-minute

With AFHQ now situated at Caserta Palace, Alec (left) and his buddies were able to enjoy sights in the English Garden on the castle grounds, so named because the garden, with its waterways and statuary, had been designed in the late eighteenth century in the English tradition that was popular at the time.

wait since putting in his original order, he "just upped and took that waiter back into the kitchen and got my own plate right away" (August 9, 1944).

In response to her continued complaints that he didn't write her often enough, he explained that "it gets to be a problem to say something when every day is just as boring as the one before, and so what with my lazy habit of sleeping in the evening why your letters suffer. I am trying to reform and bring it up to a daily basis" (August 8, 1944). He started to provide her with a few more

More GIs enjoying the sculpture near the top of the gardens in Caserta.

details of his daily work, whatever he could share without getting censored. First, he reported, "Today was just like every other day except that I was at a place trying to make a radio run off of a generator when in walked a big shot [his term for anyone who was above him in the Allied military/wartime hierarchy, regardless of nationality] and caught me at it. He said something to me, but I couldn't understand what it was but judge that it was hello in his language" (August 6, 1944). Alec also mocked some of the more frivolous requests he got:

> Sometimes someone asks me about the voltage or how to connect a transformer or some other question, possibly about a job, and I say, "Let them wait" and so they wait. The whole trouble is I am not very sympathetic with the people at this place, what with their requests for white wire to match the walls when all we have is red [and] quiet signs so that the big shots won't be disturbed by a truck going by, and all the time we have others who have to put up with the noise of gunfire on the front. (August 8, 1944)

Or, "I have to paint my poles green now so as not to spoil the view for some of the big shots, but then I guess we are supposed

Allied soldiers enjoying their local swimming pool, La Peschiera Grande, originally designed to teach Bourbon princes naval warfare strategies. This view is from the castle end of the pond looking up toward the large network of ponds and fountains extending up the hill beyond the castle.

to keep a big shot happy" (August 9, 1944). And occasionally he explained about the dangers of electrical work, some humorous, some deadly:

> This electricity stuff is dangerous now and then. A high wire fell down around here today, and an Italian got curious about it and that was the end of him. There is a great contrast between the way the Italians work and the way we do. They had to see the wire, then go for their engineer, then back to the office, and then out to fix the wire, and if we hadn't been here they would have done it on foot and gotten the work done tomorrow or the next day. Speaking about electricity, the funniest thing we had was an Italian who was sprinkling dust with a hose and having a hell of a lot of fun swinging the hose around until he sprayed some electric wire, then pop it knocked him flat on the ground and was he a surprised and foolish looking wop.*[7] (August 9, 1944)

He also had some choice comments about the "big shots" he was working with:

---

* According to Wikipedia, the term "wop" originated in the early twentieth century, deriving from the Southern Italian dialect term "*guappo*," meaning thug, pimp, or swaggerer. It is used pejoratively but not with as much negative connotation in the 1940s as in the twenty-first century.

Another view of La Peschiera Grande; this one faces back toward the castle.

I have to go over and check the voltage tonight just to see how things stand because I raised it to try and make the bulbs a little brighter, as someone in the states sent us 160-volt bulbs and we have 150. It's just something to add to my troubles along with the fact that the Italians don't care too much what high voltage they give you and so let it drift all over the map.

I had my big transformer working today, which is good because I said tomorrow night and it is well to be early on something like that. My rush job on the big shot's light came back today, as the raised voltage was too much for it, so now I have to do something about that or get hell. Sometimes I think they should leave all the big shots at home so that they would be comfortable and they could officiate by telephone, but that would never do, as home was never like what they want here. (August 10, 1944)

He also reported that he had been surprised to meet an old professor of his from college days:

A funny thing: I met a colonel today who taught military when I took it at OSU, and here he has been with this outfit for 15 months and I haven't ever seen him before. Sometimes I wonder if I ever get around or if I just stay holed up like a hermit. One of these days I am going to hole up, though, and be a hermit, only I am going to be a married hermit and you're going to be Mrs. Hermit, and we will have a hermitage all of our own and maybe some little hermits. (August 9, 1944)

August continued to be hot and humid, and Alec's daily routine seemed to be much more of the same: movies with his buddies, some occasional poker, and lots of electrical work. His health seemed to be improving, and his optimism was also returning because of the Allied progress in France. He reported an interesting conversation about the war: "An Italian lieutenant said today he was through fighting—he said they could take him out and shoot him, but he wasn't going to fight for any side because it was just a waste of energy because regardless of who wins, Italy will be in a hopeless way. I suspect that after the war the U.S. will feel the effects of it, too, with less cars for people to run around in and high taxes to take their excess money away" (August 14, 1944). Of course, he continued to ply his Mary with sweet words of love, such as "I love you with all my heart, if you can love with the heart, and if not, I love with all that a person has to love with and for" (August 14, 1944). Or "It's very important to me to make love with you because I love you so much and because you belong to me personally and to no one else. . . . I like lovemaking and think it's more fun than anything else—what I think is second best fun is playing and going places with you. It all comes down to that you are my fun and my pleasure; you are my love and make my life worth living" (August 26, 1944). He also tried occasionally to amuse her with whatever humorous anecdotes he could muster:

> Today was another uneventful one except for an amusing little incident. There have been a couple of Italian women around several times asking about having their lights turned on, and today they showed up with a letter, written by some soldier I presume, saying that they showed the boys a good time but they really needed lights because it was so hard to find them in the dark. We all got a big laugh out of that because obviously the girls didn't know what the letter said. (August 22, 1944)

Unfortunately, by the end of August, he was having more medical issues, this time with his digestive system:

This week I have been having a bad case of indigestion. The doc at the dispensing seems to have taken a great interest in it for some reason or other, and so I got a real x-ray picture of it, about 10 altogether, and they watched it work and found that it is working too fast, which they say is a sign of eating too fast or some kind of nervousness. I suppose I could be nervous because the setup here makes me so mad I almost blow up over nothing—but when I told the fellows around the office about nervousness they all laughed because I have a reputation of not letting anything bother me. The reason I don't get very excited over any of the work is because it's so unimportant and it doesn't make any difference if they send me out of this place. Personally I'd like to get away, but if I did, I suspect they would let me lay in a replacement pool and that would be worse.

Back to my stomach—I am always hungry even shortly after eating and now I am supposed to eat food at meals with no liquids and drink liquids between meals when I feel hungry. The doc says that I shouldn't use medicine because that would get to be a habit and wouldn't get at the real cause. He stopped me in the mess hall today and said to come up to see him again and he wanted to make a few more tests. I must be an interesting case, but it's annoying to feel hungry all of the time.

Soldiers cooling off in the Fountain of the Three Dolphins at one end of the first pool in La Peschiera Grande.

Really, what I need is a rest cure with you. I never have liked this Italy and have never felt too good here (many of the others are feeling this way here, too). I guess the dirt and the filth and the mosquitoes and insects and dampness make it an unhealthy place to be. In the summer you sweat like everything, and in winter you can't get warm. (August 31, 1944)

This might have been the start of the ulcer problem that would prove to be significant in his later years.

It was in the summer of 1944 that he started to talk about the local swimming pool that was just across from where he worked, a pool he described as so cold that he jumped right out again the first time he went in, but he found it cooled him down for quite a while afterward and made him think he might like to live somewhere

Alec sitting in front of the Fountain of Diana and Acteon in the gardens at Caserta

that he could have a pool in his backyard, saying "it's a lot of fun when the weather is hot, and it makes me feel a lot better than I have for a long time. It takes that tired feeling away" (September 2, 1944). This was definitely not your average local swimming pool, though. While he never identified the pool by name, his photos included several images of soldiers swimming in pools and fountains on the grounds of Caserta palace, so his swimming pool was actually a huge and elegant water feature, designed by Luigi Vanvitelli as an integral part of the palace gardens, combining the tradition of the Italian Renaissance garden with elements from the gardens at Versailles. All the pools, streams, and fountains at Caserta were fed by the Carolino Aqueduct, which was originally built in the mid-eighteenth century to serve the water needs of not only the palace but also the city of Naples and all the farms in the surrounding area. The water originated from springs in the hills above Naples and the conduits were mostly underground, which would account for the chilly water Alec noticed.[8] Alec's swimming pool would have been the Peschiera Grande (literally, the large fish pond), a pool of water more than 1,500 feet long, with the Fountain of the Three Dolphins at one end, from whose mouth came the mountain spring-fed water from the aqueduct.[9] The network of pools and fountains also included a miniature mock castle and was originally used for naval war games for the young prince Ferdinand IV of the Bourbon dynasty. In fact, the fountains and waterways, complete with statuary on all levels, extended almost two miles up the natural hillside surrounding the palace gardens, and it would seem that centuries after those eighteenth-century princely war games, they continued to provide recreational opportunities for many Allied soldiers awaiting their next real war assignments.

In early September, Alec reported that "Things have been moving so fast that they have started interrupting the radio programs to give us the latest flashes. Just a few moments ago they said we had crossed the Belgium border and we are almost to the German border. It sounds good for you and me, Mary; boy will I enjoy getting you in my arms after this is all over" (September 2, 1944). In fact, things were progressing very quickly for the Allies in the Mediterranean and southern Europe. In the Mediterranean, the US Fifth Army launched an assault on September 8 against the Gothic Line north of Florence, Field Marshal Albert Kesselring's last major line of Nazi defense in Italy. The British Eighth Army took Monte Altuzzo on September 17, San Marino on the

The war was now going well for the Allies, but there were still many infrastructure challenges to be attended to. Alec (left) with another unidentified engineer, possibly his friend Fennel.

nineteenth, Marradi on the twenty-fourth, and, as Julius Caesar had done in 49 BC, reaching the proverbial "point of no return," they crossed the Rubicon in northeastern Italy on August 26. On September 2, Germans began to evacuate the Aegean Islands; on the twelfth, they evacuated Rhodes and other Greek islands in the eastern Mediterranean; on the twenty-first, they evacuated the Peloponnesian peninsula; and on September 27, they evacuated western Greece entirely.

In France, Patton's troops took Verdun, and the Canadians liberated Dieppe on September 1. On the second, the Allies crossed into Belgium; and on the third, the British Second Army liberated Brussels. On September 9, General de Gaulle formed a provisional French government that included communists. More victories in France included Le Havre on the twelfth and Calais on the thirtieth. On September 10, the first allied patrol crossed the German frontier near Aachen, the westernmost city in Germany on the border with Belgium and the Netherlands, and on the fifteenth, the US First Army reached the Siegfried Line east of Aachen—a 392-mile long defensive line of bunkers, tunnels, and tank traps, built between 1938-40 along the western border of the old German empire (the border with the Netherlands in the north, and Belgium, Luxembourg, France, and Switzerland in the south), but not used in combat until reactivated by Hitler in late

Alec was happy to receive this photo from his "luscious wif," taken at her parents' farm in rural Clackamas County, Oregon.

August of 1944. On September 16, Paul Goebbels, Reich minister of propaganda for the Nazis, pushed all Germans to resist the Allied onslaught "with the utmost fanaticism,"[10] but by the twenty-fourth, British troops had crossed the German border near the lower Rhine. Things were moving fast enough that even at AFHQ, they were having trouble keeping track of all the developments, especially since, as Alec reported, rumors were rampant:

> We sure are hearing rumors about Germany flying around here thick and fast. If we could believe 1/10 of them, why I would be on my way home now, but then they are never confirmed and we have to wait for information from AFHQ, which is a laugh sometimes. For example, I heard a captain say they put a pin on their official war map because it was in the newssheet. The true reports do look very good for us, though. (September 6, 1944)

Though the war was going well in the field, the utilities engineers at AFHQ were still faced with infrastructure challenges on a regular basis in both Naples and Caserta:

> I got one of my big generators connected today and pushed the remote control button and it started up without a hitch, and

then I threw the switch from city power to the generator and it worked like a charm. The only trouble is that it is too small and so it requires a person to operate it. If I could have gotten one large enough, I could have made it completely automatic and it would have started by itself when the power failed. (September 6, 1944)

Clearly the good reports were doing wonders for his spirit as well, and he was especially pleased to report that he had received a package of candy and three letters from Mary, one of which held several photos that he treasured: "I received the picture of my luscious wif and the pictures of the farm, and my wif looks good enough for a full course meal and the farm a good place to enjoy the meal with all the trimmings of love" (September 4, 1944). Little did he know then that in spite of the recent momentum in the fighting, it would be another year before he would be able to return home to his beloved.

14

LIFE IN CASERTA WHILE FIGHTING CONTINUES IN EUROPE

FALL 1944

While the Allies were definitely making progress against Germany in northern Europe, the fighting in Italy in the late summer and autumn of 1944 continued to be surprisingly challenging, with the Nazis showing much more resistance than anyone expected and the weather refusing to help in any way. This created a second miserable winter for the soldiers stuck in what some US officials called a "wretched deadlock" where the strategy seemed designed not to win but merely to endure.[1]

Though he didn't write home about it until later in September, Alec was able to take a leave early in the month and went to Rome to do some sightseeing. It was only about seven or eight weeks since the Nazis had been driven out and the city liberated, so it's possible that he was also involved in helping with infrastructure challenges in that city, but he was not officially "on duty" at the time of this trip, and his letters about the visit seem more like a tourist adventure than a working vacation. There was a fairly large gap in the letters between mid-August and mid-September, and Mary definitely complained of a gap in September, so this was most likely the time period he was writing home about. His first mention of the trip was a humorous anecdote about the chaplains who were part of his travel group:

We of the engineers are plagued by the chaplains a lot, and
I have to tell you about what happened on this trip to Rome.
As they were going through the catacombs they were warned
by the priest that if they took any souvenirs they would be
excommunicated. The Episcopal chaplain said, "That wouldn't
affect me because I was excommunicated 400 years ago."
(September 19, 1944)

He sent Mary a package of items purchased in Rome, and he
described one as something he "strongly suspect[ed] was made
from stolen materiel left around due to bomb damage" (October 5,
1944) and promised to write her more about the trip soon. The item
in question was likely a tall brass vase that looked like it might
have been made from a large artillery shell of some sort that Mary
used in later life for her bearded iris bouquets or other tall flower
stems. In the promised letter with more detail about his trip, he
explained that he had been hanging out with war correspondents
while he was in Rome, which he found quite fascinating:

> I had quite a vacation there and saw all the sights. I lived
> at a hotel with some war correspondents and it was some
> experience. A few of them are just like the movie idea, always
> wisecracking and drinking, and some of their friends are the
> movie type that talk about their various husbands and have
> that sophisticated manner the movies depict of people who
> have lots of money. Some of them have quite a bit, too—one
> well known person receives $500 a week for his work, which I
> found out because he was trying to check up on his money via
> telephone and cable because he hadn't received any for a while.
> Several of them were persons whose names I recognized and
> it was interesting talking to them. Some of the reporters were
> women and it surprised me how young they seemed—in their
> early twenties. I really had quite a time and also drank more
> liquor than I usually do. Sometimes I could feel it, but really I
> wasn't quite drunk, just a little woozy in the head. I felt swell
> because I had so much exercise and the long walks brought
> my legs back into shape, but I suppose they will get soft again
> around here. (October 5, 1944)

Of the 1,600 reporters allowed to wear the armband embla-
zoned with the letter "C" for war correspondent during WWII, only

During Alec's visit to Rome about eight weeks after the city was liberated from the Nazis, there were lots of other Allied soldiers in the city. Some visited the Colosseum, just as if they were regular tourists.

127 (less than 1 percent) were women. In an article for *National Geographic News*, Mark Jenkins wrote: "World War II opened doors for American women in a number of ways. Some would close again; others remain barely ajar. But those 127 flung one door wide open and emerged from those muddy, bloody campaigns having proved that in reporting war, women were the equal of men. It wasn't easy. Wherever they went, these 'gal correspondents' had to hustle harder than their male colleagues. For theirs was a double war: the war against the enemy, and the war against the system. They had to fight red tape, condescension, disdain, outright hostility, and downright lewdness."[2]

Alec mentioned when he got back to Caserta after his Rome adventures, that he was sure he wasn't going to get as much exercise and admitted that he felt best when he was able to get out walking a lot. He also told her about his recent visit to the ruins of Pompeii, which were much closer to Naples than to Rome but something he hadn't seen before. He also sent her some photos in addition to his description of the day trip:

> I have told you about Rome but haven't as yet mentioned
> Pompeii. It takes about three hours to walk around the ruins
> of the town. . . . It was a beautiful day when I was there and

I took what ought to be some very good pictures. I bought a tea set (cloth), which was made by the orphan girls at a very beautiful church near Pompeii. It's much smaller but I think it's about as beautiful as St. Peter's. All it lacks is the depth to produce grandeur. About Pompeii—those people believed very much in hot love, and I almost bought a set of pictures taken from some of the walls showing different ways to do it, but after looking at the pictures and then thinking about you, I decided they weren't quite the thing to send you. They don't appear so bad when seen along with the ruins, but as pictures alone they are just vulgar. So you'll just have to wait till we make our world tour together to see what I am talking about. As far as the rest of Pompeii, it is interesting because of its age and because it must have been a beautiful place in its day. (October 15, 1944)

Clearly, Alec had visited the ruins of one of the most famous brothels in ancient Pompeii, one that had finally been excavated in the eighteenth century and was called the *Lupanare* (Latin for wolf's den). A famous feature of the Lupanare was its erotic wall paintings, each depicting a different position for sexual intercourse. The paintings are believed to have been part of an advertising board for the various specialties that were available to clients.[3]

Castel Sant'Angelo in Rome, also known as the Mausoleum of Hadrian.

St. Peter's Basilica in Vatican City, which remained neutral during the war.

Once Alec returned to Caserta and to his regular routines at AFHQ, it also meant a return to his speculation about what he might want to do after the war was over. He thought about lots of different options:

> I see where I'll be able to go to school for a year and perhaps I'll do that because as for engineering I am very rusty and need a brush up. First, though, we are going to have a long vacation and relax and travel just as we feel and when we feel. I would still like to live in Brazil if I could make enough to live on down there. Personally, I think teaching in a college would be fun, as it would leave 3 months out of the year free for vacations, but really I am not at all settled in what I want to do except make love to you and be happy in your arms. (August 31, 1944)

The Servicemen's Readjustment Act, more popularly known as the GI Bill, had been signed into law by President Roosevelt on June 22, 1944, guaranteeing returning servicemen different kinds of financial assistance after the war, college tuition stipends being only one aspect of the bill, and Alec had clearly heard the news.[4] However, he often mentioned that he was still rather unsure of what he might really want to do when the war was over: "I don't exactly know what I want to do after the Army. Some days it's one thing and the other days it's something else. I am not particularly pleased with the kind of engineer I am because I know so little about it and have forgotten so much. I know we have lots of love to catch up on, and other than that I am unsettled. We will just have to see" (October 5, 1944). He also admitted that "I haven't got much interest in anything except my wif. Sometimes I wonder if I am even interested in engineering. I know I am not satisfied with what I know about it and sometimes I think I would like to have been a doctor, but I don't have the personality and possibly not the ambition. I suppose the best place for me would be at a college or lab, and I am not in the least prepared for either of them" (October 8, 1944). He also thought about studying lighting and optics, and in November of 1944 asked Mary to send him books on both.

He explained to her the likelihood that he would not be getting another promotion in the Army any time soon because there were already two captains in his outfit, and if there were going to be a promotion soon, it would probably go to the other first lieutenant who was from the same outfit as his current major. He said that didn't bother him much, as long as the electrical stuff continued to work smoothly. He also shared that he believed he had good standing within the point system for after the war: "I am fairly well up on the list I imagine, except for medals and brats. I don't know if you knew it or not but I have a service star for being in a combat zone, which is a joke in that I received it for living in a combat zone by about 200 yards" (October 8, 1944). He also said he had a combat star for driving too close to the front at Cassino (about an hour outside of Naples) without actually knowing how close they were until a couple of exploding shells suddenly woke him and the other soldier he was with to exactly where they were (October 29, 1944). The Advanced Service Rating (ASR) Score, to which he referred, was a scoring system that awarded points to a soldier and was used to determine which ones were sent home first. At the end of the war in Germany and Italy, a total of 85 points would have been required for a soldier to be allowed to return to the States. Points were awarded for months of service (+1 point each), months overseas (+1 point each), campaign stars worn on theater ribbons (+5 points each), awards received (+5 points each), and for children at home under the age of 18 (+12 points each, up to three). My best calculation is that in the fall of 1944, when this letter was written and half a year shy of the

St. Peter's Square from the steps of the Basilica. Though the Nazis had been gone for several weeks, there was still an Allied helicopter patrolling the skies above Rome.

The view of St. Peter's Square from the cupola of St. Peter's Basilica. There are 231 stairs to the first level where the saint statues decorate the roofline. It is another 320 steps up a narrow corkscrew staircase to the top of the dome and this famous photo opportunity.

official end of the war in Europe, Alec had accumulated approximately 67 points (32 months of service; 25 months overseas; 2 campaign stars, one each for North Africa and Italy) and would easily have accumulated at least another 14 points, possibly more, before Hitler finally capitulated in the spring of 1945. If a soldier had fewer than 85 points, he could expect to continue to serve in the Army and would most likely have been sent to fight the Japanese. The problem with the ASR Score was that it rewarded rear echelon troops like Alec who had been overseas a long time even though they had never seen combat. Many supply troops had served two or three years overseas, whereas it was unusual for a combat infantryman to actually survive that long.[5]

While the war trudged on in Italy that autumn, with little in the way of resolution, it continued to advance with more definitive results in Eastern Europe, where the Germans evacuated Belgrade on October 19 and began to evacuate Albania on the twenty-eighth. In northern Europe, the Allies began a 60-hour truce at Dunkirk to allow the evacuation of civilians on October 3. On the tenth, the Americans' 24-hour surrender ultimatum to Germans at Aachen was rejected, and the city finally fell to the US First Army on the twenty-first, becoming the first German city to be captured by the Allies. On October 14, Rommel committed suicide after having been implicated in the July 20 bomb plot against Hitler.

In the absence of much news to report that Mary wouldn't already have known, Alec continued to defend his short letters with a self-deprecatory explanation that was definitely starting to sound familiar:

> Mary, I love you as my only sweetheart and only wif, but I don't seem to have anything to say. Perhaps if I had a few drinks I might loosen up a little; usually when I do I can write a great number of pages. It must be a sign of lack of mental capacity to be so blank that one page becomes difficult. I have been living in a vacuum since I left you anyway. I used to know a great deal of what was going on in the world, but now it's only the war news. It will change, though, one of these days. I will know you and the pleasures of having you near me and being next to you. . . . Goodnight, my love. Let's dream together of our life together. (October 6, 1944)

Just a few days later, he wrote pessimistically about the possibility of ever finding peace in the world, even once the war was over.

> Mary, my love, you have someone way over here in Italy who thinks of you and wonders how you are and wishes he were in your arms. It's getting to be too long. It was too long when we separated but now it's getting so bad that this war just has to finish so that we can be together again. It makes me a little annoyed to hear them talking about peace already when I don't think there ever will be peace that we will see in our time. Just as soon as nations are in a position we will have another war because there is too much inequality between peoples and therefore they are subject to the talk and swaying of power-mad leaders. . . .
>
> There will be a chance after this war is over to . . . try to make up for all the love we have missed. You know love is a great comfort when we are alone, but it can't in any way compare with love when we are together because then it seems that we really become one and it's a potent union that we make. They are really hammering Germany and it shouldn't be long until it will be over and we will be making love to each other and having a perfect time and our own special happiness. (October 8, 1944)

When he wasn't worrying about the future or the length of the war, he continued to question his good fortune in finding and marrying her:

> You know, wif, I think I know you very well, but I don't understand you and probably never will. I can't see why you should have picked me out and I can't even understand why a woman, particularly you, should want to be bothered with a male, particularly me. Males are not very interesting, and American males are not very good looking. They have too large or too small heads, too large or too small a nose. I have noticed some of the officers who think they are quite the tops as lady-killers, and they are a queer assortment of shapes. Frenchmen have a more uniform appearance.

Enough of that—what I want is the appearance of my wif in a dim light while I am letting my hands drift slowly around her head and down across the smoothness of her throat and further down to upper wif, and I want to feel her breath close to my face and draw her in tight so that the very beating of her heart becomes a part of me. You must know, wif, that you are my passionflower, and without you close to me to keep me warm inside I am all alone, and without the thought of you I would be lost. So pep up and say a curse against the Germans for separating us and think of tomorrow and how bright the sun will look when we are facing it together. (October 17, 1944)

He admitted that even though it continued to be a mystery to him, he thought it was a good thing that they got married and how fortunate they were to have found each other.

He was very frustrated and getting impatient to get home, telling her his morale was low because "It looks like the Germans will last the winter—the damn nuts" (October 26, 1944). He continued to be frustrated about his workload and cynical regarding the expectations of others, complaining that, "Some of my electricians were taken away from me, and they will expect as much work as ever. It's the old Army efficiency game: 'Don't put a man where he trained to go, put someone there that knows nothing about the job'" (October 9, 1944). He was also working on sound equipment

Alec at the base of the Egyptian obelisk in St. Peter's Square. Built around 2500 BCE, it was brought to Rome by Caligula in 37 AD and moved to this location in 1586 under the direction of Pope Sixtus V.

for those big shots and told her he finally got the general's juke-box fixed by using an electric fan motor and a pulley system, but because the power cycle system in Italy was so inconsistent, it broke five records at first because of being out of sync: "That should be a small loss, though, as all the big shots have to do is order some more by air. As you can see I am sort of proud of the juke box even if you are the only one there that I can tell about it, because it wouldn't be good to let other people know how I am fighting this war" (October 29, 1944). He also shared a rather rare positive story about one of the big shots his unit worked with who was thinking about more than his own comfort:

> I wonder if I told you about the stoves. We were putting them in at the request of big shots when one of our lieutenants asked a particular big shot where he wanted his. Well, this big shot called in an assistant lieutenant and asked him if the combat troops had all the stoves they needed—received a no—turned to [our lieutenant] and said "No stoves will be installed in this area until combat troops have theirs. I am issuing orders for all stoves to be returned to the depot, and furthermore, I don't want a stove." So now it gives me great pleasure when some big shot's aide calls up and raises hell because of no stove for me to tell him in no uncertain terms, "no stove." I love to get huffy with some of the huffy ones. (November 4, 1944)

He was also frustrated with some of the things others, presumably her co-workers at the shipyards, were telling Mary about the military overseas:

> The big shots do live very high over here and a lot of the men feel that they are forgotten by the people at home . . . and a few blame the administration, but I think he is wrong in saying that all blame the administration. Most of them blame the Army and the system it has built up around the officer caste. Anyway you have to watch me for I am peculiar and don't have very much use for Republicans and particularly Dewey. I don't like his mustache and the way he attacks anything and everything, right or wrong. Incidentally when he said in a newsreel that it was the administration's fault that we're forgotten over here, there was an uproar of boos and hissing. (October 26, 1944)

Alec's photo of the ruins of Pompeii with Vesuvius in the background.

This letter was written in the midst of the fall 1944 presidential election in the United States, where Roosevelt, a Democrat, eventually won an unprecedented fourth term in the office. His challenger was the moderate Republican governor of New York, Thomas Dewey. With a war going on and going well for the Allies, Dewey did not attack Roosevelt's policies. However, he did question President Roosevelt's abilities to continue in office by continually referring to FDR as the "tired old man."[6] But negative campaigning didn't do Dewey any good; he lost the election.

In the midst of the autumn of 1944, his second in Italy, Alec suddenly found himself hospitalized yet again, this time for something they suspected at first might be syphilis, but which was eventually diagnosed as trench mouth. In late October, he had gone to the dispensary to get something that might alleviate the pain he was experiencing because of canker sores, and they had immediately put him under observation because he had too many for a "normal person" and they were worried that he might be contagious. When he told his buddies he would be sent to the hospital, they started kidding him, saying they "had been expecting it because I hadn't had a rest since Rome. They are always kidding me about the amount of resting I do because I really have it very easy" (October 29, 1944). Trench mouth, also known as periodontal disease, was very common for soldiers during WWI and got its name from the stalemates that kept soldiers in the trenches for long periods of time and without good oral hygiene, where gun care was more important than gum care.[7] During WWII, medical personnel had antibiotics with which to treat the infections, and it was less common, but the condition, which came from poor dental hygiene, had not been eliminated altogether, and soldiers like Alec who liked their candy above all other foods, were often the first to be affected. Risk factors for the disease included poor nutrition, poor dental care and hygiene, compromised immune system, and stress, all of which could have been at play in Alec's situation.[8]

While he was in the hospital, his letters got longer and he reported that he had actually read at least one book, *Honey in the Horn*, which was one of Mary's favorites. It was a Pulitzer Prize-winning novel, written by H. L. Davis in the mid-1930s, about homesteading in the Oregon territory in the first decade of the twentieth century.[9] He told her he especially liked "the remark about the woman having a baby every time her husband shook out his overalls" (November 2, 1944). While in the hospital Alec talked often about being in the mood to make some brats and was clearly trying to reassure her that they had plenty of time to make a family once he returned:

> I read an item in *Time* that said the least time between babies was one year so you can still have a big family if you have a need to. It is going to be rather difficult on our brats, though, with us as parents and the way we will live after we are together and not staying in one place or getting a better job it if means less time for us to be together. I imagine the brats making fun of us for being so lovey-dovey, but I won't mind as long as it is you that I am lovey-dovey with because you are my private love and I want everyone to know it, and if I embarrass you in the show that's too bad because I am going to do it when I get to your side, and you and the public are just going to have to put up with me. It's been a long time since I have tasted you and when I get near why it's going to be hard not to eat you right up all at once instead of keeping you for a little chewing for the rest of our life. I'll keep you, though, and I thank my guiding star that you will let me because it will mean so much happiness for me and I hope all that you expect. We had a taste of what two years together was like, and now I want the eternity that we are married for. (November 2, 1944)

While still in the hospital, Alec complained to Mary about the state of the world around him:

Mary, I am disgusted, disgusted with the world, with its people and with myself, disgusted with having been taught the value of monogamy and chastity and then having two years of forced living which do not lend themselves to that tracking, disgusted with a religion that says after it's over treat your enemy as a brother, but keep your gun ready as some of your own people may turn communist and you can do a good deed (and have fun doing it) dispatching them to hell, disgusted with some of my friends here who can't see that race prejudice is a function of the mind and not a matter of heredity, and I am disgusted with myself for so little a thing as going to the dispensary for some canker sores and getting myself shut up in a hospital when if I had only waited they would have gone away by themselves. I am disgusted because I am out of candy, having eaten my ration this week, and I am just plum down in the dumps. (November 3, 1944)

They kept him hospitalized for a total of ten days this time, most of that time in isolation, probably because they had a hard time diagnosing his situation.

Even though he had a camera with him, Alec continued to send Mary an occasional postcard of his surroundings. This is an image of the small castle in the gardens of Caserta that was created so the young Bourbon princes could "play" while learning the art of warfare.

When he got out in early November and enjoyed his first shower in almost three weeks, he went to the movies with his buddies and then returned to the same routines and the same slow progress of the war in Italy that had been frustrating him for many, many months already. Meanwhile, in early November, German forces stopped the Russian advance and established a firm line west of Belgrade on the second, but Marshal Josef Tito's Yugoslav resistance forces (now allied with the Russians) controlled the whole border between Yugoslavia and Greece as of November 6. German forces evacuated Skopje on November 13, and on the twenty-third, the Allies declared Macedonia (on the Greek-Yugoslav border) free of Germans. Also in November, fighting continued in Belgium, the Netherlands, and France. For the first time in the history of the Third Reich, Hitler failed to appear in Munich on November 8 to address 'the Old Fighters' on the anniversary of the 1923 Beer Hall Putsch. Speculation mounted as Himmler read a speech in the Fuhrer's place. On the sixteenth, the US First and Ninth Armies launched a new attack east of Aachen, and the US Third Army crossed the German frontier on the eighteenth; the French First Army captured Muhlhausen in Alsace, and the French Second Armored Division took Strasbourg on the twenty-fourth. On November 20, Hitler departed for Berlin from his headquarters in East Prussia, which he had occupied since the beginning of the war with the Soviet Union in June 1941, never to return. But in spite of the Allied momentum, Hitler and the Nazis would not capitulate for another nearly six months, and it would take another several months after that to formally shut down AFHQ before Alec and other support troops in Italy could finally return home to their loved ones.

15

LAST MONTHS OF THE WAR IN EUROPE

NOVEMBER 1944 – APRIL 1945

In spite of the Allied progress in northern and eastern Europe, the fighting in Italy continued to drag on, and Alec returned to his regular routines in Caserta after leaving the hospital in early November of 1944. He also returned to his regular excuse-making for what Mary called his too-short letters, identifying himself as a "short-winded person" by nature, and proposing a solution that probably made her smile:

> I think one of these days I am going to get a little tight just so that I can write you a good letter. You see, when I am tight I am not so bashful and so easily embarrassed so that I can scratch emotion all over the pages without the least turning red or having my mind blank out because of my timidity in dealing with the female (meaning you) of the species (meaning people, white class A1). That makes me think of how I would have to order you through a mail-order house—stock no. W3525NE16 [her parents' address in Portland where she stayed while he was overseas]. Human being, white, female, age 28-29, origin—Oregon, parents good, disposition excellent, character perfect, distinguishing mark—mole on tummy ¾" diameter, size just right, quality superb, desirable characteristics—most lovable person in the world to match Human being male #MAPO512 [his military APO address]. Quantity one each, shipment air express.

Does the above sound all right to you? I surely wish that I could get on the radio and make an order like that, particularly the shipment part. It really would be fun to have you meet me here in Europe so that we could start out to see the world together. (November 3, 1944)

He had read several books while in the hospital and suggested that "if they [kept] me in a hospital long enough, I might become a literary man" (November 4, 1944). He had also gone back to noting how many letters he got from her and how many days between getting letters. This became a rather interesting chronicle of his emotional state as well, and as more time away from her passed, he seemed to return to a similar obsession about the timing of letters to that he had experienced when he was first overseas. In early November, he got eight letters in a single day, and though he was rhapsodic about his good fortune to have current news from her, he also admitted that the letters were:

> . . . a poor substitute for getting it direct from your lips. What I should like to get from your lips is a multitude of luscious kisses, a few of passion. It would be joy just to be with you

Alec was frustrated at having much to do but without much help, other than his Italian crew. Though the requests he was getting for lighting help weren't critical to the fighting itself, they kept him pretty busy, so perhaps that's the reason for the tongue-in-cheek sign on his desk.

and I know of no way of describing how good it would feel to have you so close that I could feel the warmth of your body. It used to make me just tingle to have you near me, and I know from the way I feel now that I'll not only tingle but also sizzle when we get together again. It gives me goose flesh just to think about it now. (November 4, 1944)

Four days later he got three letters from her, two the following day, but in another week, he complained that he was having a very bad day because there were no letters at all from her "so there is nothing to cheer me up and only tomorrow to look forward to and hope" (November 14, 1944). A few days after that he confessed that he was getting "a little anxious" because while he actually received a letter that day, he hadn't had any letters from her in the last three days, admitting that even when there were no delays, he was "always anxious for your letters" (November 16, 1944). He had also noticed that only a few letters ever made it to him in what he called "record time, [but] then the rest take about a month and sometimes more." Later in the month, he admitted he was feeling much better because he got another new letter from her but insisted that "three whole days without a word from my love are just three too many" (November 23, 1944). At the end of the month, he explained why he enjoyed visualizing her writing a letter to him:

> Your letters are so important to me. They are the bright part
> of my day and they arrive (when they do) just after lunch,
> but alas for several days now there have been none, and so I
> am wondering about what you might be doing: how you are,
> how Pete is, what you look like. Have you changed? . . . I look
> at a picture and say no, you look just the same, and then at
> another and I say, well a little bit. I know my appearance has
> changed but my feeling about you hasn't. It has only increased,
> or I have only become more aware of it.

> It's my bedtime again, my love, and I wish it was yours, too,
> that we might go together. It will be exciting to do just that
> again. Good night, my precious, my little gem of love and the
> jewel in my heart. I love you as always. (November 29, 1944)

After getting out of the hospital, it seemed that he really did try to write longer letters, as requested. Or perhaps it was because his work seemed less urgent as the war went on. To fill those letters, he shared his most recent musings about their relationship and the future they might want to create for themselves after the war:

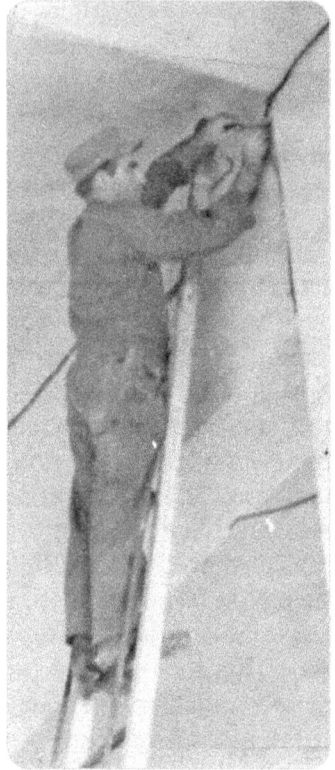

One of Alec's Italian helpers running some wire for one of their lighting jobs.

> I want you to know that you are my love and my wif and my mistress. I know that I am very fortunate in having your love and particularly that my wife and mistress is the same person. It is so much better that way. I hear some of the men complaining about how women are all unfaithful and they tell their experience to prove it. The trouble is they seem to blame the women when a lot of it is just the war. It would be very hard I should think for a young girl to be true to a person she hardly knew for two or three years, and you would be surprised how many men here don't know their wives at all. . . .

This war makes a mess of things, but I imagine the human race will keep going anyway and have its babies and wars for some time yet. . . .

Anyway, my love, we will have our life together and try to make our brats a little more understanding and maybe someday there will be enough sense in the world to stop the expense of all our excess energy on war. I am glad I'm living now and not 50 years ago, but I should rather have lived 50 or 100 years from now because I think there will be so much more known then, perhaps even about being happy. I think we have found the solution to it between ourselves, but there are so many that haven't that we are caught in the whirlpool of the multitude, and all we can do is try to keep on the outside edge and keep each other and try to pass on what we have to our children. It's a difficult thing to pass on, but I think it can be done. (November 7, 1944)

Once he was back to his regular routine, Alec continued to share a few tidbits from time to time about the work he was doing at the palace or in the city of Naples:

My frequency converter is all ready to function now and tomorrow morning is the big test. It is to eliminate the gasoline generators, which cause us so much trouble. I think I complained once before about someone sending 60-cycle stuff over and causing all kinds of trouble for me. I must tell you about my frequency converter, though. It's a large generator driven by a large motor and belt. Well, the belt wouldn't stay on the middle of the pulley, and we fooled around and then I got a bright idea. I took a piece of tape and ran it around the pulley where I wanted the belt to run and that did the trick. I am always proud when I get a bright idea like that, but then I am proud of most of my ideas—especially the one when I married you, but that required your cooperation so I can't take full credit for that. (November 9, 1944)

In the winter of 1944, Alec grew a moustache, which he named "the tickler."

The following week he told her that even though not much was happening, "I am now going into the street lighting business so I think all that is left is electric railways and the electric rail to make a complete tour of electrical problems. I have surely hit more than anyone back there would ever thought existed in the Army. It is surprising what there is over here sometimes in that line" (November 13, 1944). He also returned to complaining about working with the locals and facing reduced staffing in his unit:

> I had quite a time today with the electricity. The extra connection that I made for increased power went sour and so I had to cut back to the main transformer and there was too much load, so I cut the motor switch and stopped the elevators and incidentally a few lights that shouldn't have been connected on that circuit, and boy did I create a storm over the telephone, and then at the same time a transformer in town blew a fuse and we had calls from all over the area. You should have heard me when someone called up about the elevator and I told them that they were for freight only. Anyway, it is straight for tonight but will probably all start over again tomorrow night because I can't get a new city connection with the number of men they allow me for the work. They expect me to do the work with Italians but I don't have enough GIs to supervise them and you would be surprised what happens when you leave an Italian to do the job alone. One day we had an Italian put a lamp in one office and an officer there asked the Italian to put a light in his room across the street. The Italian did just that only he took lamp cord and ran it from the office window to the window across the street and that is bad. Oh, well, it's quite a job at times, and the one that demands the most service is the one who recommends cutting the number of men. (November 14, 1944)

Sometimes there were also humorous anecdotes to be shared: "Actually nothing happened today—some general pinched himself on a toilet seat so we fixed that in a hurry, but otherwise no excitement" (November 26, 1944). And it seemed his electrical department had gotten involved in entertainment endeavors at AFHQ, including a theatrical production of Thornton Wilder's *Our Town*, put on by soldiers, both British and American, the WACs, and members of the Air Transport Command (ATC), those responsible for transporting equipment, supplies, and personnel from the United States to the various overseas combat theaters during WWII:[1]

> There is a lot of electrical stuff used by the gang that puts on the play and because I have given them a lot of things to help we had a box shared among the bunch from the utilities. It was quite an advertisement for my electrical department tonight, too, because the city power failed and I couldn't even start my generator because this afternoon when the power failed the generator switch broke and discharged the starting batteries, and it takes at least 10 hours to recharge them so all I could do was sit and take a ribbing from the boys. We knew about the generator before the show and on top of that the converter supplying the movie house broke a piece out of the pulley, and so one of the electricians called off a visit to the show because he didn't want to take a chance on seeing only half when there was no generator available and a broken pulley on the converter. (November 28, 1944)

Before the end of November, he told Mary that his commanding officer, Major Karas, "was taking the same rest cure I had" (November 18, 1944). But by the end of December, it became clear that Karas did not have trench mouth at all. Instead, he was eventually sent home for mental/emotional reasons, something Alec called "mental fatigue" but didn't explain any further. During WWII there was certainly more awareness of what was then called "combat fatigue" than there had been during WWI, and the military had started to require psychiatric screening for those going to fight in the war in 1940 in hopes of minimizing soldier collapse,[2] but there were still some in the military who denied that it was a real problem—most famously Patton and his aforementioned infamous slapping incidents during the Sicilian Campaign. In any case, most of the awareness during and right after WWII focused on combat troops, and very little had been written about how support troops might also have been affected, though clearly some of them were.

In spite of having told Mary he didn't like Dewey's mustache, it seemed Alec had grown one of his own that winter, possibly while in the hospital, and sent a photo to Mary, perhaps to deflect her concern over the fact that he had lost quite a bit of weight

Alec loved the new black leather jacket Mary sent him for Christmas 1944, and he wore it all the time.

while working overseas, which she had noticed in some of his photos. He called it "the tickler" and assured her it would come off before any more photos were taken of him. It appeared Mary was happy with his renewed commitment to longer letters home, and told him so, but he still didn't think much of his ability to write or to tell her how much he loved her:

> Well, my sweet, I am out of noble words, and in spite of all your statements I don't think much of my letters. In fact letter writing irks me because it lets me know just how dumb I am when I sit and try to think of something to say. I can say I love you, and I do mean it, and if I didn't say it when we were together why you should have hauled off and hit me with the frying pan, because it is so true and I really want you to know it all of the time. (November 18, 1944)

In fact, in his quest to find new ways to tell her about his love for her, once he even put large brackets around half an empty page of paper, with a note inside saying "censored love" (November 14, 1944). He also mentioned the holidays and once again hoped that this year would truly be his last "combat Christmas in Europe," and he encouraged her to "keep your chin up and a tight sweater in the closet all ready and waiting for your hub. You know

I like tight sweaters. There are a lot of other things I like, but the main one is just being with you" (November 26, 1944). He also said that while fur coats might feel soft and feminine to their wearers, he much preferred sweaters, especially because he "love[d] to see what's under the sweater show up" (December 17, 1944), which he knew embarrassed her.

In early December of 1944, the Allies continued to advance into Germany. The Ardennes Offensive, better known as the Battle of the Bulge, the costliest action ever fought by the US Army, which suffered over 100,000 casualties, began on December 16 and continued through January 25. Early in the battle, Americans from the 106th Infantry Division surrendered in the Schnee Eifel, a heavily wooded plateau with many deep ravines and valleys on the German-Belgian border, in the most serious US reversal in

Alec on the beach in the early spring of 1945. It was still cold enough to wear his new leather jacket.

Europe. Nearly two-thirds of the division—approximately 6,000 men—were marched off into German captivity before the end of the first week of battle, though the Allies ultimately thwarted the Germans before the end of January 1945. In southern Europe, Athens was under martial law on December 4, and on the fifth, the British Eighth Army took Ravenna and cut the rail link to Bologna. Continuing heavy casualties and autumn rain in northern Italy halted the Allied drive north, and the second winter in Italy was as dreadful as the first, leading to "another wretched deadlock in which the campaign 'sank to the level of a vast holding operation,' as the official U.S. Army history put it."[3] Italians returning home found their towns destroyed and fields fouled by landmines, and the ongoing Allied strategy in Italy seemed designed not to win but simply to endure.[4]

After many long letters in November, there was a two-week gap in Alec's letters in early December, but when he wrote again, he was happy about having just received a leather jacket from Mary, presumably his Christmas present. He liked it, said it was a "swell" fit and looked expensive, and that it creaked when he wrote to her while wearing it (December 15, 1944). He reported that he was busy again, but in an interesting new way:

> I have been very busy the last couple days particularly designing and getting a clubhouse wired with a fancy lighting system. It's all for the war effort you know, even if I doubt it myself sometimes. Anyway it gives me good experience and a chance to use my own ideas. It's gotten to the point now where I haven't enough electricity to furnish all the lighting that the generals want. It's partly my own fault in that respect because I started it by putting in the first indirect lighting, and it has gone from high generals down to low generals and now to WACs. This club, though, is going to be fancy. . . . I even have a professional architect interested in it so I hope the lighting turns out good because it looked well on paper. (December 15, 1944)

Before Christmas, Alec reported to Mary that he had a new boss. Field Marshal Harold Alexander, another Brit, replaced Wilson as Supreme Commander at AFHQ until the end of the war. In spite of the fact that Alexander had served as Eisenhower's deputy commander in North Africa, commanded the Allied ground forces for the Sicily invasion, and led the Allies in the taking of Rome, which had been the first Axis capital to surrender,[5] this change didn't make Alec particularly happy. He had a few things to say about his feelings on the matter, more about Alexander's management style than his military prowess:

> As you know we have a new big boss and like all of them he is starting with a storm. I have often wondered why each new boss always has to start cleaning house as though the old one didn't keep it well and then let up and let things drift back to the same old system. I guess that is the world all over. Not much happened or could I have done anything about it if it did because all I had was Italians and can they get things messed up. I suppose it is my fault, but I have printed instructions on

a card in Italian next to the equipment and still they won't do it right and then the bosses fume. Why even one day their movie stopped when the city power failed and that had to wait till the generator warmed up. Oh that was terrible; almost lost us the war. (December 17, 1944)

In spite of the reversals at the onset of the Battle of the Bulge, Alec still held onto the hope that he would be home soon and continued to imagine how their reunion would be:

It is going to be a bit strange when we do meet, but I know that won't last long because there is a craving inside of me that won't let me be a stranger. And when we do start to knowing each other again it is going to be an exciting time—something that I am looking forward to more than anything I have looked forward to before. Really now it seems more important than getting married though that can't be because if we hadn't why it wouldn't be our reunion to look forward to. It's a good thing to be married to someone you love. I love you and I love being married to you and know that it was an important day in my life when we met each other. Just think what a little thing might have done to our meeting. It's enough to scare me when I think how easily we might never have met, and I would have missed all the happiness you have for me. (December 18, 1944)

He also complained of being in a bad mood, probably related to the bad news about the 106th from the Ardennes Forest as well as staff reductions:

The news isn't so hot today, and besides that they want to take a good electrician away from me and leave a deadbeat that doesn't know a wire from a pipe, so I am not in any too good of a mood; perhaps you can remember my bad moods at home when I was tired and wanted to rest and you wanted otherwise. . . . I wonder if I ever told you that you are a master at making love. I love your love and wish it could be more personal. Letters have an advantage in one respect, though. They give more of an insight into each other's thought than we would ever have gotten out of personal messages of love. It just seems that when one of us writes a letter we put more substance into it, which if we were together we would be enjoying each other to such an extent that opinions and beliefs would be subordinated. I like both ways, but I would rather enjoy myself than be intellectual, particularly I should rather enjoy myself with you. . . .

My stomach has been kicking up again a little and last night I slept with the heating pad I got for last Christmas and it kept hot all night and also helped my stomach so that tonight it feels fine again. What I need is a rest cure with you to get settled down from the strain of this long separation. I never believed in war, at least not for us. I can see where we couldn't avoid it and I don't see any way that junior can avoid another one, for the more I see of these Europeans the more I think that all they understand is the use of guns to settle their differences both between and amongst their own groups. (December 20, 1944)

Alec continued to complain to Mary about the situation in Italy and how much he disliked being there.

Alec asked Mary specifically for this picture of her in her fur coat, even though he was much more interested in what was underneath that coat.

He wrote again before the end of the month about the boredom of his situation, saying, "Today was dull, nothing at all happened. The lights went out a few times, and I got ribbed about it, but paid no attention. It isn't my fault and there wasn't anything I could do anyway. You can't keep lights going without electricity, and that is something I haven't got too much of. Also these people don't seem to realize that we aren't back in the States, and I am now deep in requests for indirect lighting" (December 22, 1944). The day after Christmas was equally boring: "Today was uneventful. I forgot an appointment and so the Col. heard about it and said that job should be No. 1 priority. I have to laugh at that because with the few GI electricians I have, why it would just mean stopping some other job. I have the GIs spread so thin now that when someone has light trouble that an Italian can't fix it just doesn't get fixed until the night man comes on duty" (December 26, 1944). A couple of days later, he reported, "The only real break in the monotony was that the lights all stayed on, that is most of them. But then we did have some trouble about heat. One of the 'combat boys' complained of the cold, and that kept us hopping" (December 28, 1944). In his last letter of 1944, he told her he was going to put on his dress uniform to go to a big dance because if he didn't go, his CO might notice, though he'd rather she was here to have fun with him instead. He also asked her to send him a photo of her in her fur coat, saying that every woman should be allowed at least one for her morale but admitted he would actually rather see her out of it (December 30, 1944).

In the late winter and early spring of 1945, the Allies continued their push into German territory. By February 4, Belgium was reported to be completely free of German troops, and on the ninth, British and Canadian troops smashed the first of the main defense zones on the Siegfried Line. On February 17, the US Third Army launched a new offensive into Germany and broke through another eleven-mile front on the Siegfried Line. On February 24, Hitler addressed his party leaders in Berlin on the 25th anniversary of the proclamation of the Nazi Party but refused to allow the speech to be reported on or broadcast to the public. Heavy fighting continued through the month of March as the Allies continued their advance into Germany, the Germans began pulling out of Holland, and the French First Army crossed the Rhine for the first time since Napoleon. In southern Europe, the Germans completed their withdrawal from Greece and Albania by mid-January. On February 22, the US Fifth Army took the Upper Reno valley in northern Italy between Bologna and Florence, and by March 8, secret negotiations had begun in Switzerland between the German High Command and the American Office of Strategic Services, a wartime intelligence agency and predecessor of the CIA, for an early surrender of German forces in Italy.

In April of 1945, the fighting intensified in northern Italy, and near the end of the month, the Allies took Bologna, Mantua, Verona, Genoa, and Venice in quick succession, Mussolini was captured and executed by Italian partisans in Milan on April 28, and on the twenty-ninth, the German armies in Italy signed surrender terms at Caserta. "The 608-day campaign to liberate Italy would cost 312,000 Allied casualties, equivalent to 40 percent of Allied losses in the decisive campaign for northwest Europe."[6] To the north, fighting continued in Holland, southern France, and Germany, with the Allies holding the upper hand and moving relentlessly forward. On April 28, Hitler married his mistress, Eva Braun, in Berlin. He also dictated his political testament, justifying the political and military actions of his 12-year rule, exhorting the German people even in defeat to adhere to the principles of National Socialism. On April 30, in his Führerbunker in

Berlin, Hitler and Braun committed suicide, he by gunshot and she by poison; on the same day, over 30,000 POWs and political prisoners were freed near Munich and in northern Germany. The liberation of the concentration camps, begun by the Soviets at Auschwitz in January of 1945, was finally completed in April as well, and the German High Command signed an unconditional surrender to the Allies on May 7, 1945, in Reims, France.

During this tumultuous period, there are only four letters from Alec to Mary (one in late March and three in April), mostly about routine day-to-day business at AFHQ. None of these few letters from the spring of 1945 actually mentioned the end of the war as it was happening, with the exception of one small postscript on April 17, 1945: "The news has the fight moving right through Germany and it looks good, though it has to look very good now because I was fooled last year. Love again and again, Alec." Nothing in the letters told of how each of them found out about the end of the war, but it's likely that they heard the news of Hitler's suicide on the radio. Since the signing of the unconditional surrender happened at Caserta on April 29, effectively ending the Italian Campaign, it's likely Alec would have been asked to be sure the electrics would be working properly for the event, though the formal laying down of German arms didn't happen until May 2 throughout Europe and may not have been public news until then.

As officials began planning for the inevitable victory celebrations throughout the US, they also faced a challenge: how to celebrate victory in Europe while continuing to keep the troops and home front workers focused on and motivated to finish the fight with Japan. Many communities adopted a "V-E Day Code of Conduct" in an effort to tamp down excessive enthusiasm and keep citizens focused on the work ahead. Portland, Oregon, where Mary lived, was one such place, and in a radio address in early May, then-governor, Earl Snell, called for a subdued reaction:

> He asked Oregonians to join him in a prayer of thanksgiving for the victory in Europe and a prayer for early victory in the Pacific. Snell reminded citizens that "we must not forget that our boys are still out in the far Pacific fighting for our freedom at this very hour." He called on Oregonians to set even more production records "until the Japanese join their comrades of Nazi tyranny in unconditional surrender."[7]

When V-E (Victory in Europe) Day arrived on Tuesday, June 8, 1945, Portland churches were open for special services. Most downtown businesses were closed, especially liquor stores, but all city offices, courthouses, post offices, and schools were open. Highlighting the rededication to finishing the war, the shipyards were open and, according to *The Oregonian* newspaper, they "operated with renewed zeal. While absenteeism was normally a chronic problem, on V-E Day the 'Swan Island yard reported even more than the normal complement of workers on the job,'"[8] so it's very likely that Mary went to work at the Port on Swan Island on V-E Day.

16

COMING HOME, SETTLING IN

MAY 1945 AND BEYOND

Though many celebrations, like those in Portland, OR, were subdued, on May 8, 1945, both Great Britain and the United States celebrated V-E Day, and "cities in both nations, as well as formerly occupied cities in Western Europe, put out flags and banners, rejoicing in the defeat of the Nazi war machine."[1] Though she never wrote about it in any of her many short stories, Mary was undoubtedly

Alec and his buddy (possibly Fennel) took a trip about an hour south of Naples to Sorrento once the war was over and before they were sent home again.

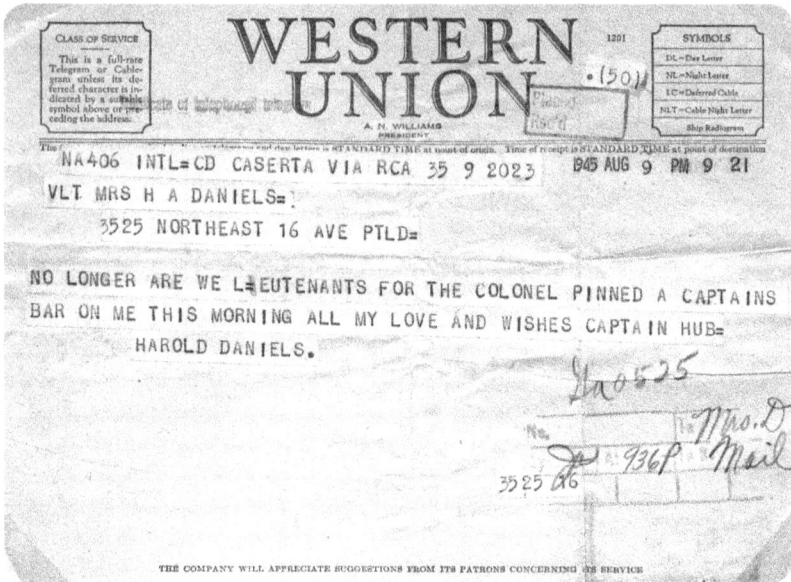

WESTERN UNION

NA406 INTL=CD CASERTA VIA RCA 35 9 2023   1945 AUG 9 PM 9 21

VLT MRS H A DANIELS=

3525 NORTHEAST 16 AVE PTLD=

NO LONGER ARE WE LIEUTENANTS FOR THE COLONEL PINNED A CAPTAINS
BAR ON ME THIS MORNING ALL MY LOVE AND WISHES CAPTAIN HUB=
HAROLD DANIELS.

Alec was promoted to captain in August of 1945.

relieved to hear the news and to join the celebration. Given the local focus on the war in Japan, she might also have been anxious that her beloved hub could be on the way to Japan before coming home, but that was not the case. Alec was not approved to leave Europe immediately and was asked to remain in Italy for several more months, aiding with the dismantling of AFHQ, which was a better option than being sent to the Pacific. This turn of events probably gave them both some peace of mind, in spite of the delay of his homecoming. Though the correspondence is rather thin for 1945 compared to previous years, a few important things come to light.

On June 5, 1945, the four Allied powers in Europe—the United States, the United Kingdom, France, and the Soviet Union—signed a declaration on the defeat of Germany that divided the country into four temporary occupation zones; on June 6 (the one-year anniversary of D-Day), Eisenhower ordered a holiday for all troops in Europe; and on June 7, after months of Alec writing that he wished she could join him in Italy to start seeing the world together, Mary surprised him with a phone call. She was taking him up on his invitation, hoping to make the arrangements to visit as soon as possible. Her call startled him into action, and he made a few calls to ascertain the procedures and approvals needed to set up her transport overseas and what complications or delays she might expect along the way.

> I have also asked the commanding officer of my whole set up, above [Colonel] Northrup, what he will advise with reference to my position, and he is going to look into it and give me an answer. Perhaps by tomorrow I'll be able to send you the definite information. (June 7, 1945)

Three days later, he had to tell her the unfortunate results of his queries:

> I sent a cable today telling you to stay home. It took me some time to think it over to the point to do it, but here is the situation. They have suspended all travel of dependents for an indefinite period to make way for relocation. That means you would likely be stuck in Paris for a while. . . . The guess of the political adviser here is 6 or 9 months. He recommended I bring you over if I could get you to Caserta. To do that you would have to have a job. There are none here because they are closing down. The nearest place would be Naples and there is a big possibility there would be more there by the time you arrived. I would have had you come anyway if I was sure of being here till next year, but I am not, and as yet the Colonel can't give me a definite answer on it. So I finally decided it was better to call it all off. The new regulation only came out Saturday (June 9th) so that is one reason I haven't let you know before, and another was that I wanted you over here. . . .

> Well goodnight, my lovely one. It seems as though we get beaten every way we turn, but we are still well above many who have lost everything. I love [you], dear, I really do. (June 10, 1945)

Mary kept copies of many of Alec's cables in her scrapbook, but the one he referred to in this letter about her not coming to Italy didn't get saved. It would not be hard to imagine her ripping it up in frustration after receiving the bad news.

Though it was clear that Alec couldn't get a definitive answer on how much longer he would be needed at AFHQ, his routines didn't seem to change much in the first months after the surrender

Important Information

FOR

MEMBERS OF THE U.S. ARMED FORCES ON LEAVE

IN SWITZERLAND

General information concerning
Food rationing in Switzerland
Export restrictions when leaving the country
a.s.o.

Welcome to Switzerland!

When I was in the States, I found a sign of welcome at every door, so nothing gives me more pleasure now than to call out to our friends from across the waters: "Welcome to Switzerland".

We know what you have done for us and are grateful for all the sacrifices you have taken upon yourselves to bring back freedom to the peoples of Europe. We shall be happy to make you comfortable in Switzerland during your visit. May all your wishes come true and may you not be disappointed in your expectations. Don't make comparisons, but simply let the impressions gained sink into your minds, discard the chaff from the wheat, gather experiences of beauty, and take the best side of the Swiss and their country. Do away with any possible prejudice and make us feel that you are at home in our country. It will be gratifying to us if the memories you retain are deep and lasting; we shall be honored if you recognise our trust in the freedom of democracy, our endeavor to work for peace and understanding among nations; we shall be glad indeed if your visit strengthens your belief that any nation, however small, can contribute to harmony among mankind.

1

Many of the GIs at AFHQ traveled to Switzerland while waiting for their turn to be sent home. Alec was no exception.

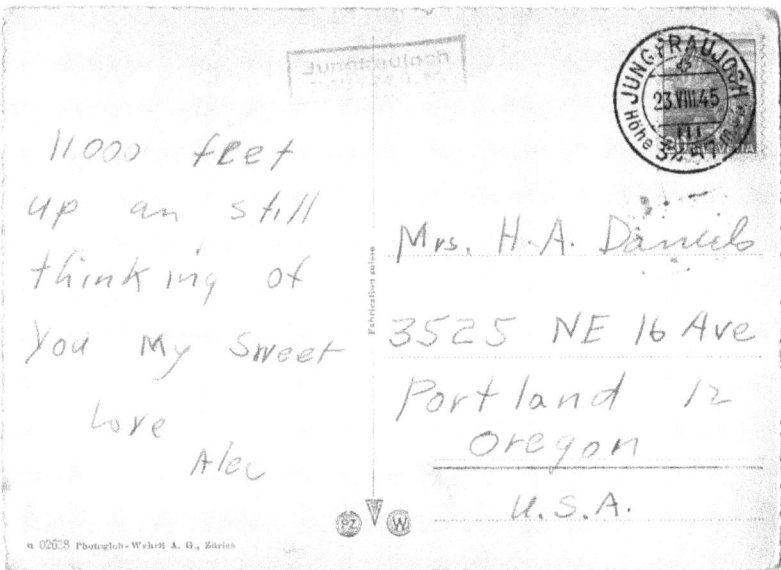

Alec sent this postcard to Mary from the top of Jungfraujoch.

One of Alec's many photos from his trip to Switzerland in August 1945.

of the Nazis. He continued to be frustrated with his Italian helpers and their behavior:

> A couple of my Italian electricians got mixed up with the MPs last night for improper passes and so spent most of the night in jail. I got them out this afternoon. They complained that the rats were so big they couldn't sleep, as they had to stay awake to keep from being bit, but they liked the food, which happened to be "K" rations, the kind you said you didn't like. . . .
>
> There are some that seem all right, but most of them are a sly and dangerous bunch that you don't dare turn your back

on. The only thing they understand is force of some kind, and we are supposed to be above that. They steal the switches off the walls of the buildings we fix. To prevent that we left the switches off till the buildings were to be occupied. Then they dug the wooden blocks out of the wall, which we had set to mount the switches. I guess it was done for spite for our not giving them a chance to get the switches. This was done by those who work for us, which is what makes it bad because we can't catch them, and if we did why the problem comes up: if you fire them where will you get some more? That is our soft policy that makes it that way. (April 24, 1945)

He was also frustrated with the Army and what he had read about "American efficiency" (a term coined in the early 20th century by Frederick Winslow Taylor that was sometimes cited as one of the reasons for America's victory in WWII[2]):

Sometimes one wonders why people want anyone to give them advice. We are just getting around to making a major electrical repair that I recommended nine months ago and had it turned

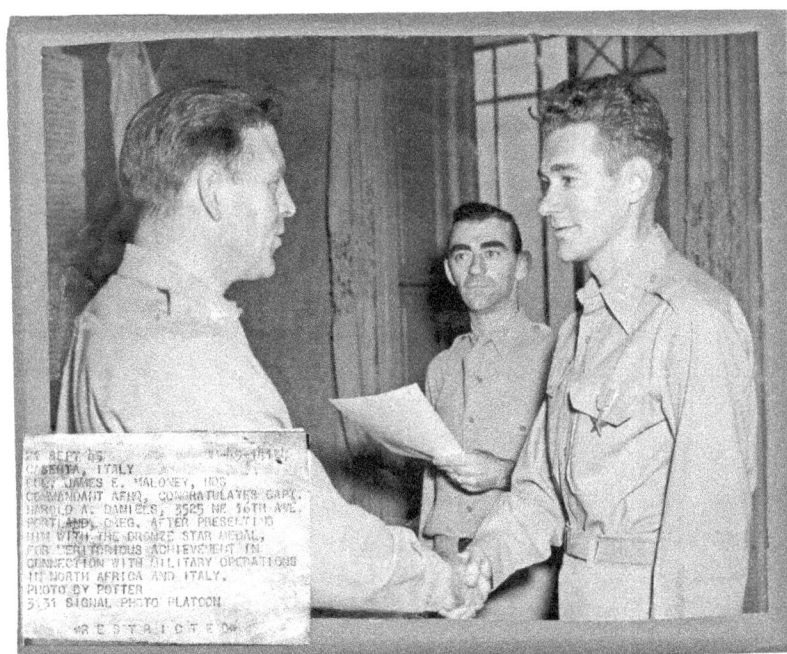

Alec was awarded the Bronze Star for his work at AFHQ in September 1945.

Mary kept Alec's medal in this frame on her bedroom wall for the rest of her life.

down, and so we have had unsteady lights all that time, and now we are going to make the change anyway. When I read the article about American efficiency I wonder. I rather think it is American push because we definitely aren't efficient in the way things are done. We go out and do it, and if there is any trouble it is just done over again. (June 7, 1945)

Alec continued to be frustrated with and unhappy about their separation. He admitted that he often breathed in her letters, which he said smelled "nice," to reassure himself that he still had his "special female" waiting for him at home (April 17, 1945). He also admitted things were better when he could stay busy, but there wasn't as much to do now that the war was officially over,

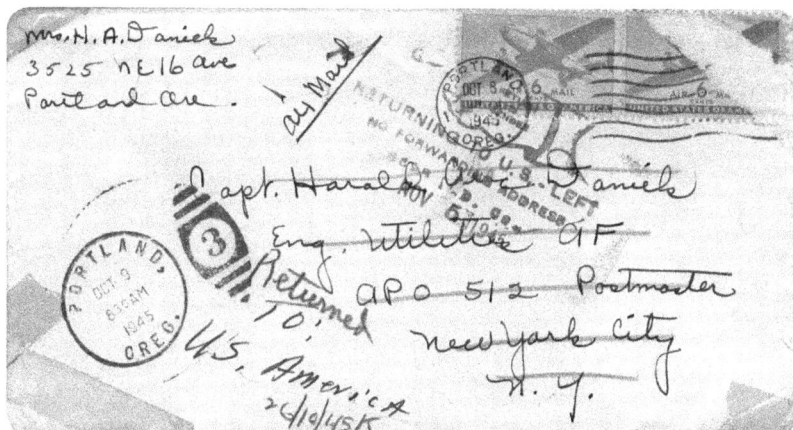

Mary's last letter to Alec in Italy was returned to her because he was already cleared to start the long journey home.

and it sounded like depression, not simply exhaustion, might have been affecting his letter-writing. "Last night I missed writing to you because I was blue. The same is true tonight so don't expect much [in this letter]. I am homesick for you, my love; it is just one of those spells I have when there isn't enough work to keep me busy, and the time hangs on my hands" (April 24, 1945). As he closed that same letter he confessed, "I love you dearly as you well know, and I am getting more impatient with the separation every day. Please include your hub in that which will make you happy. He really needs you, Mary—more than you might realize" (April 24, 1945). He also continued to wonder about his future and reiterated something he had told her a number of times before: "I am still wondering what I might do some time a long time from now when I get out of the Army. I'll have to give that some real thought. Right now I haven't the slightest idea what might be attractive. The main thing is that I want to be happy with you" (August 5, 1945).

He did a little sightseeing, perhaps to take his mind off the fact that Mary would not be able to join him and just how little there was for him to do, even though the Army couldn't give him a definitive answer about when he'd be able to go home. He took an overnight trip with one of his buddies to Sorrento, on the southern end of the Bay of Naples, in July of 1945. And in early August, he told her that another Army buddy had recently returned from an inexpensive tour of Switzerland, so he thought he'd take

While they never did as much world traveling as Alec had envisioned while overseas, one of the first things they did after his return to the States was to hop in the pneumonia box and head for Mexico City.

advantage of that opportunity fairly soon as well. At this point in Alec's story, it seemed that he might have abandoned letter-writing almost altogether, instead using cables (many of which Mary placed in a scrapbook she kept during the war) and an occasional phone call to start the planning for his return home. In early August, he cabled some exciting news from Caserta: "No longer are we lieutenants for the colonel pinned a captain's bar on me this morning. All my love and wishes, Captain Hub" (August 9, 1945).

His promotion took place on the same date when the Allied bombers dropped "Fat Man," their second atomic bomb, on the Japanese city of Nagasaki, only three days after having dropped "Little Boy" on Hiroshima, though none of the correspondence mentioned this coincidence.[3] Many years later, Mary wrote a story about the impact of hearing the news of the bombings while she was visiting a college friend on her days off:

> I was in Seattle that weekend in August when the PI [*Post-Intelligencer*] and the Seattle Star headlines told of a new kind of bomb that had been dropped in Japan—they expected it to have great impact on the war. . . . Yes, it worked. And it had brought

Mary on an Aztec pyramid, probably either the Pyramid of the Moon or Pyramid of the Sun, in Teotihuacan, near Mexico City.

the war to an end as they hoped it would. For the first time in four long years, we let out a national sigh of relief.

On August 14, 1945, only three and a half months after the Nazis had capitulated in Europe, Japan surrendered unconditionally to the Allies, effectively ending the war and bringing the hostilities to a final and highly anticipated close. Since then, both August 14 and August 15 have been known as "Victory over Japan Day," or simply "V-J Day." The term has also been used for September 2, 1945, when Japan's formal surrender took place aboard the USS *Missouri*, anchored in Tokyo Bay.

Alec took that trip to Switzerland in late August and sent a postcard to Mary with the image of Jungfraujoch, a mountain in Switzerland also known as the "Top of Europe," and inscribed a simple handwritten message, "11,000 feet up and still thinking of you, my sweet" (August 23, 1945). Jungfraujoch is a glacial saddle in the Bernese Alps in western Switzerland, connecting two higher peaks, Jungfrau (13,642') and Mönch (13,474'), and its railway station at 11, 371' is the highest railway station in Europe.[4] Alec was quite taken with the Swiss Alps and took many photos. He also brought her a lovely gift, a beautiful jewelry box that was a detailed wooden model of a Swiss chalet, with an edelweiss flower pressed inside a small Swiss tourist brochure. Mary kept her jewelry in the box for decades.

Even though Alec had spent most of the war downplaying his abilities to Mary, the Army clearly saw things differently, and on September 21, 1945, he was awarded a Bronze Star "for meritorious achievement in connection with military operations in Italy and North Africa from 15 December 1942 to 1 August 1945" (Bronze Star Citation). The citation continued:

> As the officer in charge of all electrical installations in connection with the operations of Allied Force Headquarters, Captain Daniels was solely responsible for furnishing and maintaining the electrical power necessary for the operation of the complete headquarters. Upon several occasions, it became necessary for him to create various electrical facilities which required inventiveness and initiative on his part. His ability to organize and to arrive at exceedingly difficult decisions on the spur of the moment, in many instances, made it possible for very important installations to have the necessary electric power to carry on operations. The superb knowledge of electricity, which Captain Daniels possessed, accompanied by this ability to put it to practical use, was of inestimable value in solving the complex problem of electrical supply.

By early October, Alec's cables were definitely suggesting that he would be coming home soon, though it appeared to have taken several tries, and several missed phone calls, for him to get a firm date for his Atlantic crossing. Finally, on Sunday, October 14, 1945, he cabled Mary, "Reporting depot Monday; with luck see you within three weeks; your voice sounded same as I remember; I like it and love you." Once he was back in the US, there were still some uncertainties about his final destination, and he cabled her again on Friday, November 9, 1945, from Lincoln, NE, where he was presumably making a stop on his train trip to the Pacific Northwest: "Expect to arrive Tacoma 7 am Monday; do not know whether debark at Tacoma or Ft. Lewis." This would have given Mary the time to arrange to get to Tacoma somehow over the weekend, and her parents would likely have offered to drive her there, given the uncertainty about exactly where he would be getting off the train. However, it's more likely that she would have simply hopped in the pneumonia box (their woody station wagon)

Army of the United States

CERTIFICATE OF SERVICE

This is to certify that

CAPTAIN HAROLD A DANIELS   O 378 002   CORPS OF ENGINEERS

honorably served in active Federal Service

in the Army of the United States from

26 MARCH 1942   *to*   6 MARCH 1946

Given at SEPARATION CENTER   FORT LEWIS WASHINGTON

on the SIXTH *day of* MARCH *19*46

J WILLARD WAGNER
LIEUTENANT COLONEL   AGD

Alec arrived back home on November 10, 1945, but he was not formally relieved of duty until March 6, 1946, for a total service in the US army of almost four years.

with Pete in the back and a tight sweater in her suitcase, and taken off up the highway on her own. In fact, it seems more likely that she would have wanted their reunion after three years apart to have been totally private. They were both such shy and private people that they would not have wanted what would most likely

MILITARY RECORD AND REPORT OF SEPARATION

BOOK **150** PAGE **409**   CERTIFICATE OF SERVICE   OFF

1. LAST NAME - FIRST NAME - MIDDLE INITIAL			2. ARMY SERIAL NUMBER	3. AGE, GRADE	4. ARM OR SERVICE	5. COMPONENT
DANIELS	HAROLD	A	O 378 002	CAPT	CE	RES

6. ORGANIZATION	7. DATE OF RELIEF FROM ACTIVE DUTY	8. PLACE OF SEPARATION
/FORCES HEADQUARTERS, HQ COMMAND, ALLIED	6 MAR 46	SEPARATION CENTER FORT LEWIS WASHINGTON

9. PERMANENT ADDRESS FOR MAILING PURPOSES	10. DATE OF BIRTH	11. PLACE OF BIRTH
3525 NE 16TH AVENUE PORTLAND, OREGON	24 JUN 1915	PORTLAND, OREGON

12. ADDRESS FROM WHICH EMPLOYMENT WILL BE SOUGHT	13. COLOR EYES	14. COLOR HAIR	15. HEIGHT	16. WEIGHT	17. NO. OF DEPENDENTS
SEE ITEM 9	BROWN	BROWN	6'0"	160 LBS.	1

18. RACE			19. MARITAL STATUS			20. U.S. CITIZEN	21. CIVILIAN OCCUPATION AND NO.
WHITE	NEGRO	OTHER (specify)	SINGLE	MARRIED	OTHER (specify)	YES NO	ELECTRICAL ENGINEER
X				X		X	

MILITARY HISTORY

SELECTIVE SERVICE DATA	22. REGISTERED	23. LOCAL S. S. BOARD NUMBER	24. COUNTY AND STATE	25. HOME ADDRESS AT TIME OF ENTRY ON ACTIVE DUTY
	YES NO X	NONE	NONE	MANETTE, WASHINGTON

26. DATE OF ENTRY ON ACTIVE DUTY	27. MILITARY OCCUPATIONAL SPECIALTY AND NO.
26 MAR 42	ELECTRICAL ENGINEER 7611

28. BATTLES AND CAMPAIGNS

ROME ARNO, NAPLES FOGGIA

29. DECORATIONS AND CITATIONS

BRONZE STAR MEDAL, EUROPEAN AFRICAN MIDDLE EASTERN SERVICE MEDAL WITH 2 BRONZE STARS, WORLD WAR II VICTORY MEDAL

30. WOUNDS RECEIVED IN ACTION

NONE

31. SERVICE SCHOOLS ATTENDED	32.	SERVICE OUTSIDE CONTINENTAL U. S. AND RETURN		
		DATE OF DEPARTURE	DESTINATION	DATE OF ARRIVAL
FORT RILEY, KANSAS		26 SEP 42	ENGLAND	8 OCT 42
33. REASON AND AUTHORITY FOR SEPARATION				
RELIEVED FROM ACTIVE DUTY RR 1-5 (DEMOBILIZATION)		19 OCT 45	U S A	10 NOV 45

34.	CURRENT TOUR OF ACTIVE DUTY					35.	EDUCATION (years)	
CONTINENTAL SERVICE			FOREIGN SERVICE			GRAMMAR SCHOOL	HIGH SCHOOL	COLLEGE
YEARS	MONTHS	DAYS	YEARS	MONTHS	DAYS			
0	9	26	3	1	15	8	4	4

INSURANCE NOTICE

IMPORTANT   IF PREMIUM IS NOT PAID WHEN DUE OR WITHIN THIRTY-ONE DAYS THEREAFTER, INSURANCE WILL LAPSE. MAKE CHECKS OR MONEY ORDERS PAYABLE TO THE TREASURER OF THE U. S. AND FORWARD TO COLLECTIONS SUBDIVISION, VETERANS ADMINISTRATION, WASHINGTON 25, D. C.

36. KIND OF INSURANCE			37. HOW PAID		38. Effective Date of Allotment Discontinuance	39. Date of Next Premium Due (one month after 38)	40. PREMIUM DUE EACH MONTH	41. INTENTION OF VETERAN TO		
Nat. Serv.	U.S. Govt.	None	Allotment	Direct to V.A.				Continue	Continue only	Discontinue
X			X		31 MAR 46	30 APR 46	$ 6.90	X		

42.	43. REMARKS (This space for completion of above items or entry of other items specified in W. D. Directives)
RIGHT THUMB PRINT	ASR SCORE (2 SEP 45) 91 LAPEL BUTTON ISSUED

44. SIGNATURE OF OFFICER BEING SEPARATED	45. PERSONNEL OFFICER (Type name, grade and organization - signature)
Harold A Daniels	GLENN D KELLY CAPT AC Glenn D Kelly

WD AGO Form 53-98
1 November 1944

This form supersedes all previous editions of WD AGO Forms 53 and 280 for officers entitled to a Certificate of Service, which will not be used after receipt of this revision.

Given that the army lost their records of Alec's service in a fire in 1973, this is the only remaining record of Alec's military service during WWII.

have been a passionate reunion witnessed by anyone, even—or perhaps especially—those family members closest to them.

One of the very first things Mary and Alec did after his return from Italy was to take a trip to Mexico, one of their favorite vacations. They encountered a film crew while there. It was obviously a vivid memory for Mary because, decades later when she was in her seventies, she wrote about that adventure in a story she called "John Wayne—A Love Story" because he had made several movies in Mexico. By that time, one of the actresses she wrote about was in her eighties and the other already deceased:

> I offer, for what it's worth in news value, the fact that in 1945 in Pueblo, just south of Mexico City, my husband and I came onto a production company that was making a movie starring Esther Williams. She was down there on her honeymoon, having just married Ben Gage. That afternoon we ran into them out shopping, and she was happily carrying a small wooden chest she had just purchased. That evening, at a nearby table in the hotel, Mary Astor and a companion were dining [most likely her then-fiancé, Thomas Wheelock]. He was making a show of ordering the wine, sniffing the cork, swirling a bit in the glass and tasting it, and rejecting it and getting a second bottle, which seemed to suit him. Mary Astor looked interested and so did we all. So I could write about that if anyone wanted to read it, but you have to strike while the iron is hot. I wonder, though, if anyone even remembers them now—Esther and Mary.

In addition to traveling to British Columbia, Mexico, and many of the western states, they also tried, unsuccessfully, to

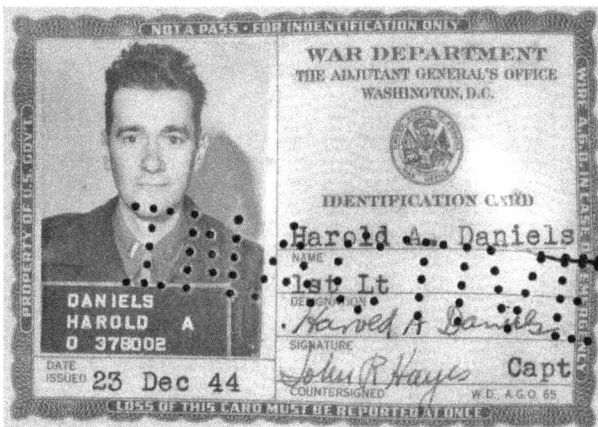

Alec's military ID card was punched "inactive" when he was relieved of duty, and Mary added the card to her wartime scrapbook.

start a family. This may, in fact, have been one of the reasons they never did the amount of world traveling Alec had hoped for in his letters. Mary never wrote a word about the excruciating anguish the long-separated couple must have felt while struggling with infertility in those post-war years. In spite of declaring during the war that he'd be happy to have Mary support him, Alec eventually went to work for Crown Zellerbach, a pulp and paper company, in Oregon City, OR, in the late 1940s. He was employed as an electrical engineer at a newsprint paper mill for more than 30 years. It's not clear where Mary and Alec lived in those first few years after the war until they moved to Lake Oswego, OR, in 1948, or possibly early 1949, living first in a small lakeside cabin that today is a boathouse. It was there that they adopted their first child, a girl. In 1950, they moved up the hill to a larger house, where they adopted their second child, a boy, in 1952 and settled happily into their family life. They stayed in that house for the rest of their lives.

17

ALL ELSE IS AFTERMATH

A DAUGHTER'S REFLECTIONS

Mom and Dad rarely talked with us kids about their experiences during the war, nevertheless there were occasional echoes of the things they shared in their letters and stories throughout my growing up. As their daughter, I've attempted to collect a few of those thoughts together for the readers of Mary and Alec's story.

I remember my dad as a funny, smart, and cheerful fellow who was not like other dads, mostly because he didn't play actively with his kids the way many other dads we knew did. I didn't realize it at the time, but I know now the reason for his inactivity was that he was in near-constant pain from rheumatoid arthritis. During my youth, I never thought of him as being a particularly athletic or physical kind of dad. He was happier to help me with my math homework than to indulge my tomboy tendencies in sports, and he had hopes that I would follow in his footsteps and become an engineer. He worked hard and was always on call for the mill if anything went wrong with #9, Crown's crankiest newsprint paper machine. He was apparently the only one on the entire plant staff who could get it going again when it broke down, which was often. I also recollect that while his military service had trained him to use weapons, Dad seemed uncomfortable with his birdshot rifle and only went hunting to sit in the woods and enjoy the peace and quiet. I recall that both of my parents came to all of my musical and theatrical performances, including one very experimental, hippy, multi-media musical in San Francisco after college graduation that involved nude cast members coming out to sit with the audience during the final song. I will never forget just how many shades of red Dad turned when one of the actors sang directly to him while he tried to look everywhere but at her.

Mom was creative, was never afraid of trying new things, was almost as good as Dad at small appliance repair and soldering, knew lots about mushrooms and all the other plants we had in our large yard, and could always suggest a book from the shelves or take us to the library whenever we asked her those questions children always have for their parents about how and why things happen in the world. Though a teacher/librarian by temperament, Mom didn't work outside the home. Instead, she was a PTA member, possibly even an officer, very active with the AFS (American Field Services) organization, especially when it came to exchanges with students from Mexico, and she also led my Camp Fire Girl troop for a while, putting her extensive crafting abilities to the test with a gaggle of pre-teen girls. She taught me to sew and knit and a little bit about cooking and baking, though she never pushed me to focus solely on the domestic arts. Instead, she taught me that girls could do just about anything they wanted when they grew up, though I never did share her passion for mycology or polar exploration.

When asked for a general memory of our parents, my younger brother, Toby, remembers them through the lens of his many athletic events as a student and comparing them favorably to the "out of control" parents he'd experienced as a high school track coach and when coaching his own sons in community athletic endeavors:

> In subtle ways, Dad was quite involved with my activities. Not as much as Mom, but in ways which were very much noticed and appreciated. Both of them attended virtually every one of my athletic events. I can hardly remember an event which they did not attend, even going to football games when I was a rally [squad] member.

> They were "perfect" parents in this way. They did not care whether or not I won or lost. They didn't care how many points I scored or how fast I ran. Most importantly, they never yelled or carried-on as fans. I've mentioned to friends many times that

Dad bringing home the new baby (me), with a view of Oswego Lake in the background.

> Mom and Dad sat in the stands and just watched, which . . .
> was wonderful. (email, August 25, 2018)

"Perfect parents" indeed. Perhaps because they understood that parenthood wasn't a given, ours wanted to be good at the job and were actively engaged in our lives as much as possible. Luckily for us, when Mom and Dad finally had to give up the idea of making their own "brats," as Dad had often referred to their hoped-for children in his letters, and they decided to consider adoption instead, help was close at hand. They had the good fortune to be close friends in the early 1940s with the doctor who became head of obstetrics at a major Bremerton hospital after the war. Betty and Ray Creelman had been their neighbors and closest friends while Dad worked at the shipyards before being sent overseas, and though they no longer lived in Bremerton, with Ray's help and guidance, they eventually adopted two children at birth: me in 1949, and my brother in 1952. When I finally met my birth mother, years after both Mom and Dad were gone, she told me that Ray had reassured her before my birth that the people who would raise the child she couldn't keep were good people who had been his neighbors and were still his good friends, and he promised that frightened teenager that he would keep an eye on her child to be sure all was well, a kindness she remembered for the rest of her life. He was as good as his word, though I never knew about what he had promised until many decades later. He may have made the same promise to my brother's birth mother for all we know. Betty and Ray were lifelong friends of our family.

Though our parents were open with my brother and me about the fact that we were adopted, the only thing Mom ever wrote about either adoption was an undated poem I found in a box after her death. My brother likes to think it's about him, and I'm quite sure it's about me:

Motherhood

They brought me this baby—
Such breathtaking perfection!
Tiny pink nails on tiny jointed fingers—
Sweet fuzz for hair, and little shell-ears.
Then the knowing overwhelmed me,
That from this moment on I could steal for you.
I could kill if by doing so it would mean
Important differences in your well-being.
Now I understood the animal mother,
Who, in the face of threat
Ingests her offspring—
Saying lovingly, "Go back into the warm dark
From whence you came and be forever safe.
Now is not a good time to be born."
And so to shield you from danger, from the sorrows of life,
Could I be like her?
Yes! I, too, would
If I could.

Having been raised in rural Oregon by parents who maintained their small farm outside town well into the 1950s, even after moving the family into the city of Portland in the 1930s, Mom would have been familiar with the opossum. Opossums are one of the species that devour their babies if they believe they cannot protect them. I once witnessed a mother opossum that had just been hit by a car in front of a friend's house, her pouch full of newborns. As she was dying, she was also trying to ingest her offspring—the only way to keep them safe. While Mom was fierce about her human children, she never forgot Pete, the dog, who she characterized as her first child in one of her stories and who was my protector and companion for the first six years of my life. I often tell people that my older brother was a German shepherd, and our family was rarely without a dog or two, usually big ones, for the rest of Mom's long life.

Mom and Dad never did build that whimsical house Mom wrote about and they dreamed about while living in Bremerton before the war—the one with secret doors and multiple levels—though they did find a charming old farmhouse to buy after the war on an acre of land full of fruit and nut trees. They raised us there and lived in that house nearly all the rest of their lives. Mom told me that they made a renovation plan in the 1950s when we kids were young, but they never did complete the job, though I remember helping my dad re-roof the house with cedar shakes when I was old enough to climb the extension ladder. Dad also rewired the house, and he installed a drinking fountain in the kids' bedroom because he got tired of getting up at night to bring us a drink of water. He was, after all, a utilities engineer.

In the early months of his overseas adventure, Dad often wrote home about the free movies that were provided to the American GIs abroad, which reminded me of the fact that after the war my parents were definitely movie buffs, enjoying foreign films as well as the usual mainstream movie hits. One of my strongest and strangest movie memories with them is going to see a surreal silent foreign film at a small movie house on Cannery Row when we were visiting my grandparents in Monterey, California, probably in the late 1950s or early 1960s. A few of that film's macabre images lingered in my imagination long after the film itself had become a distant memory. I learned later that the film was most likely the groundbreaking 1929 surrealist film, *Un Chien Andalou* by Luis Buñuel.

Dad also wrote often about the music he heard on the radio, which surprised me at first because my memory of his musicality was that it was more or less non-existent. His favorite song was "Home on the Range" and he couldn't manage to carry even that simple tune in the proverbial bucket, no matter how large, and I have his own tape recording to prove it. Mom, on the other hand, was quite musical and loved singing along to big band jazz and Broadway musical recordings, and encouraged musical interest in both her children, so I suspect Dad's interest in music was entirely because of her love for the songs of the time. However, his love for radios and desire to tinker with that technology was indisputable.

Writing about the romance between them was probably the most interesting and challenging part of this story. I don't know many children, regardless of their age, who have much interest in their parents' romantic inclinations. In fact, most of the people I've ever asked about it don't want to know any details. As an adopted child, it's easy to believe your parents never made love. Because they were very private individuals and were both raised by parents with very Victorian sensibilities about showing their feelings, I grew up without seeing many overt signs of affection between my parents. So, it was easy to believe that their marriage was more about friendship than romance. I remember from helping Mom give herself perms when I was in high school that she had naturally straight, fine, silky hair, so I can appreciate the sensuality Dad was expressing when he wrote about loving to run his hands through her hair, even as my childhood-self doesn't really want to think too hard about what he meant by "among other things," when writing about romantic activities he missed between them.

I do recall feeling a bit jealous as a teenager of the love my parents so obviously had for each other. One very vivid memory was seeing Dad when he returned from getting what might have been his first cortisone shot at the clinic, which took away his chronic rheumatoid arthritis pain for a few days. I watched him dance and romance Mom around the kitchen that afternoon, something he almost never did in sight of the kids. But as awkward as I felt watching them, I was completely convinced that it was not an act because the love between them was palpable in a way I'd never seen before. At a time when I was particularly needy, I was a little upset that they paid more attention to each other than to their kids for those few pain-free days. But as an adult, I know now that's the way it should have been, and I feel blessed to have had such a stable example of a solid marriage to learn from as I grew into my own adulthood. That loving and stable relationship was one that my brother and I both tried to emulate in our own marriages, though I have to admit it took me two tries to get mine right.

One memory triggered by Dad's "boy with a donkey" story in Chapter Ten was particularly interesting to me because during my childhood, we made several trips to Mexico, which gave Mom the idea—in spite of her fear of horses due to a terrifying wild horse stampede she experienced as a child when camping with her family—that having a *burro* might be fun, though it turned out to be more challenging than she bargained for. I recall watching Mom pulling hard on the rope as she tried to get the recalcitrant Koko to move from one grazing spot to another in our large yard. I even remember one day seeing her blue skirt flashing by out the window as the feisty burro pulled her by the rope tether at full speed down the center of our street, only veering off at the last minute when a car was coming from the other direction.

As far as I know, Dad never wrote much after the war, other than an occasional letter when I was away at college, mostly wondering what I was doing, and he definitely never talked about his wartime experiences to his kids. This reticence to discuss the war was common in my parents' generation. Perhaps it was their upbringing, or perhaps they simply didn't want to burden their children with their unpleasant memories, but it was not specific to the two of them; many in "the Greatest Generation" never shared their war stories once they came home. Mom continued to write regularly when we were younger, though as far as I know she never had any stories published in spite of the one revise and resubmit request during the war years. Her writing when we were growing up consisted mostly of letters to the editor of our local paper or for projects to do with volunteer groups she became involved with. I never realized at the time that her involvement with AFS reflected her anti-war sentiments. I knew that it was a way for her to maintain her interest in other peoples and cultures, but it was only recently by reading the AFS-USA website that I understood that the organization's stated mission was to work "toward a more just and peaceful world by providing international and intercultural learning experiences to individuals, families, schools, and communities through a global volunteer partnership."[1] Or, as paraphrased by a friend recently, "to eliminate war." So affected was she by the trauma of war that Mom once told me she refused to believe in a god that allowed WWII to happen.

While both parents rarely touched alcohol, I remember that we never went very long without a supply of Coca-Cola in the fridge. Unfortunately, Dad's abiding love for Coke, which he referred to numerous times in his war letters, was one of the precipitating reasons for his visit to the hospital where he ultimately died in 1972, the year after I finished college. Many years of washing

Mom and Dad traveled to Mexico often in the years after the war, leaving the kids with Mom's parents, who had moved to Pacific Grove, California, until we were old enough to come along.

down his aspirin for arthritis pain with a Coke eventually gave him a terrible ulcer, which led to his death nearly three decades after the war. He went into the hospital for what should have been a routine ulcer surgery, but complications kept him hospitalized for close to a month, punctuated by a second and more intricate surgery, followed by the pneumonia infection that claimed his life just weeks after his fifty-seventh birthday. Even near the end of his life when he was being fed with a tube because his intestines couldn't digest regular food, what he talked about most often was how he really wanted a steak—and a Coke.

Of course, the sad irony is that some part of his spirit, the aspect of his persona as a young man who wanted to see the world, to be spontaneous and adventurous, was eventually somehow crushed by his experiences during the war. Though he never talked with me when I was a young adult about his reasons for no longer wanting to travel, it's possible that the responsibilities of his post-war life made it harder than he had originally imagined, especially after children came into the picture in the late 1940s and early 1950s. But Mom always maintained that the war experience, especially being so close to the combat zones, was the thing that had broken his adventurous spirit and possibly led to his early death. Unfortunately, many of the other men in his generation who had fought in the war didn't live to see sixty, either. Though he decried a settled life after the war in his letters home from overseas, Dad worked for the same company from the late 1940s until his death, and though he rose through the ranks to a quasi-management position, he definitely settled into a fixed routine once he was back in the States. Our vacations were always planned far in advance because of his responsibilities at work, and there was little spontaneity involved in any of our family travel. Thankfully, cell phones had yet to be invented, so on family outings, he was able to escape from the near-constant weekend phone calls when things went wrong at the mill.

After Dad died, Mom eventually returned to work once again at Meier & Frank, the same department store she had worked in during the war, this time in the book department. Then in her late fifties and trying to make a new life for herself without her partner of over thirty years, she had no interest in the job leading to anything else and actually turned down several promotion possibilities—buyer and department manager—in favor of simply selling books, something that gave her great pleasure until her eventual retirement over a decade later. She also continued to volunteer regularly at the local library, usually shelving big art books because none of the other volunteers wanted to get down to work on the lower shelves so close to the floor.

Mom once joked with me, saying that she was meeting more men at the senior center than most of her friends who were all complaining about not finding interesting men to talk to and that it was because she took a class on earthquakes and volcanoes that didn't interest the rest of the ladies. However, she was not interested in finding another man. Though there was a time after her close friend Betty Creelman died that I hoped Mom might connect with and possibly marry Ray Creelman, that ever-helpful and always-friendly doctor, she never had another romantic interest after Dad's death. She didn't share anything with me about how she had adjusted to her grief and loss, something I regretted when my own husband also died unexpectedly and much too young. But she certainly did model for me how to live a solo but fulfilling widowed life into old age, and for that, I will always be grateful, though I was never able to tell her so since she died before my tragedy happened.

When Mom attended creative-writing classes at the local senior center, she started mining her memories to write numerous short essays and stories. Many of these were about her childhood, her family, her upbringing, or about the community we lived in, but the war figured strongly in several of them. One of those untitled stories described how Dad had been called up for the Korean War (1950-53), but that he had flunked a hearing test and didn't have to go, which she called a "small miracle." She also wrote about the fact that their children didn't have to go to the Vietnam War. I didn't have to go because women weren't allowed to fight, and I was in college, both of which would have qualified me for a draft deferment. If I'd been a man, though, my birthday would have meant a single digit draft number, and I would definitely have been called up if I had left college before the war ended. Instead, Mom wrote that her daughter "spent turbulent college years join-ing protesting groups instead of doing what you're supposed to be doing at college, and that is having fun, going to dances, and getting engaged." My brother "was too young to be caught up in a war. The lucky ones can go through life being a little too young or a little too old to go to war." I remember understanding that if Vietnam had continued long enough to put my brother in jeopardy of being conscripted, Mom was prepared to send him to Canada to avoid the draft.

Her wartime letters to Dad did not survive, but I know the war experience had a powerful impact on Mom's memories, and she eventually wrote several stories about those feelings. In one of them, she explained:

> It is possibly true that if you are of active service age in a time of war and you are called to duty, then those years of high excitement, churning emotions, anguish, fear, loneliness, camaraderie are the climax years of your life and all else is aftermath. So, if those are your twenties, all the rest of your life you may be looking backwards. We, the generation who served in World War II, both actively as members of the armed forces, and inactively as their wives, lived through separations as long as four years, the men on one side of the oceans and the women on the other.

In another, she wrote about a book she recently read that defined the three greatest tragedies in our country's history as the Civil War, the great flu epidemic of 1918, and the Great Depression. However, she took exception to the last of those choices. As someone who lived through the Depression, she felt that after the initial shock, people were still close enough to their pioneer roots to see that solutions to the problems could be found if folks were willing to use their heads and their hands. Instead, she strongly believed that WWII was

> The third greatest tragedy in our country's experience. Over five hundred thousand [Americans] died in this war [and the overall death total, both military and civilian, was actually between 70-85 million]. . . . Should we not stop and wonder why it is we set such a low value on male human life that we can afford to toss it away as casually as a tree drops its leaves in the fall? Shall we hope that perhaps there won't be a fourth greatest tragedy?

And finally, in another story, she imagined a confrontation with Mother Nature about wars and the future of the world:

> Tell me, Mom, will there ever be a time when we'll be finished with wars?
>
> Frankly, I watch and wonder, too, and grieve for my poor misguided children. I had such great plans that have come to naught. I sent you a man who could have solved your problems with arthritis. You shot him at the battle of Shiloh. . . . I had a lad who could have wiped out the common cold. You killed him in France in 1915. He was German, by the way. I had a promising candidate for the solution to cardiac arrest, but he went into the Pacific Ocean when the [USS] Sculpin shot his ship out from under him. So yes, I will keep in mind the fact that you have many needs, and I shall keep trying to find people who can help find the answers, but I shake my head at the hazards my great gifts to you face when they are among you. You seem so intent on destroying each other. I wait and wait for you to mature, and I begin to wonder if it will ever happen. All that brainpower thrown into the ocean, cast upon the winds. One of these times I may sigh for one last time (yes, I'm thinking about it), and I may say but, alas, it all seems useless, and shut down altogether.

Dad never talked much about the war, but he did let me put on his uniform jacket for this photo with my brother, Toby, likely taken in the late 1950s.

Mom told me that during the 1950s some of the Army wives she knew decided to destroy their war letters, perhaps because the raw and vulnerable nature of their contents seemed too intimate to reveal to others or perhaps because they were reminders of such a difficult time in their lives. She said that, ultimately, she couldn't go through with destroying all of them, but she may have destroyed some, which could account for some of the gaps in what was undoubtedly a regular correspondence. It's not clear to me whether she actually started to destroy some of the letters and then couldn't continue, or whether many letters from this period simply went astray in other ways. I suspect it's a bit of both. She also sent me a few she thought I might be interested in when I was living away from my hometown area in the late 1980s and throughout the 1990s, so she clearly didn't think of them as any kind of "collection" to be preserved.

At some point in her later years, Mom inked her own calligraphy copy of a Chinese poem that remained framed on her bedroom wall until she passed away, just a few weeks shy of her ninety-first birthday in 2006. I never knew how or where she found it, and I did not truly understand the significance of this poem for her until doing the research and preparation for this book. I close with its words, words that clearly sustained my mother, perhaps during the war, but also for some or all of the nearly 35 years she survived after my father's death. It has, for me, become emblematic of my parents' love story during the war and throughout their life together. I can imagine my mother hearing these words in her mind uttered by her own beloved soldier husband:

A Chinese General to His Wife Two Thousand Years Ago
by General Su Wu

Since our hair was plaited and we became man and wife
The love between us was never broken by doubt.
So let us be merry this night together,
Feasting and playing while the good time lasts.

I suddenly remember the distance that I must travel;
I spring from bed and look out to see the time.
The stars and planets are all brown dim in the sky;
Long, long is the road; I cannot stay.

I am going on service, away to the battle-ground,
And I do not know when I shall come back.
I hold your hand with only a deep sigh;
Afterwards, tears—in the days when we are parted.

With all your might enjoy the spring flowers,
But do not forget the time of our love and pride.
Know that if I live, I will come back again,
And if I die, we will go on thinking of each other.

NOTES

Introduction

1. Smithsonian Institute online, "Letter Writing in World War Two," National Postal Museum, accessed January 30, 2015, https://postalmuseum.si.edu/VictoryMail/letter/index.html.

Chapter One

1. Daryl C. McClary, "Puget Sound Naval Shipyard," HistoryLink.org Essay 5579, posted November 4, 2003, http://www.historylink.org/File/5579.

2. US Geological Survey, *An Introduction to Hood Canal*: 1, accessed November 11, 2016, https://wa.water.usgs.gov/projects/hoodcanal/data/HC.pdf.

3. "Olympic National Park, Washington," National Park Service, accessed November 11, 2016, https://www.nps.gov/olym/planyourvisit/weather-brochure.htm.

4. Wikipedia, s.v. "Tacoma Narrows Bridge," accessed April 25, 2016, https://en.wikipedia.org/wiki/Tacoma_Narrows_Bridge.

Chapter Two

1. Larry Roberts, "History of Fort Leonard Wood," *Engineer*, Summer 2008, 4-6, http://www.wood.army.mil/engrmag/Maneuver Support Magazine/PDFs for Summer 2008/Roberts.pdf.

2. Roberts, "History of Fort," 4-6.

3. Wikipedia, s.v. "Waynesville, MO," accessed November 12, 2016, https://en.wikipedia.org/wiki/Waynesville,_Missouri.

4. Encyclopedia Britannica Online, s.v. "Ozarks," accessed November 12, 2016, https://www.britannica.com/place/Missouri-state.

5. Kee Malesky, "The Journey from 'Colored' to 'Minorities' to 'People of Color,'" New England Public Radio, last modified March 30, 2014, http://www.npr.org/sections/codeswitch/2014/03/30/295931070/the-journey-from-colored-to-minorities-to-people-of-color.

6. Henry Louis Gates, "Many Rivers to Cross" PBS Learning Media Blog. 2013, http://www.pbs.org/wnet/african-americans-many-rivers-to-cross/.

7. U.S. Army Center of Military History, "Diversity in the Army," accessed May 10, 2016, http://www.history.army.mil/html/faq/diversity.html#african.

8. National WWII Museum online, "African Americans in World War Two: Fighting for a Double Victory," accessed May 10, 2016, https://www.nationalww2museum.org/sites/default/files/2017-07/african-americans.pdf.

9. State of Missouri Official Manual, *The Role of the Negro in Missouri History* (State of Missouri, 1973), https://law.wustl.edu/Staff/Taylor/manual/civrits.htm.

10. Constitutional Rights Foundation, "The Southern 'Black Codes' of 1865-66," accessed August 1, 2018, http://www.crf-usa.org/brown-v-board-50th-anniversary/southern-black-codes.html.

Chapter Three

1. K. Lawrence, "American Armed Forces Airmail during World War II, Part 1, 1941-43," Linn's Stamp News, April 7, 2014, https://www.linns.com/news/us-stamps-postal-history/2014/april/american-armed-forces-airmailduring-world-war-ii-p.html.

2. Lawrence, "American Armed Forces Airmail."

3. National WWII Museum online, "Take a Closer Look at V-Mail," accessed April 27, 2015, http://enroll.nationalww2museum.org/learn/education/for-students/ww2-history/take-a-closer-look/v-mail.html.

4. Lawrence, "American Armed Forces Airmail."

5. For all dates specific to WWII actions in the European Theater, I compiled for myself a research chronology made up of information from various online historical sources, including historynet.com, On This Day at History.com, the National WWII Museum website, Worldwar2.net chronologies for both western and southern Europe, and information gleaned from the first two volumes of Atkinson's *Liberation Trilogy*. Throughout the book, I will not note specific sources for date references unless direct quotes from specific articles or other expanded information about the event itself are also included.

6. Allan M. Winkler, "The World War II Home Front," *History Now*, Issue 14, Winter 2007, https://www.gilderlehrman.org/history-by-era/world-war-ii/essays/world-war-ii-home-front.

Chapter Four

1. Laura Sparaco, "American Soldiers Arrive in Great Britain, January 26, 1942," National WWII Museum online, posted January 26, 2012.

2. Wikipedia, s.v. "This Gun for Hire," accessed November 13, 2016, https://en.wikipedia.org/wiki/This_Gun_for_Hire.

3. Olive-Drab.com, "WWII Army Officers Uniforms," accessed November 14, 2016, https://olive-drab.com/od_soldiers_clothing_ww2_officers_army.php.

Chapter Five

1. Elizabeth Landau, "Why Do We Use Pet Names in Relationships," Scientific American, February 12, 2015.

2. Ken Burns and Lynn Nowak, PBS Home Video. "The War" (2006).

Chapter Six

1. John J. McGrath, *The Other End of the Spear: The Tooth to Tail Ratio in Modern Military Operations*. Combat Studies Institute Press, Fort Leavenworth, KS, 2011: 19.

2. McGrath, *The Other End of the Spear*, 5.

3. Rick Atkinson, *An Army at Dawn: The War in North Africa, 1942-43.* (New York: Henry Holt and Company, 2002), 195.

4. Atkinson, *Army at Dawn*, 237.

5. Atkinson, *Army at Dawn*, 196.

6. Atkinson, *Army at Dawn*, 247.

7. Wikipedia, s.v. "Officer of the Day," accessed October 5, 2016, https://en.wikipedia.org/wiki/Officer_of_the_day.

8. Atkinson, *Army at Dawn*, 262.

9. Atkinson, *Army at Dawn*, 250.

Chapter Seven

1. Atkinson, *Army at Dawn*, 281-300.

2. Atkinson, *Army at Dawn*, 323.

3. Atkinson, *Army at Dawn*, 293.

4. Atkinson, *Army at Dawn*, 196.

5. United States History online, "U.S. War Bonds," accessed October 19, 2016, https://www.u-s-history.com/pages/h1682.html.

6. Women in the Army online, "Creation of the Women's Army Corps," accessed October 17, 2016, https://www.army.mil/women/history/wac.html.

7. Mattie E. Treadwell, *The Women's Army Corps.* Center of Military History US Army, Washington, DC, 1954: 381.

8. Richard R. Lingeman *Don't You Know There's a War On? The American Home Front 1941-1945.* G.P. Putnam's Sons, New York, 1970: 161.

9. Atkinson, *Army at Dawn*, 399.

10. Atkinson, *Army at Dawn*, 390.

11. Robert A. Newton, "Battle for Kasserine Pass: 1st Armored Division Were Ambushed by the Afrika Corps at Sidi Bou Zid," in *HistoryNet.com* (World History Group, n.d.), previously published in *World War II*, September 2002, http://www.historynet.com/battle-for-kasserine-pass-1st-armored-division-were-ambushed-by-the-afrika-corps-at-sidi-bou-zid.htm.

12. Atkinson, *Army at Dawn*, 411.

13. Atkinson, *Army at Dawn*, 443.

14. Atkinson, *Army at Dawn*, 530-33.

15. Rick Atkinson, *The Day of Battle: The War in Sicily and Italy, 1943-44.* (New York: Henry Holt and Company, 2007), 5.

Chapter Eight

1. Arthritis Foundation online, "Rheumatoid Arthritis," accessed March 9, 2017, http://www.arthritis.org/about-arthritis/types/rheumatoid-arthritis/symptoms.php.

2. Wikipedia, s.v. "First Lieutenant," accessed February 7, 2017, https://en.wikipedia.org/wiki/First_lieutenant.

3. Military.com, "Army Officer Ranks," accessed February 7, 2017, https://www.military.com/army/officer-ranks.html#officers.

Chapter Nine

1. Atkinson, *Army at Dawn*, 534.

2. Atkinson, *Army at Dawn*, 538.

3. Atkinson, *Day of Battle*, 21.

4. Andrew J. Birtle. "Sicily 1943," U.S. Army Center of Military History, last updated October 3, 2003, https://history.army.mil/brochures/72-16/72-16.htm.

5. Atkinson, *Day of Battle*, 50.

6. Atkinson, *Day of Battle*, 29.

7. Atkinson, *Day of Battle*, 29-30.

8. Atkinson, *Day of Battle*, 29-30.

9. Atkinson, *Day of Battle*, 48.

10. Atkinson, *Day of Battle*, 68.

11. Atkinson, *Day of Battle*, 109.

12. Atkinson, *Day of Battle*, 123-25.

13. Birtle, "Sicily 1943."

14. Atkinson, *Day of Battle*, 128-155.

15. Atkinson, *Day of Battle*, 156-70.

16. History.com online, "Battle of Kursk," 2009, https://www.history.com/topics/world-war-ii/battle-of-kursk.

17. Atkinson, *Day of Battle*, 195.

18. Atkinson, *Day of Battle*, 202-238.

19. Atkinson, *Day of Battle*, 241-42.

Chapter Ten

1. VI Corps of Combat Engineers online forum, "What Was Your WWII Pay?" posted November 30, 2012, http://www.6thcorpscombatengineers.com/engforum/index.php?/topic/7766-wwii-soldiers-pay-with-responses-from-the-vets-themselves/.

Chapter Eleven

1. History.com, "Italian Campaign," 2009, https://www.history.com/topics/world-war-ii/italian-campaign.

2. Holocaust Encyclopedia online, s.v. "Italy," last updated March 23, 2010, https://www.ushmm.org/wlc/en/article.php?ModuleId=10005455.

3. Atkinson, *Day of Battle*, 252.

4. Atkinson, *Day of Battle*, 245, 247, 256.

5. History.com, "Italian Campaign."

6. American Cleaning Institute online, "Soaps and Detergent History: 1900 to Now," accessed January 21, 2017, https://www.cleaninginstitute.org/clean_living/soaps__detergent_history_3.aspx.

7. Rebecca Onion, "Some Choice Bits of Slang from American Soldiers Serving in WWII," *Slate*, November 11, 2013, http://www.slate.com/blogs/the_vault/2013/11/11/military_slang_terms_used_by_soldiers_in_wwii.html.

8. Atkinson, *Day of Battle*, 270.

9. Atkinson, *Day of Battle*, 298.

10. Brian John Murphy. "Patton's Ghost Army," *America in WWII online*, 2005, http://www.americainwwii.com/articles/pattons-ghost-army/.

11. Atkinson, *Day of Battle*, 312.

12. Atkinson, *Day of Battle*, 318.

Chapter Twelve

1. Atkinson, *Day of Battle*, 445-452.
2. Totally History online, "Operation Shingle," 2012, http://totallyhistory.com/operation-shingle/.
3. Atkinson, *Day of Battle*, 348.
4. GlobalSecurity.org, "Gustav Line," accessed July 16, 2017, http://www.globalsecurity.org/military/world/europe/de-gustav.htm.
5. Atkinson, *Day of Battle*, 432-441.
6. Atkinson, *Day of Battle*, 431.
7. Atkinson, *Day of Battle*, 431.
8. IMDb online, "Princess O'Rourke," accessed March 8, 2017, https://www.imdb.com/title/tt0036277/.
9. IMDb online, "A Guy Named Joe," accessed March 8, 2017, https://www.imdb.com/title/tt0035959/?ref_=nv_sr_1.
10. Reggia Di Caserta online, "History of the Palace and of the Bourbon," accessed March 10, 2017, http://reggiaofcaserta.altervista.org/en/palace/history/.
11. Atkinson, *Day of Battle*, 484-94.
12. Sara E. Pratt, "The Most Recent Eruption of Mt. Vesuvius," *Earthmagazine.com,* March 17, 2016, https://www.earthmagazine.org/article/benchmarks-march-17-1944-most-recent-eruption-mount-vesuvius.
13. Atkinson, *Day of Battle*, 483-84.
14. Atkinson, *Day of Battle*, 507-9.

Chapter Thirteen

1. Kathi Jackson, *They Called Them Angels; American Military Nurses of World War II*, Praeger, Westport, CT, 2000: 58.
21. MedicineNet.com, "Medical Definition of Sandfly Fever," accessed April 9, 2017, https://www.medicinenet.com/script/main/art.asp?articlekey=31320.
3. William A. Reilly, Roberto F. Escamilla, and Perrin H. Long, "Sandfly Fever," in *Infectious Diseases*, ed. John Boyd Coates, Jr. and W. Paul Havens, Jr., vol. 2, *Medical Department, United States Army Internal Medicine in World War II* (Washington, D.C.: Office of the Surgeon General, Department of the Army, 1963), http://history.amedd.army.mil/booksdocs/wwii/infectiousdisvolii/chapter2.htm.
4. Lingeman, *Don't You Know*, 155.
5. Lingeman, *Don't You Know*, 156.
6. Sharon H. Strom and Linda P. Wood. "What Did you Do During the War, Grandma? Women and World War II," Brown University Library, 1995, http://cds.library.brown.edu/projects/WWII_Women/WomenInWWII.html.
7. Wikipedia, s.v. "Wop," accessed March 10, 2017, https://en.wikipedia.org/wiki/Wop.
8. Reggia Di Caserta online, "The Fountains of Caserta," accessed March 9, 2017, http://www.reggiadicasertaunofficial.it/en/garden/fountains/.
9. Chronicles of Carlo, "A Walk in the Garden of the Royal Palace of Caserta," accessed March 9, 2017, https://carlodeviti.wordpress.com/2016/09/05/walk-in-the-garden-of-the-royal-palace-of-caserta/.

10. World War-2 Net, "War in Europe," accessed March 10, 2017, https://www.worldwar-2.net/timelines/war-in-europe/war-in-europe-index.htm.

Chapter Fourteen
1. Atkinson, *Day of Battle*, 580.
2. Mark Jenkins, "'Gal Reporters:' Breaking Barriers in World War Two," *National Geographic* accessed March 20, 2017, http://news.nationalgeographic.com/news/2003/12/1210_031210_warwomen.html.
3. AncientOrigins.net, "The Houses of Pleasure in Ancient Pompeii," posted August 1, 2015, https://www.ancient-origins.net/ancient-places-europe/houses-pleasure-ancient-pompeii-001925.
4. History.com, "G.I. Bill," 2010, https://www.history.com/topics/world-war-ii/gi-bill.
5. Custermen.com, "The Point System or Advanced Service Rating Score," posted October 25, 2008, http://www.custermen.com/AtTheFront/Points.htm.
6. History Central online, "1944 Election Results Dewey versus Roosevelt," accessed March 26, 2017, http://www.historycentral.com/elections/1944.html.
7. European Federation of Periodontology online, "Trench Mouth – The Great War Periodontal Disease," posted November 17, 2014, http://www.efp.org/newsupdate/trench-mouth-gum-disease-periodontology/.
8. Medical Look online, "Periodontal Disease," accessed March 25, 2017, http://www.medicalook.com/Mouth_diseases/Periodontal_disease.html.
9. Wikipedia, s.v. "Honey in the Horn," accessed May 20, 2017, https://en.wikipedia.org/wiki/Honey_in_the_Horn.

Chapter Fifteen
1. Wikipedia, s.v. "Air Transport Command," accessed May 25, 2017, https://en.wikipedia.org/wiki/Air_Transport_Command.
2. Carol Schultz Vento, "World War II Psychiatric Wounds of War," Defense MediaNetwork, last modified May 2, 2012, https://www.defensemedianetwork.com/stories/world-war-ii-psychiatric-wounds-of-war/.
3. Atkinson, *Day of Battle*, 580.
4. Atkinson, *Day of Battle*, 579.
5. History of War online, Field Marshal Harold Alexander, 1891-1969," accessed on April 9, 2017, http://www.historyofwar.org/articles/people_alexander_harold.html.
6. Atkinson, *Day of Battle*, 581.
7. Oregon Archives online, "Victory at Last: Oregon Celebrates the Final Acts of the War," accessed May 29, 2017, http://sos.oregon.gov/archives/exhibits/ww2/Pages/after-victory.aspx
8. Oregon Archives online, "Victory at Last."

Chapter Sixteen
1. History.com, "V-E Day is Celebrated in America and Britain," accessed April 21, 2017, http://www.history.com/this-day-in-history/v-e-day-is-celebrated-in-america-and-britain.

2. Christopher Lehmann-Haupt, "The Man Who Invented American Efficiency," *New York Times Archives*, posted 1997, http://www.nytimes.com/1997/08/11/books/the-man-who-invented-american-efficiency.html.

3. Atomic Heritage Foundation, "Bombings of Hiroshima and Nagasaki-1945," posted June 5, 2014, http://www.atomicheritage.org/history/bombings-hiroshima-and-nagasaki-1945.

4. Wikipedia, s.v. "Jungfraujoch," accessed April 20, 2017, https://en.wikipedia.org/wiki/Jungfraujoch.

Chapter Seventeen
1. AFS-USA, About AFS, accessed May 28, 2017, http://www.afsusa.org/about-afs/.

SELECTED BIBLIOGRAPHY

The sources included in this list are the ones from which I learned a significant amount of detail about WWII. Though they are cited in the endnotes, I did not include here any source from which I extracted simple facts or definitions, such as encyclopedias or on-line historical sites that gave me event dates, military term definitions, or other simple data. The sources listed here are those with more detailed descriptions and insights about the progress of the war in Europe, specifically events in North Africa and Italy.

"African Americans in World War Two: Fighting for a Double Victory." National WWII Museum online. Accessed May 10, 2016. https://www.nationalww2museum.org/sites/default/files/2017-07/african-americans.pdf.

Atkinson, Rick. *An Army at Dawn: The War in North Africa, 1942-43*. New York: Henry Holt & Company, 2002.

———. *The Day of Battle: The War in Sicily and Italy, 1943-44*. New York: Henry Holt & Company, 2007.

Birtle, Andrew J. "Sicily 1943." U.S. Army Center of Military History online. Last modified October 3, 2003. https://history.army.mil/brochures/72-16/72-16.htm.

Deviti, Carlo. "A Walk in the Garden of the Royal Palace of Caserta." Chronicles of Carlo. Accessed March 9, 2017. https://carlodeviti.wordpress.com/2016/09/05/walk-in-the-garden-of-the-royal-palace-of-caserta/.

"Diversity in the Army." *U.S. Army Center of Military History*. http://www.history.army.mil/html/faq/diversity.html#african.

"The Fountains of Caserta." Reggia Di Caserta online. Accessed March 9, 2017. http://www.reggiadicasertaunofficial.it/en/garden/fountains/.

Gates, Henry Louis. "The African Americans: Many Rivers to Cross." *PBS Learning Media* (blog). Entry posted 2013. http://www.pbs.org/wnet/african-americans-many-rivers-to-cross/history/j-a-rogers100-amazing-facts-about-the-negro/.

"History of the Palace and of the Bourbon." Reggia di Caserta online. Accessed March 10, 2017. http://reggiaofcaserta.altervista.org/en/palace/history/.

"The Houses of Pleasure in Ancient Pompeii." AncientOrigins.net. Last modified August 1, 2015. https://www.ancient-origins.net/ancient-places-europe/houses-pleasure-ancient-pompeii-001925.

Jackson, Kathi. *They Called Them Angels: Military Nurses of World War II.* Westport, CT: Praeger, 2000.

Jenkins, Mark. "'Gal Reporters': Breaking Barriers in World War Two." National Geographic online. Accessed March 20, 2017. http://news.nationalgeographic.com/news/2003/12/1210_031210_warwomen.html.

Landau, Elizabeth. "Why Do We Use Pet Names in Relationships?" *Scientific American.* February 12, 2015.

Lingeman, Richard R. *Don't You Know There's a War On? The American Home Front 1941-1945.* New York: G.P. Putnam's Sons, 1970.

Linn, Lawrence K. "American Armed Forces Airmail during World War II; Part One, 1941-43." Stamp News online. Last modified April 7, 2014. https://www.linns.com/news/us-stamps-postal-history/2014/april/american-armed-forces-airmailduring-world-war-ii-p.html.

Malesky, Kee. *The Journey from 'Colored' to 'Minorities' to 'People of Color'.* Anonymous New England Public Radio. 2014.

McGrath, John J. *The Other End of the Spear: The Tooth to Tail Ratio in Modern Military Operations.* Vol. 23. Fort Leavenworth, KS: Combat Studies Institute, 2007.

Onion, Rebecca. "Some Choice Bits of Slang from American Soldiers Serving in WWII." Slate.com. Last modified November 11, 2013. http://www.slate.com/blogs/the_vault/2013/11/11/military_slang_terms_used_by_soldiers_in_wwii.html.

"The Point System or Advanced Service Rating Score." Custermen.com. Last modified October 25, 2008. http://www.custermen.com/AtTheFront/Points.htm.

Pratt, Sara E. "The Most Recent Eruption of Mt. Vesuvius." Earthmagazine.com. Last modified March 17, 2016. https://www.earthmagazine.org/article/benchmarks-march-17-1944-most-recent-eruption-mount-vesuvius.

Reilly, William A., Roberto F. Escamilla and Perrin H. Long. "Sandfly Fever." In *Infectious Diseases,* edited by John Boyd Coates, Jr. and W. Paul Havens, Jr. Vol. 2 of *Medical Department, United States Army Internal Medicine in World War II.* Washington, D.C.: Office of the Surgeon General, Department of the Army, 1963. http://history.amedd.army.mil/booksdocs/wwii/infectiousdisvolii/chapter2.htm.

Roberts, Larry. "History of Fort Leonard Wood." *Maneuver Support Magazine,* Summer 2008.

Smithsonian Institute. "Letter Writing in World War Two." National Postal Museum. Accessed January 30, 2015. https://postalmuseum.si.edu/VictoryMail/letter/index.html.

"Soaps and Detergent History: 1900 to Now." American Cleaning Institute online. Accessed January 21, 2017. https://www.cleaninginstitute.org/clean_living/soaps_detergent_history_3.aspx.

"The Southern 'Black Codes' of 1865-66." Constitutional Rights Foundation. http://www.crf-usa.org/brown-v-board-50th-anniversary/southern-black-codes.html.

Sparaco, Laura. "American Soldiers Arrive in Great Britain, January 26, 1942." National WWII Museum online. Last modified January 26, 2012. http://www.nww2m.com/2012/01/january-26-1942-american-soldiers-arrive-in-great-britain/.

State of Missouri Official Manual. *The Role of the Negro in Missouri History.* State of Missouri. 1973.

Strom, Sharon H., and Linda P. Wood. *What Did You Do During the War, Grandma?* Providence, RI: Brown University Library, 1995.

"Take a Closer Look at V-Mail." National WWII Museum online. Accessed April 27, 2015. http://enroll.nationalww2museum.org/learn/education/for-students/ww2-history/take-a-closer-look/v-mail.html.

Treadwell, Mattie E. *The Women's Army Corps.* Edited by Kent Roberts Greenfield. United States Army in WWII, Special Studies. Washington, D.C.: U.S. Army Center of Military History, 1954.

U.S. Army. "Creation of the Women's Army Corps." Women in the Army. Accessed October 17, 2016. https://www.army.mil/women/history/wac.html.

"V-E Day is Celebrated in America and Britain." History.com. Accessed April 21, 2017. http://www.history.com/this-day-in-history/v-e-day-is-cele brated-in-america-and-britain.

Vento, Carol S. "World War II Psychiatric Wounds of War." Defense Media Network online. Last modified May 2, 2012. https://www.defensemedianetwork.com/stories/world-war-ii-psychiatric-wounds-of-war/.

"Victory at Last: Oregon Celebrates the Final Acts of War." Oregon Archives online. Accessed May 29, 2017. http://sos.oregon.gov/archives/exhibits/ww2/Pages/after-victory.aspx.

The War. Directed by Ken Burns and Lynn Novick. 2007.

"What was Your WWII Pay?" 6th Corps of Combat Engineers Online Forum. 2012. http://www.6thcorpscombatengineers.com/engforum/index.php?/topic/7766-wwii-soldiers-pay-with-responses-from-the-vets-themselves/

Winkler, Allan M. *Home Front U.S.A.: America during World War II.* The American History Series. Illinois: Harlan-Davidson, 1986.

ABOUT THE AUTHOR

Rebecca Daniels (MFA, PhD) has been a university professor and has also had a creative career in the theatre. Recently retired, she taught performance, writing, and speaking in a liberal arts university setting for over 25 years. Before becoming an academic, she was the founding producing director for Artists Repertory Theatre in Portland, OR, and directed in nearly all the other major Portland theatre companies before entering academia full time in 1992. In retirement, she is now associated with Silverthorne Theatre, a small professional company in western Massachusetts. Throughout her career, her work has always been a mix of performance/directing, teaching, and her own writing. She is the author of a groundbreaking book on women directors and the effects of gender on their work (*Women Stage Directors Speak: Exploring the Effects of Gender on Their Work*, McFarland, 1996), and she has been published in several theatre-related professional journals over the years. She also has two full-length play manuscripts in progress, and her most recent work in progress includes a memoir about her personal experiences with genealogy and DNA testing that led to her finding both her biological parents in the past three years, in spite of the challenge of being given up for a closed adoption in 1949 at the age of three days old.

www.ingramcontent.com/pod-product-compliance
Lightning Source LLC
Chambersburg PA
CBHW021354090426
42742CB00009B/845